Chicken Soup for the Soul®

Campus Chronicles

Chicken Soup for the Soul: Campus Chronicles
101 Inspirational, Supportive, and Humorous Stories about Life in College
by Jack Canfield, Mark Victor Hansen, Amy Newmark, Madeline Clapps

Published by Chicken Soup for the Soul Publishing, LLC www.chickensoup.com

The publisher gratefully acknowledges the many publishers and individuals who granted Chicken Soup for the Soul permission to reprint the cited material.

Front cover photos courtesy of PunchStock/DigitalVision. Back cover photo courtesy of JupiterImages/Photos.com. Interior illustration courtesy of iStockPhoto.com/inktycoon.

Cover and Interior Design & Layout by Brian Taylor, Pneuma Books, LLC
For more info on Pneuma Books, visit www.pneumabooks.com

Distributed to the booktrade by Simon & Schuster. SAN: 200-2442

Publisher's Cataloging-in-Publication Data
(Prepared by The Donohue Group)

Chicken soup for the soul : campus chronicles : 101 inspirational, supportive,
    and humorous stories about life in college / [compiled by] Jack Canfield... [et al.].

    p. ; cm.

    ISBN-13: 978-1-935096-34-4
    ISBN-10: 1-935096-34-6

1. College students--Literary collections. 2. College students--Conduct of life--Literary collections. 3. Young adults--Literary collections. 4. College students--Anecdotes. 5. College students--Conduct of life--Anecdotes. 6. Young adults--Anecdotes. I. Canfield, Jack, 1944- II. Title: Campus chronicles
PN6071.C67 C55 2009

810.8/02/03557   2009922156

PRINTED IN THE UNITED STATES OF AMERICA
on acid∞free paper
17 16 15 14 13 12 10 09   01 02 03 04 05 06 07 08

Chicken Soup for the Soul

Campus Chronicles

101 Inspirational, Supportive,
and Humorous Stories
about Life in College

Jack Canfield
Mark Victor Hansen
Amy Newmark
Madeline Clapps

Chicken Soup for the Soul Publishing, LLC
Cos Cob, CT

Chicken Soup *for the* Soul

www.chickensoup.com

Contents

❶

~Overcoming Fear~

❷

~Love and Dating~

❸

~Trying New Things~

❹
~Good Friends... and Not~

❺
~Campus Antics~

6

~Difficulties and Obstacles~

7

~Lessons Learned~

❽

~Professors and Mentors~

❾

~Family Bonds~

⑩
~Personal Growth~

Chicken Soup for the Soul

Introduction

Dear College Student,

    The face of college has changed drastically since we published our last book created just for college students—and it seems to be evolving more every day. Tuition is higher, campuses are bigger, and the Internet and constant text messaging have made the way you find friends and form relationships even more complex. College is a thrilling but difficult time, full of fork-in-the-road moments that offer you new meanings for old vocabulary words such as perspective, growth, and maturity. It's a time for you to begin to realize who you are—as well as who you're not.

    That's why we've created *Chicken Soup for the Soul: Campus Chronicles* for you. It doesn't have all the answers; in fact, half the fun of college is finding your own answers to whatever questions you're faced with. But this book can offer you one thing: support. There are stories in here from students who have been through tragedy, like the death of a loved one, or who have been challenged and changed by a special professor or friend. Some students have written about learning to be away from home, about grappling with newfound freedoms—and about that ultimately perplexing question: What is my major? You're in the midst of all this, but don't worry—we've been there and our contributing authors have been there—so you're hardly alone.

    There are 101 brand new stories in here that we have carefully compiled with one purpose in mind—to give you something to connect to. It doesn't matter if you're sitting in your dorm room, alone for the first time and scared to death that you'll never make a single friend, or if you're awaiting your upcoming graduation day, satisfied that your college career has been everything you hoped it would be. Hopefully, there's something in here that you'll read and think, "I felt that," "I did that," or most importantly, "I needed that."

We wish you much success and happiness, both in college — and beyond.

~Amy Newmark and Madeline Clapps

Chapter
1

Campus Chronicles

Overcoming Fear

Courage is not the absence of fear,
but rather the judgment that something else is more important
than fear.

~Ambrose Redmoon

Your First Night at School

Change always comes bearing gifts.
~Price Pritchett

Ahhhh... you made it. Can you believe it? You survived the stress of senior exams, prom, SATs, college applications, scholarships, and you're finally in college. It's a little weird, isn't it?

So it's your first official night at college. Time to relax; the hard part is over: your parents are (hopefully) out of your dorm, and if you're lucky your stuff is all put away (or at least on its way out of boxes), your furniture is arranged (keep rearranging to maximize the space in that tiny room) and you are stress-free, lying in the bottom bunk (if your beds are bunked, fight for the bottom, you'll get sick of climbing up to the top by November).

Get a good night of sleep tonight. Tomorrow, and the rest of the week, will be exciting. My first week of college, my roommate and I went to a cookout, an ice cream social, met a ton of people, and gave ourselves a campus tour. Maps in hand, we energetically explored the buildings and lecture halls, literally racing each other from building to building. At that point, walking everywhere didn't seem that bad, but a week into classes, voluntarily climbing a flight of stairs was far from our list of leisure activities.

This first week is going to be a whirlwind, but take advantage of the energy while you have it. Go to everything you have time for, meet people and remember their names, and get to know your campus. Your impressions of it will change as it becomes your home, but that first impression will remain a cherished memory.

I bet you're a bit scared, anxious, and unsure, but do your best to allow excitement to overshadow all of those emotions.

Classes haven't started, exams are months away, and you're just meeting your hallmates. Be who you are. You're an adult, capable of making decisions, taking responsibility, and dealing with consequences. Be genuine, be caring, devote yourself to your studies, and to meeting people that aren't like you. You'll be surprised at how much you have in common with them. Expand your horizons, but never forget where you came from.

At college you will sleep through an 11 o'clock class, learn about things like NCAA football, international politics, dining hall food, and how incredible your parents really are. You will make lifelong friends, get an education, learn about yourself, and make memories that will be sweet for the rest of your life.

Rest well. The next few days will be full, exciting, challenge-laden, and stressful... but also fun and unforgettable. Sweet dreams.

~Amanda L. Southall

Move-In Day

The family —
that dear octopus from whose tentacles we never quite escape,
nor, in our inmost hearts, ever quite wish to.
~Dodie Smith

On Wednesday, August 20th, my life completely changed. I went from being a child living at home with my family to an adult living in my own apartment. Move-in day was filled with excitement, anticipation, fear, and sadness. While in the line at the Residence Life Hall of Prairie Crossing, I was smiling and talking about how much fun the next year was going to be. We were all joking and laughing, but inside my heart was breaking.

On the very first day of my freshman year in high school I started counting down the days until this moment, dreaming of how wonderful it would be to live on my own, away from my parents. The dream had turned into reality. Tomie, my Resident Assistant, handed me the key... but all I wanted to do was hand it back to her.

When I stepped out of the office, I had to put my happy face back on. I managed a huge smile as I showed everyone my key. Then my parents, my sister, and I started unloading the boxes and bags from my car and my dad's truck. The entire time we were taking the pieces of my life, stuffed into cardboard boxes and suitcases, away from the cars and into the apartment, my heart was shattering into a million tiny parts.

I could barely contain my emotions when we gathered the last few things from my car. I walked into my new living room, set my belongings on the floor, crawled up on my new leather couch, and cried like a child. My mom and my sister came over and held me while they dried my tears in an effort to try and comfort me. My dad couldn't bear to see my raw emotions so he walked into my new bedroom. The whole time we had been unpacking, my dad had been trying to hold back his tears as well.

I wasn't ready to live on my own, and the freedom I had dreamed about felt more like a nightmare. My parents had known all along that I wasn't ready—they'd told me so all summer—but I just didn't listen. The thought of being away from home scared me to death. All of my life, my parents had been just across the hall and my sister just around the hall corner.

The whole event began in January during my senior year in high school. I had interviewed for a very prestigious and much needed scholarship package through the Honors College at Texas A&M University-Commerce. To be completely honest, I hoped in the back of my mind that I wouldn't be picked to receive it—I would have to move away from the only home I had known for my eighteen years.

The interview went well and I was extremely impressed with the campus, as well as the apartments that I would potentially be living in. I vividly remember telling my mom that although the apartments were very nice, they would never truly be home to me if I were to receive the scholarship package. The weeks went by without a letter from the interview committee; although I knew that the scholarship would seriously benefit my family's financial situation, I was happy that I would not have to move away from home just yet.

On February 13th that year, I received the best and, at the time, the worst news in my entire life: I had been chosen as one of the fifty scholarship recipients out of the hundreds of applicants that had been interviewed. My family and I were overjoyed that I would be able to receive a debt-free college education and I was overwhelmed with all the newfound freedom I would have. Now, on move-in day, I regretted ever going to that interview and receiving my acceptance letter.

After my family helped console me and calm me down, we started to put my things away and make my new bedroom feel like home. Once all the goofy pictures of my graduation dinner were put up in my collage picture frame, I realized that living away from home might not be as bad as it seemed. I was only thirty minutes from home, and I had my cell phone, so I could call anytime I wanted. When my family left me at my apartment that night, I cried myself to sleep once again.

I am writing this during finals week of my first semester, and I have settled into college life extremely well. My fears subsided after my first trip home during the first week of school. A few months ago, I feared change and new surroundings, but now I am saddened that I have to leave all my new friends during Christmas break. Moving away from home helped me to grow and mature as a person. I've realized that fears about moving away are normal, but trust me — living on my own has been great, and since move-in day I haven't regretted receiving my scholarship package once.

~Kally E. Hinton

Freshman Orientation

*Many of our fears are tissue-paper-thin,
and a single courageous step would carry us clear through them.*
~Brendan Francis

"At this time, we ask that parents and students separate into two groups for the remainder of the day. Parents and students will be reunited at the conclusion of the campus tour."

Flocks of incoming freshmen happily abandon their parents upon hearing this announcement. I am less than thrilled at the prospect of starting college, let alone leaving my mother's side to tour the campus with the rest of the wide-eyed incoming freshmen.

"Okay Laur, I'll see you in a few hours, and remember, this is going to be a great experience for you!" Mom says, her big brown eyes alive with enthusiasm. I am amazed by my mother's resilience, considering what my family and I have been through during the past four years.

My mother disappears into a sea of overzealous parents who look as if they have ransacked the campus bookstore; many of the parents, to the embarrassment of their teenagers, are proudly sporting university attire with slogans like, "I'm a Sunny Brook University Dad."

We follow our senior tour guide. The other incoming students chatter and make casual introductions. I drag behind. How could I have believed I was ready for this? After all, it has only been a few months since I was discharged from the hospital. I am feeling better for the first time in years... but college?

My brooding is interrupted by a peppy voice. "Hi, I'm Jennifer."

The voice is attached to a freckle-faced blond girl dressed in what can only be described as hippy-like sports attire. For some strange reason, I like her immediately.

"I'm Lauren," I reply.

"Commuting or dorming?"

I fumble for my words, still caught up in my own thoughts. I would dorm, but I have spent the last four years overcoming a major depressive disorder that nearly claimed my life. I am still readjusting to living back home, in a place where I can come and go without asking for a "pass" or for a staff member to unlock the door to let me outside. I'm not quite sure I'm ready for this right now.

"I, uh, I don't know yet. My parents think I should dorm, but I don't really want to," I say in my most confident voice.

"You should definitely dorm! I'm going to, and I think it will be a lot of fun!"

I can't decide if Jennifer's enthusiasm is annoying or refreshing, but I decide to give her the benefit of the doubt. Before I can utter my less than enthusiastic reply, the tour guide announces that it is time to create our schedules.

We crowd into the Student Activity Center, or as the true, full-blown university students call it, the Sac, a nickname that immediately reminds me of the warm, safe bed at home I wish I were nestled in. We are ushered towards stiff, metal-backed chairs that hungrily await our freshman flesh. Three seniors hand out course bulletins as thick as textbooks, and slap registration forms down on the tables in front of us. All around me, papers crinkle and pencils scribble furiously. These sounds blare like an alarm clock, screaming "Wake up, Lauren!" Students seem to be moving through the process at rapid speed and I have not even opened my course catalog.

Focus, I tell myself. You can do this. Just read through the catalog and find the courses you like and a schedule that works. No big deal.

Intro to Psychology A or B, Foundations of Biology 2, Calculus, Geology 101, English, History, sections 1, 2, 3, 4, 5,6,7... the list goes on, and on, and on.

I begin to panic. How am I supposed to know what to do? I'm just relearning how to live in the real world again, and they want me to make a schedule?!

Other freshmen are handing in their materials, grinning as they rush out to meet their parents.

I cannot breathe, anxiety is coursing through my veins, and my head is pounding.

In moments, I am sobbing.

Other students abandon their tasks to stare at me, making me wish that the earth would open up and swallow me whole. One of the seniors in charge walks over to my table.

"What's the matter?" she asks gruffly.

"I... I can't do this!" I cry.

"All you have to do is make your schedule, just like everybody else," she says, clearly annoyed.

I cry harder. Then, a warm hand on my shoulder... Jennifer.

"Everything is alright," she tells the senior. "I'll help her."

The insensitive upperclassman walks away, and I feel the weight of the dozens of staring eyes lift. The other students quickly lose interest in the spectacle I've created and I can breathe again.

"What's wrong, sweetie?" Jennifer asks.

I am touched by this near stranger's concern. She hardly knows me, but seems to genuinely care.

Jennifer's kindness gives way to new tears. If crying were a major, I would have earned my doctorate in it by now.

"It is just too much; it is just too overwhelming," I say. "I... I have depression and I take medication."

Why did I say that? She probably thinks I am a freak now. But Jennifer puts her arm around me and her words reach out and wrap warmly around my soul.

"I know all about that sort of thing," she says. "My mother has depression. Besides, I think it's pretty normal to feel overwhelmed right now."

And with these words, just like that, the stigma of my mental illness is lifted for a moment and I am just a normal teenage girl with real fears about this exciting but frightening new adventure called "College."

The room is nearly empty now, and I still have no schedule. The pages before me are watermarked with tears.

Jennifer reaches out and gently places her hand on my arm. "Okay, so you said earlier you wanted to be a Psych major, right?"

And with that, this girl who was a stranger to me before this day guides me through the process, step-by-step, until I have everything in place and my schedule is complete. I am amazed at how much more clearly I can see now that the veil of anxiety and tears has lifted. "See," Jennifer tells me softly, "you knew exactly what to do — you just needed to believe in yourself."

That was the beginning of what would blossom into a powerful friendship. With a hug goodbye and a promise to keep in touch, we left Freshman Orientation with much more than our schedules. As I went to meet my mother, I decided that I would give living on campus a try... after all, I had come this far, and with a little help from a new friend, I had been reminded of the strength that existed in me. Four years later, as I graduated from the university with the distinction of Magna Cum Laude, I looked back on Freshman Orientation, on all of my fears and insecurities, and smiled.

~Lauren Nevins

People over Paper

*One's friends are that part of the human race
with which one can be human.*

~George Santayana

Everyone back home told me that one of the nicest things about college is the people you meet. They all assured me that I would make friendships that could last a lifetime. I would always smile and agree. Frankly, before I left for college, I really didn't care. I was going to school far from home, and I wasn't exactly thrilled about meeting new people. My plan for college was to get in, get my degree, get out, and get on with my life as fast as I could, not to establish an elaborate social circle.

I applied for every dorm except one, in which six guys live in two small connecting rooms. The rest of the dorms had doubles. As things turned out, I ended up in the dorm I didn't apply for—the ancient and revered Slight. All my roommates seemed to be okay guys, but I didn't really try to get to know them. I spent most of my time studying in the library and didn't get back to my room until I was ready for bed, which was considerably earlier than my roommates. No matter what song my roommates blared, or what action-packed movie they were watching, I would be tucked in my bed with earplugs and a shirt wrapped around my head, usually entertaining unpleasant thoughts about my roommates.

I have always been rather quiet and have never been able to make friends easily. My first few weeks at college reflected this. Since

I wasn't trying to make friends, I would always forget names after I met people. When we passed again and they called out my name, I would reply with an embarrassed wave and a weak hello. I would try to keep any conversations to a minimum since I felt awkward for not remembering their name and was too proud to ask them to remind me of it.

This is how things went for the first month or so. After a while, things started to change. A couple of my roommates would try and keep me talking. Soon, these two roommates and I started becoming fairly close. We began going to the cafeteria together, exercising together, and meeting in the library to study. At one point, a girl asked me what room I lived in and seemed surprised when I told her I was from Slight #12. She went on to say that she knew a lot of guys who wished they lived in my room, because it was such a cool group of guys.

During this time, I also made a commitment to remember other people's names. Whenever I would meet someone I would try and address them by their name at least three times during our first conversation. This helped, and now I was at last trying to build relations with other people. I began to rely heavily on the people God had sent into my life and I started viewing their friendship as a gift from Him.

These feelings culminated one night when one of my roommates invited me to listen to a fellow roommate practice with one of our college choirs. I almost opted out, as I had a lot of homework to do and was feeling pretty tired, but in the end I agreed. Later that evening, my roommates and some other friends picked me up from the library to drive me across campus where my roommate was to perform.

It so happened that this was my birthday, but I had kept quiet about it. So you can imagine my surprise when we entered the recital hall and the 120-member choir began to sing "Happy Birthday" to me. After the choir finished the song, we left and allowed them to get on with their practice. Back at the dorm, my friends threw a small party for me, complete with a card and cake.

I was completely shocked to find that my roommates had

arranged for the choir to interrupt their practice to sing me "Happy Birthday" and that they scraped together their funds to throw me a party. I felt totally unworthy of their kindness and proud to be able to call them friends. It was then that I realized that college means more than the piece of paper you receive at the end—it's an education in both life and people. Thanks to the friends I made, I understood that the people back home were right all along.

~Travis Shelley

Flight of Faith

The World is a book, and those who do not travel read only a page.
~St. Augustine

When my plane touches down in Guadalajara, Mexico, I disembark with a plastic-bound conversational Spanish guide and a small rolling suitcase. The agency arranging the homestay for my college-level study abroad hadn't been able to give me any details about the woman I will be living with for the next few months. So I search the crowd looking for my mysterious hostess.

For the first time, it enters my mind to question whether she will be able to speak English. Uncertainty creeps in as I realize how difficult this airport, this city, this country, will be for me to navigate alone.

I scan the crowd. I am surrounded by tall, white cowboy hats and fellow travelers bearing cardboard boxes bound with string.

Then, I see her. Short, chestnut-colored hair. Cold eyes the faint blue of glacier ice. Polyester skirt past the knees. Orthopedic shoes. She looks to be nearly sixty, with stout fingers gripping a white piece of paper with my name scrawled across it in black ink. She looks more intimidating than I could have imagined, and I have a wildly active imagination.

I move toward the unsmiling woman, my stomach tightening at the impossible sharpness of her eyes. She points to the sign, "League Aun?" she questions in a pronunciation that's new to me.

"*Si*, Leigh Ann."

She nods and lets the sign drop to her side. She looks relieved, and I feel relieved that she suddenly has shown some warmth. She is, after all, the only person in Mexico who knows, well, at least how to spell my name.

"*Mi nombre* Leigh Ann. *Soy de los montañas de Carolina Del Norte.*" My name is Leigh Ann. I am from the mountains of North Carolina. This is the extent of my Spanish.

She nods again. My name is the extent of her English.

She begins to speak Spanish, her words flowing faster than river rapids. I can tell that she is not chitchatting; she's trying to give me the information I need to adjust to life in Guadalajara, but I can't even remember how to say I don't understand.

The airport traffic moves around us. We are their obstacle, language is ours. She touches my arm, and I notice that her eyes have softened a bit more. She walks to a kiosk and after a completely indiscernible conversation with the attendant, she presents me with a bottle of juice. Then we sit surrounded by a nervous silence before taking a taxi into the city.

The first few days I live with Señora Montañas, it is impossible to communicate even the simplest things. Another American student boarder who has just arrived, Katie, becomes my translator and helps me get to and from the university where I am to take Spanish classes.

When we return after hours of scribbling in vocabulary books and sitting in on Sociology classes, Señora asks about our days. First, she addresses Katie, who always carries on a language-class-worthy conversation, then me. I simply smile, my only surefire form of communication. But still she asks every day, as if she already knows that soon I will be able to answer.

Every afternoon, an hour before mealtime, Señora plops lumps of gritty dough in my hand and demonstrates the making of *gorditas*—thick corn tortillas made through a process not unlike tossing a baseball hand to hand. As the dough takes shape, day after day, so does my voice. Over time, our conversations grow to fill the kitchen.

Then come the mariachi songs, "Aye, aye, aye, aye," she belts with gusto, watching my enthusiastic repetition with delight.

When Señora has her extended family members over for dinner, she invites me to sing or read or speak to them in Spanish, proud of my progress, however slow. Often, I pause for comically long periods of time, trying to find the right Spanish words, and the group laughs. But Señora tells them to hush, and reminds them in Spanish, "When she came she couldn't say anything. Now at least she can talk!" I am touched by the pride in the blue eyes that had, not so very long ago, been those of a stranger.

When you travel abroad for any amount of time you must have faith that you will find your way, communicate, and learn something worth more than the frequent flyer miles. More often than not, you do. And more often than not, it is because someone with local knowledge takes you into their life and teaches you.

Whenever I become nervous about traveling to an unfamiliar part of the world, I will think of Señora Montañas. As I board my plane, take my chance, and rack up more frequent flyer miles, I will find solace in knowing that there are ambassadors of goodwill like her at work in the world. As I leap across cultural divides, I will remain ever faithful that, at each destination, I will find a place to call home in a language other than my own.

~Leigh Ann Henion

Hardest Decision

Everything in life is luck.
~Donald Trump

I stared at my school catalog. I had been through all 430 pages of it five times and still could not make a decision about the one thing that would set my entire college career on course and ultimately decide what I do when I graduate. It is also the answer to the one question that everyone — and I mean everyone — asks you. It can be summed up in one word: Major.

It was already my sophomore year. I had been through all the general questions: What fields will pay me the most money? What do I enjoy? How much math do I have to take? Still, there were no answers for me. I had even taken personality tests.

Stress was now starting to set in. I had professors, counselors, and the all-important parents asking me if I had chosen. Every day I dreaded getting the phone call from Mom.

Her greatest worry was that I would not make it out. She believed that I would spend the rest of my time taking classes here and there, wasting money. Trust me; I did not want to be stuck in college forever. I wanted to graduate. College was fun, but not fun enough for me to stay past four years.

Anyway, back to my dilemma. I came into college thinking that I would major in Communications. It had been my dream to be a sportswriter. I knew that it would be hard for a female to get into a male-dominated field, but I was going to do it. I was going to show all those male writers that I was just as good as they were. This would also be an opportunity for me to show off all the sports knowledge that my dad had taught me. That was my dream until I got the acceptance letter that stated I was not qualified for that major. Well, that dream went down the drain quickly.

It was on to Plan B. I thought about History. It sounded fun! I have always been a fan of European history, especially British. I had read countless books on all their monarchs; Henry VIII and Elizabeth I being my favorites. I knew random facts about British history that my friends always made fun of me for. Now I could see all those facts coming in handy. I could see myself excelling in this field.

I thought about History for a few days. I eventually got excited and leaked the idea to my dad.

"What are you going to do with a degree in History?"

"Um..." He had me there. I guess I really hadn't thought that one through. What was I going to do with a degree in History?

"Are you going to be a teacher?"

I really did not want to go into teaching. Maybe it had to do with seeing just how much teachers have to go through. No, thank you!

So, then it was on to Plan C. Plan C including asking my mom for help. Let me tell you right now — it was so not the thing to do. Her suggestion came from an article that she had read in one of her magazines that talked about the job market and what job positions were needed the most right now.

Her answer: Nursing.

My answer: No.

There was no way I was going to be a nurse. I could barely go to the doctor's office without getting freaked out about getting a shot. How was I supposed to give them to other people? On top of that, I don't do so great in hospitals. Once when I had to watch my brother get stitches, I almost passed out. I couldn't handle seeing him in pain while the doctor tried to close his cut. The nurse had to hold him down. Yeah, nursing was not an option.

So, there I was, back at square one. What if I tried the "pick a random page" trick? I gave it a try and the result was: Mathematics.

I couldn't help but laugh, because math is the last thing I've ever wanted to do. I gave it another go and this time: Chemistry. Yeah, that's not going to happen either. I almost failed my high school chemistry class.

"I give up!" I shouted, and tossed the book across the room. It hit the wall with a loud BANG and landed open on my bed, as if daring me to look again. Should I look? I figured it was probably just some dumb subject that I struggle with, like Biology or Political Science. Still, a small part of me wanted to see.

I slowly got up from my computer chair and walked over to my bed. There on the page was one word that caught my attention: English.

I had never thought about that major before. It included both things I love: reading and writing. I found a winner! I quickly picked up the book and scanned the English section, noting all the great classes. British Literature, Study of the Novel, and Intro to Shakespeare all grabbed my interest. I could do this and enjoy it! Why didn't I think of this sooner? It had been right in front of me the whole time. I wanted to be a writer when thinking about Communications and wanted to read when looking into History.

I quickly picked up the phone and dialed my mom. I didn't even give her a chance to say hello.

"I found it!" I shouted with joy.

~Robyn Schroder

Blood Drive

Panic at the thought of doing a thing is a challenge to do it.
~Henry S. Haskins

All right, so I am basically a chicken. The idea of having a hypodermic needle jammed into my arm makes me shudder and the thought of having my blood siphoned away causes a pale, sweaty mask to form on my face. As a member of my university's student service organization, I have enthusiastically recruited others to donate their blood to the American Red Cross, and smiled thankfully when they signed their pints away.

As for giving my own blood, that was always another matter. Every year, the excuses I gave to avoid it became wilder with each blood drive. Mononucleosis worked a couple of times, hepatitis, medication, etc.... The best one I came up with was "rolling veins." While I did a grand job of fooling everyone else, I felt uneasy lying to myself. I knew that eventually I would have to go through with it.

This year's blood drive marked a turning point and I decided that it would be better to die on the donor's cot than to go on living with the guilt harbored in my chicken veins. Besides, my friend Ruth promised to give blood at the same time and I figured I could always hold her hand if I really got scared.

The appointed day came when the big semi truck arrived on campus. At my eight o'clock class, Ruth informed me that she had a funeral to go to later that day and couldn't make it. I would have to face this one alone. As my appointed time approached, I hobbled to the parking lot. I walked inside the trailer and surveyed the blood-mobile setup. There was plenty of juice to drink, but I would have preferred a shot of something stronger.

I took a seat in a row of chairs against the wall while I waited for a nurse to call my name. When she did, I got up and walked over to where another nurse methodically asked me preliminary questions from a sheet. This was it; there was no backing out.

"Have you ever had grphnxlty?"

"No."

"Xaklytany or krvanp?"

"No."

"Are you or have you been pregnant in the last six months?"

"Ummm...."

"Please step this way."

Another nurse pricked my finger to see if my blood met the minimum daily requirements. As she popped a thermometer into my mouth, I garbled, "Will this hurt?"

"No. Just relax. Good, your blood is red and your temperature is normal. Please step over there." She pointed to a place where another nurse was standing next to an elevated cot.

"Hi there," she said. "Would you please lie down?"

"Sure, lady."

"You seem a little edgy. Have you ever given blood before?"

"No, I'm a first-timer." I thought about Ruth, who bailed on me. I asked hopefully, "Will you hold my hand?"

I climbed up on the cot and saw Smith lying on an adjacent one, already bleeding into a bag. From his looks, I thought about walking out. But it was too late.

"Hold onto this and squeeze your fist slowly," the nurse ordered.

Attempting to defuse the situation with some humor, I looked at her and said, "Hey, if you strike oil in my veins, I'll split the profits with you!"

"Very funny, young man. That's the first time I've heard that one — today!"

"Oh, sorry."

The whole experience was over as smoothly as it began. After the nurse put a bandage on my arm, I left the donors' table for the one with cookies and juice. There was a whole group of people like me who had just finished donating blood. They were all milling around, munching and joking with cookie-filled mouths. One fellow was commenting about the nervous types who put on a show and try to act brave when they step into the bloodmobile. I laughed along nervously.

Walking out of the trailer, I felt like a real hero. After all, I did give a whole pint of my very own precious blood. And I had a bandaged arm to prove it. The fact that millions of people donate their blood every year didn't matter at that moment. All I cared about was my personal glory, regardless of how short-lived it might be.

~David Hyman

Campus Chronicles

Love and Dating

We choose those we like;
with those we love, we have no say in the matter.

~*Mignon McLaughlin*, The Neurotic's Notebook

Heathcliff in Jeans

*My love for Heathcliff resembles the eternal rocks beneath—
a source of little visible delight, but necessary.*
~From Wuthering Heights by Emily Brontë

When I was a teenager, I was a hopeless romantic. I was a Romeo and Juliet, Heathcliff and Catherine, *liebestod* (love in death) sort of romantic. Love wasn't real unless it was a dark passion. After reading *Wuthering Heights* far too many times, my idea of the perfect love was the ruggedly handsome Heathcliff, banging his head against a tree trunk, begging his love to haunt him for the rest of his days. What could be better than a man who loves even your ghost?

I went to an extremely small international high school in Nairobi, with only twenty-five guys in my senior class. Needless to say, there wasn't much of a selection, and I graduated without having any romantic experiences. College would be the place where I would realize my romantic destiny.

When I got to freshman orientation, I ended up spending a lot of time with the son of one my dad's former colleagues. Short and more than a little goofy, I couldn't imagine him shouting my name into the sunset, his face strained with the intensity of his passion. But he did pay me a fair share of flattering attention, and I decided to give him a shot. When he kissed me a few days later, injecting his tongue into my mouth and letting it sit there like a paralyzed slug, I realized that he was no Heathcliff. Perhaps, love just wasn't as grand as my favorite authors had convinced me it would be.

The rest of the year didn't yield any promising entanglements—most of my suitors were frat boys or, in at least one case, an unfortunately creepy guy who wrote poems about me. I would be returning to Kenya for the summer and I didn't have a single romantic story to spin to my high school friends.

Of course, that was when I met him—the night before leaving for the entire summer. We'll call him Heathcliff. Tall and dark-haired, Heathcliff had a wounded past, which only made him more intriguing. Though I had only just met him, I wanted to soothe him and help heal his deep wounds. We talked through the night and went on a leisurely midnight drive through the rural roads surrounding our school. And it certainly didn't hurt my growing infatuation that, upon discovering I had not yet learned to drive, he immediately insisted I get behind the wheel of his car. "Ah, this is it," I thought. "This is what Emily Brontë was thinking of." And it was—the thrilling, exuberant, and frightening high I had been waiting for. When he kissed me at the end of the night and told me that he looked forward to spending time with me the next year, I could swear I almost swooned.

And then I had to leave... for the entire summer. When I finally returned to the U.S., I couldn't wait to reconnect with Heathcliff, who I had only spoken to a few times over the summer. I had grand plans for our reunion—I imagined that our first midnight drive would be repeated countless times. I dialed his number on my cell phone with trembling fingers. No guy had ever made me feel this way before—no one had made me experience this aching sense of anticipation and desire.

When Heathcliff finally answered his phone, though, I could tell something was off. He didn't seem to be the same cool, witty, sensitive guy who had charmed me so many months past. He claimed that he was now the owner of two businesses that he had formed over the summer. Because of this, he would not be returning to college. He was too busy running his business and cruising around in his brand new Camaro. Not only did Heathcliff not sound like the guy I had been dreaming about for months, he also didn't sound like a completely sane person. I left our conversation feeling confused and not a little bit stupid. Had I imagined everything? Did I create Heathcliff from thin air?

In spite of this, I wasn't quite willing to give up. I tried to justify his odd behavior: Maybe the phone call had been a fluke? Maybe he was just joking around and I was too dense to get it? I called and left him a message, pledging to myself that I would give up if I didn't hear anything back.

One day, my friend, Sarah, called with some juicy gossip. She'd talked to Heathcliff's old roommate, who said that he had spent the entire summer on drugs—hard ones. Of course, instead of convincing me to stay away from him, this news made me want to help him all the more.

A few weeks later, I got a call, and when I heard the husky voice at the end of the line, I knew immediately who it was. Heathcliff! My heart sped up. He explained that he had spent the past month in the hospital. He had bipolar disorder and his summer had been consumed by a long, manic free-for-all. He had done drugs and spent money he didn't have (that explained the Camaro). He said he'd turned things around now.

We started dating. I was certain that my love would turn him around. I gave him all I had, telling him my every secret and even arranging to bring him to Kenya for a month over the summer. Though his unstable behavior often made me cry, loving him meant being in pain, and I had convinced myself at the tender age of nineteen that losing him would mean the end of me.

A year later, he broke my heart, not only by rejecting my love, but by starting to do drugs and party again. And though at first I thought I couldn't live without him, I eventually moved on. I didn't embrace a life of revenge and anger, I didn't commit suicide, and I didn't join a nunnery. Instead, I lived one day at a time, discovering for myself what it was to be an adult and what it was to be a person on my own terms instead of someone else's. I lost my first passionate love, and I am happier for it.

I learned that Heathcliff is not all he's cracked up to be.

~Angela Polidoro

Freshman Nuptials

*Love is a gross exaggeration of the difference between one person
and everybody else.*

~George Bernard Shaw

By the end of the first week of college, I already had five different husbands.

Sure, we weren't really married—and only one or two knew my name—but my hypothetical marriages kept me awake in my classes, and that was good enough for me.

The whole five-husband business came about as a way to contain my initial crushing. I figured that if I chose a boy from each of my classes I would not spend so much time scoping the student center or library for other potential boyfriends. Though in hindsight, I still found a guy to gaze at nearly everywhere I went on campus.

I had this theory going into college that every boy I met would be worth marrying. I chose a small private school which, according to my naïve, freshman mind, meant that every boy I met would be a good one—one who my parents would approve of, one who would have the same interests as me. But that wasn't always true. Finding that husband was a lot harder than I had imagined.

I got sick of most of my "husbands" by the end of week three. My Speech husbands (I had an extra one as a backup) both had serious girlfriends. My Gen. Ed. husband reminded me too much of my ex-boyfriend, though he was the most intelligent of the five. My News Writing husband looked like a younger version of Mulder from the sci-fi classic *The X-Files*, and the spare husband I passed on the way to class (husband five-point-five) turned out to be a racist. The only husband that stuck was Caleb, my Communications husband, who already had a girlfriend. He was my favorite.

Caleb lacked one attribute that all my other husbands seemed to have in overwhelming amounts—arrogance. Caleb was your typical sit-in-the-back-of-the-room, carefree, bearded junior college guy. He didn't pretend to know all the answers in class; he accepted whatever came his way. Even when my professor patted him on the backside to teach us about inappropriate nonverbal communication, he barely cracked a smile. I liked this guy.

Most of the time, I crushed from a distance. Meaning I would give him a half-smile if we made eye contact, or I initiated small talk if I deemed it appropriate. When I was really desperate, I would simply observe him through the reflection on my laptop screen in class—he only sat two rows behind me. But one morning I made my presence known to him more than I wanted.

On a Friday in October, our university had a special choir and band concert to replace the typical chapel service. I left my dorm room to meet a friend at the fountain in the middle of campus before heading to the concert. I went out the back door and followed the sidewalk to the fountain. The sidewalk connects to another pathway in the middle, and that pathway happens to lead to a boys' dorm. But not just any boys' dorm—it was Caleb's hall. Just as I neared the intersection, Caleb exited the side door of his building. I noticed he was wearing a three-piece suit, clearly a member of the choir or band, on his way to perform. My gaze shot to my feet and I dawdled.

Maybe we won't meet up. Maybe his pace is just fast enough and mine is just slow enough that we'll miss each other completely.

Caleb and I met side by side.

Of my five husbands, Caleb is the only one with whom I've exchanged words. So, if I ignored him while meandering down the sidewalk, I would have seemed like a jerk or just terribly shy. I'm neither. So I said something, the only thing that seemed to fit the occasion: "Lookin' good." I turned to him and awkwardly smiled.

He looked back at me and said thanks matter-of-factly, as if I'd just complimented his shoes and not just revealed my secret attraction. My eyes found the ground once again. We crossed paths, not saying another word.

After that, I expected Caleb to mock me in class or ignore me completely. But nothing happened; he must have forgotten it had occurred. We still made small talk and I occasionally caught a distorted glimpse of him through my computer monitor, but the luster faded and my heart moved on. I began searching for husband number six.

Okay, so I'm starting to realize that college isn't all about finding the one I'm going to marry. That may seem very obvious to most people, but after meeting numerous married college sweethearts, it's hard to believe otherwise. Maybe I will meet my "real" husband here, or maybe I won't. But I know that a relentless search is not worth it. College presents numerous opportunities just as important as a male-female relationship — friendships, parties, road trips, education, freedom. I'd miss out on a lot of those if I had a guy glued to my side.

So for now, and for the rest of my college career, I'm not going to care as much about locating my next husband. Now I can wear sweats and watch movies all Saturday or spend hours studying for an exam with no distractions. And I'm okay with that. Husbands number seven, eight, and nine can wait.

~Lauren Sawyer

A Name among Thousands

When you realize you want to spend the rest of your life with somebody,
you want the rest of your life to start as soon as possible.
~Nora Ephron, When Harry Met Sally

I was a junior in college at Arizona State University in Tempe, Arizona. I had been dating a senior, and in May I found myself attending his graduation from ASU's School of Business. We were sitting high in the stadium, watching a very long ceremony and I was bored. The procession of students seemed endless, and the air horns were giving me a headache. It would be at least another hour until his name was called.

To pass the time, I began thumbing through the directory of graduates looking for my boyfriend's name. A name other than the one I was looking for caught my eye. Brian Geiger. My favorite uncle is a Geiger, and in all my years in Arizona, I had never met anyone with that last name. It jumped off the page at me. Laughing, I pointed it out quickly to my mom, and then kept searching through the thousands of names. Little did I know I had just picked out my future husband's name — nor did I know that fate would introduce us a few short weeks later.

The next month passed without much incident. I was working as a research assistant in a university science lab, and because I was employed by ASU, I had a summer pass to the campus gym. My relationship with my boyfriend had deteriorated since graduation, so I spent a lot of time at the gym playing volleyball. A group of us played every Tuesday and Thursday. That day, I had signed up for research lab time but didn't feel like being alone in a sterile science lab. I decided to stop by the gym and see if the regular crew was there to play.

The minute I walked in, I noticed a new guy playing on the far court. Wow. He was amazing! He hadn't seen me, but all I saw was him. I felt my face flush, and I knew I had to meet him. Luckily, I did. By the end of the afternoon, there were only enough people left for two teams of three. I was supposed to go to work at the lab, but that would have left uneven teams. I knew I should leave, but I still hadn't officially accomplished my goal of meeting this new man. When the game was over, the new guy, Brian, and his friend, Matt, asked me to go with them for drinks. Volleyball and drinks gradually became a weekly routine: just Brian, Matt, and me. However, it wasn't until a few days later that I actually realized who this Brian guy was.

In order to check out a volleyball, students use their ID cards. When the ball is returned, the ID is given back. One afternoon, I had checked out the ball, but I had to leave before everyone was ready to quit. So my new cute friend, known simply to me as Brian, gave me his ID to exchange for mine. On the walk down the hall, I looked at his name. I got chills. It was Brian Geiger.

If he had graduated, why was he at the campus gym? I later found out that he had intended to move back to his home state of Illinois immediately after graduation, but he couldn't bring himself to leave Arizona. And he had persuaded the gym to let him have a free summer membership. I was stunned. ASU didn't give out free memberships. He never should have been there. We never should have met. I hadn't ever put a lot of stock in destiny, but I was becoming a believer.

By August we were dating. He took me to meet his parents and we laughed that we were all in that same stadium, watching that same graduation ceremony. I knew after four months that he was the man I would marry. Looking back at the graduation ceremony, I am now fully convinced that I didn't notice his name by chance. It was just too unlikely. Thousands of names, and I saw his, which was later to become mine.

~Lisa Geiger

Dreamboat

The heart has its reasons that reason knows nothing of.
~Blaise Pascal

E ven when the sun was out of my eyes, I was totally blinded—by him. Sitting on the sidelines of the field in the evening summer heat, I listened as the other girls nearby whispered about him. Whispered about his wind-swept shaggy hair, about the way he jumped and ran and moved. I looked over at them, and we shared a knowing look. Everything about him was so perfect. In fact, he was so unattainable I figured I could stare as much as I wanted. So I kept on staring.

It was my friend Jeff's idea that I come to play Frisbee that first time. We had been working out at the gym together the summer between sophomore and junior year of college, and he was trying to get a few girls to join his mostly-boys bi-weekly Ultimate Frisbee game. I was feeling shy and nervous and had been holed up in my room for the first half of the summer, coming home from work only to read novels in my comfy green chair. I was scared to commit too fully to life back at home in the room I had inhabited since I was four years old. I thought I was only biding my time while I was living with my parents, waiting for my real college life to begin again in September. I turned out to be very wrong.

At my second Frisbee game, I was the only girl playing, but I wasn't scared. I was defending a big, doofy-looking guy who couldn't run very fast and I was determined to prove myself to all the boys there by keeping him from even touching the coveted little disk. Sweaty and beet-red, I tried to keep my eyes down. I wasn't there to make friends, only to get a little exercise. That's when he caught my eye for just a second.

"How ya doin', Maddy?" he asked, the dreamy one who jumped what seemed to be miles in the air to catch the Frisbee, the one all the girls had been whispering about. I just smiled. Words wouldn't come out of my mouth.

The next week, he came up to me, his hair wet with water he had poured on himself to combat the summer sauna we were playing in, and I scrambled to make myself presentable in some way. I brushed my bangs off my forehead and caught some sweat, but tried to ignore it. He was talking to me. Nothing else really existed.

He said he wanted to pick my brain, that he needed me to help him out with something his sister was working on, and he said he wanted to "send me some questions." It sounded oddly like an excuse to talk to me, but it couldn't be. Absolutely not. He was dreamy, and I had slipped back into my sad, shy, single life that included only work, home, and falling asleep watching TV on my best friend's couch.

That night, I awoke with a start from a dream I had. In it, I was on the Frisbee field, my breath heavy and labored. I stopped and turned and there he was. I was prepared to stare, to be invisible, to simply be around him. But he was looking back at me. I woke up from the dream and tried, in vain, to fall back into it.

On my last day of Frisbee, he picked me for his team—but I hadn't heard from him about any "questions" or anything of that sort. I was sad about it, although I hadn't really gotten my hopes up. This dreamboat, I had decided, was out of my league. Ten thousand leagues out of my league. When the game was over, I went to retrieve my car keys and my water bottle, knowing I was going to be unable to come to Frisbee for the rest of the summer. I looked over at him sitting on the bench—in that moment, something compelled me to walk over. I thought I would be overcome with fear as I approached him, but I was oddly calm.

"Hey," I started, "Are you going to send me any questions?"

He glanced up from the bench, squinting, looking like a model in a photo spread. My heart skipped a beat. I couldn't believe that after this day I wouldn't see him again. We would go back to our separate colleges, back to our separate worlds, and that would be that. We would most likely never reconvene at home again.

"Actually," he started, "I would rather..."

"Just not send questions?" I cut him off mid-sentence, trying to save face. Of course he wasn't going to try to contact me. Of course. What was I thinking?

"... ask you them over dinner sometime." I was shocked. Dreamy had asked me on a date. A real, live, take-me-out-to-dinner-and-a-movie date.

"Sure," I said, surprising even myself with my nonchalance. "Do you have my phone number?"

Four months later, I was lying on my couch in my dorm room, on the phone. My feet in the air, I rolled around and twirled my hair, listening to the voice on the phone recount what sounded like the plot of some teen movie, but was, in fact, my real life.

"You know," he said, "there was a bet going between me and Mike."

I giggled. "What about?"

"It was a bet to see who could win you on the Frisbee field. I almost gave up. I never thought you'd go out with me."

I smiled a huge, luminous smile that the owner of the Dreamy voice on the line couldn't see. Although I knew I had won the ultimate, shaggy-haired prize, I also knew that his Frisbee bet had taught me another lesson — that I was worthy of real love and affection from someone who liked me for all the reasons that I liked me. Because for the first time in my life, I had been someone's dreamboat — and I hadn't even known it.

~Madeline Clapps

A Semester in London

Travel and change of place impart new vigor to the mind.

--Seneca

Istepped off the plane and was blindsided by an epiphany: I had completely lost my mind.

Insanity was the only explanation for what I had done. It didn't help that all of the people who had so kindly bestowed travel advice upon me had never before been to Europe. The foremost of these advisors being, of course, my mother, who has never ventured more than twenty miles from her driveway after experiencing turbulence on her first and last plane ride back in '67.

I arrived in London wearing the thickest, itchiest wool turtleneck of all time. My mother, the world traveler, had warned me that London would be "bone-chillingly" cold. Not true. With the combination of my extremely long hair, the horrid humidity, and the five pounds of wool on my back, I was sweating profusely before I even left the airport. Not to mention the red rash spreading on my neck from the wool.

The next bit of priceless wisdom I had received was not to take a cab anywhere because it would be too expensive. However, I can tell you that after trudging up and down hilly, cobblestone roads for three hours while carrying everything I owned—there was no price I wouldn't have paid to have the feeling back in my arms. Finally, just as I could see my new college in the foggy distance, I collapsed on the nearest park bench.

As I sat in the rain, surrounded by two suitcases, three duffle bags, a backpack, a video camera, and a purse, I gazed at my future home and thought, "How in the world did I end up *here*?" Unfortunately, I knew the answer—and as you might imagine, it had a little something to do with a boy.

We met in the college bookstore. I stopped in to buy what turned out to be some frighteningly large British literature books. As I was staring at the pile of books and seriously contemplating a change of major, a voice greeted me from behind the counter. He asked if I was an English major and we chatted for a few minutes. My overly jealous boyfriend at the time, who was standing next to me, probably would have called it flirting; however, I didn't think too much of our initial meeting.

It was fall. Every Thursday, we would cross paths as I walked to my Spanish class. Before I knew it, I began looking forward to that class more and more. We didn't talk very much, just kind of looked at each other and exchanged a sarcastic remark or two. This continued until we both showed up at a meeting to write for the school newspaper. We ended up hanging out in his dorm that night... and all of the nights after that.

I listened while he played guitar and sang me his favorite songs. I read him stories and shared my aspirations of becoming a writer. He told me about all of the crazy places he had lived and the people he had met. We talked about life and all of the stuff that made us who we were. It was almost as if I was a different person inside those walls, and everything I hated most about my life didn't seem to matter as much. It was safe and happy, and I hated leaving. But we couldn't have been more different. I was the cautious observer and he was the adventurous risk-taker; nonetheless, he got me. And in a way that I couldn't fully realize then.

So we lived happily ever after, right? Well, as much as we wanted to be together, I knew deep down that he had dreams that needed room to breathe, and I would never be able to move away from my family, who needed me. Despite all of his convincing, I was stubborn. Or maybe I was just scared.

One snowy night, it was particularly hard to leave his dorm. I finally closed the door and started running up the hill to my car, when all of the sudden he yelled for me to stop. As we stood there shivering, with the snow falling around us, he summed up what seemed to be the root of my unhappiness. He told me I was unhappy because of fear. Fear of disappointing others, of not meeting expectations, of failure, and even of success — that is what kept me from pursuing my dreams. He said that if I didn't stop living for everyone else and the people who held me back, I would become just another girl with a lot of potential.

Many times he had told me about his experience studying abroad and how it was one of the greatest things he ever did. I had shot down the idea on several occasions, but he kept bringing it up. By this time, it was far past the registration date for spring semester in London, but he said if I was serious about going he would make it happen. He said that sending me away would be the most difficult thing he could do, but he wanted the best for me. I had never even flown before, and now I was considering packing up my life and moving to a foreign country. Not to mention the depression that my mother would inevitably slip into when I told her I was leaving. I also knew that if I left, he would not be there when I returned.

But as fate and guts would have it, three weeks later I boarded a plane to London and began a semester that changed my life. And *that*... is how I got there. I guess you could say it was all because of a boy in a bookstore.

~Britteny Elrick

Puzzle Pieces

I've learned that people will forget what you said,
people will forget what you did,
but people will never forget how you made them feel.
~Maya Angelou

"**J**ust do what you do." That's what Matt would always say to me when trying to decide what to do in a situation, but this is not the only phrase that is permanently engraved in my mind....

Matt and I met through friends, and there was something about the way that he made me laugh that made me want to see him again. The next time we hung out, we spent hours talking interspersed with some kissing. He walked me to the door, kissed me goodnight, and ended by saying "I can't wait to call you tomorrow!" with a giant grin on his face. As I walked home at four o'clock in the morning, I thought to myself, "Crap, I'm going to fall in love with this boy, and I'm pretty sure I could spend the rest of my life with him."

After a first date, and two weeks of hanging out almost every day, Matt was officially my boyfriend. A week later, he said those three little words that I had been waiting to hear all my life: I love you.

We were crazy in love. Like two pieces to our own puzzle—a perfect fit. We were that couple; holding hands all the time, making out in public, dancing too much, unable to keep our hands off each other. Most important was our constant laughter, even when I was curled up in his arms watching a movie. I was genuinely happy. Not just because I was in love, but because I was me, and he loved me for me. I didn't have to play stupid games or put on make-up or shower after I went to the gym. I didn't have to put on a show. I was just being myself, and I felt more secure in my own skin that I had ever felt because of Matt: my Matty.

Summer break came, and in the fall he was going to spend the semester in France. But that didn't scare us. We spent the summer months traveling between his home and mine, eating great food, and doing absolutely nothing together. We talked about the upcoming semester, and at this point we both knew that we were going to spend the rest of our lives together.

He called it a "serious, serious" relationship—and I was done. Done dating, done with the mind games. I had given my heart to him completely. I had met the person I was going to marry, build a family and grow old with. Throughout all of that, I knew that Matt would love me no matter what.

We spent the day before he left in Manhattan, running errands, having lunch, and enjoying each other's company. We had decided to take a break for the semester, knowing very well we would get back together when he returned. We knew the time distance and our different schedules would put a strain on our relationship, so it was not worth ruining something that we knew was great and would last a lifetime.

We kissed goodbye in the middle of Grand Central Terminal. His arms wrapped tightly around my waist, and mine around his neck. His last words to me were "I'll always love you, don't forget that!" He dropped his sunglasses over his eyes, and I did the same as tears rolled down my cheeks. We turned and walked our separate ways. I described that day as the perfect goodbye, and it was. Little did I know it was the last time he'd ever hold me in his arms.

We talked via Skype, and I sent him e-mails reminding him that I still loved him. On Monday, September 29th, we video chatted, and I walked away from the conversation feeling great, knowing that everything was going to work out okay. That was the last time I ever spoke to my Matty.

I'll never forget Friday, October 3rd. My friends sat me down in a bedroom, telling me I couldn't go into work yet. I knew something was wrong. We waited in silence. When the door opened, my good friend, who was the president of Matt's fraternity, came into the room, and I knew. Brad sat down on the edge of the bed, and looked at me with such sad eyes.

"Amanda, I have some bad news," he said. "Matt passed away this morning."

I shook uncontrollably, sobbing into my best friend's arms. The next two weeks were a blur. I could not function. I did not understand. I was in a daze, and still cannot recall a lot of those days. I did not go to class. I passed most of my days in his fraternity house with boys who had become my family. My friends told me when to shower, eat, and sleep. When I showered, I washed my face with my body wash, or washed my hair twice because I couldn't remember if I had washed it or not. I wore all black, my face pale from my emptiness.

The day of the funeral shattered my hopes that it had just been a dream. It was a Jewish funeral, so they lowered him, my Matty, the boy I was going to marry and love forever, into the ground. I shook uncontrollably, clutching my friend's arm to remain standing. I cried hysterically, and I can't remember when I took my turn to shovel dirt onto his coffin.

The next thing I knew, I was digging my nails into my friend's suit and sobbing into his shoulder. I couldn't feel my legs, and attempted to use my arms to hold myself up. As my tears started to slow and my breathing returned to normal, I looked around to see all of his fraternity brothers crying, most of whom could barely look at me. I was given many hugs, and slowly it was time to leave.

Almost three months have passed, and I'm doing better. I'm still in love with him, and I know I always will be. How could I not always hold a place in my heart for someone so incredible? Matt brought me to life; he sparked something in me that made me want to be a better person. Even though I lost the love of my life, I gained an entire fraternity of boys as friends and family.

"Just doing what I do" wasn't the big lesson that I learned from loving Matt, and then losing him in the worst way. It taught me to live my life, and live it to the fullest. I'm grateful for every moment, and I make sure to do what's going to make me most happy, which means laughing as much as possible with people who are important to me.

Don't let life pass you by. It's way too short and in an instant it can be taken away. Try something new, even if it's as small as a tasting new food — or as great as falling in love.

~Amanda Romaniello

Experiment

All life is an experiment.
The more experiments you make the better.
~Ralph Waldo Emerson

My freshman year of college, I experimented. But not in the sense that would make most parents squeamish. In high school, I found my niche. I had a set group of friends, I was a member of clubs, I was a part of sports teams, I wrote for publications, and I felt comfortable knowing I had a place I belonged.

In college, I entered as a guppy in a sea of students who meant nothing to me. In this new world, I was undefined, and I immediately searched for a place where I fit in. I tried out for the cheerleading squad, to no avail. I tried out for the dance team and left tryouts intimidated. So I moved on to Plan C. Second semester of freshman year I decided to take a swing dancing class. I wanted to meet new people and I figured what better way to do so than in a completely forced social setting. This was the best decision I made throughout my college years—next to refraining from going out and drinking that Tuesday night before my big test, and deciding not to spend the night with the fraternity boy who asked me to his formal.

Swing dance class met every Tuesday and Thursday in the basement of the university gymnasium. I could not have been more nervous—a little freshman, unsure of what to wear for swing class, what shoes to bring, or who my classmates would be. I didn't know the first thing about swing dancing. The class consisted of about seven girls and four boys, one of whom caught my eye. Standing at 6'2" in his jeans, tight T-shirt, and sneakers, I knew I had seen him before but I couldn't place him. Then I realized that he was in my communications class the previous semester. He was the outspoken one who sat in the middle of my row and was always on his laptop. I remembered being impressed by him and his quick, witty responses when the teacher called on the student least likely to be paying attention. That was how I remembered Eamon Brennan. The story of how we fell in love is much more remarkable.

Swing class began with the choice of a partner. Rather than being forward and running over to the cute boy to ask him to dance, I waited on the side of the room to be selected. Unfortunately, one of the socially awkward boys in the corner decided to make his way over to me and asked if I'd be his partner. As I glanced at Eamon, who had made eye contact with me, I felt the urge to say "I'd rather dance with the sexy boy over there " but instead I said, "Sure "

Luckily, I soon found out you switch partners, moving clockwise after every count of eight. Three partners later, I was in Eamon's arms... literally. We officially introduced ourselves and danced as if we had been friends, maybe even more, for years and years. Our eyes locked and even when we weren't partners we made eye contact across the room. Our secret glances were betrayed by the mirrored walls, and the chemistry could be felt across the room. Two or three weeks went by with us exchanging flirtatious glances, and one night after class Eamon asked if he could walk me home. I ecstatically accepted and so began our series of dates.

Eamon and I have been dating for nearly two years now and my college experience has been greatly shaped by my decision to take that swing dance class.

I wasn't looking to find love when I enrolled in a swing dance class and I wasn't looking to find a lifelong hobby. I was exploring my options. The best advice I can give a college student is to experiment. Don't experiment with sex, drugs, and rock and roll—but experiment with the things that will matter in ten years. Experiment with the things that help you find your own current in a sea of swimming fish.

~Jamie Miles

Have No Fear

Moving on is simple. It's what you leave behind that makes it so difficult.
~Anonymous

W ords of advice to high school seniors preparing to embark on the infamous college journey: Have no fear. Worst case scenario, you end up sitting on the stoop of a grand, New England building, drunk off cheap beer, crying about a boy while listening to Joni Mitchell on your iPod.

It had been a little over a year since Nathan and I had finally ended our mess of a relationship. He was wrong for me in every way, but I was nineteen and thought I was madly in love. Rather than love me for who I was, he treated me badly, which only fed into my insecurities. That year was ripe with epiphanies, all of which helped me to realize that what my friends and family had always told me was true: A guy like Nathan didn't deserve a girl like me, and our separation was for the best.

I was a late bloomer, and it wasn't until junior year of college that I really felt myself coming into my own. I was free from a relationship that had made into someone I was not, and I began to dedicate my free time to friends and activities that made me truly happy. My heartache had nearly vanished. I had met a few nice guys, nothing serious, but that was fine with me. I didn't want to fall back into the mentality of needing someone else to make me happy.

Girls repeatedly and proudly declare that they fall for the bad boys. I know because I used to be one of them. Let me save you years and years of grief right now—you are the only one who will finish last if you don't pick the nice guy.

On a deliciously warm spring night in Boston, my friend threw a party. I remember standing on the tiny balcony outside her room and peering down at the crowd of college students that had gathered. Below me was a sea of baseball hats emblazoned with the letter "B," short skirts, and high heels. I closed my eyes; all the voices seemed to fuse together in one intoxicated rant. I let the noise drone on, enjoying the feel of the warm wind playing with my hair, when suddenly a girl's voice broke free and I heard a very distinct, "Nathan!" My eyes flew open, and I traced the voice back to a blond girl waving at someone. I allowed my eyes to follow the invisible line to the person on the other end and sure enough, it was Nathan. My Nathan.

I watched as they greeted each other, him swooping her into a hug, and her face beaming on the other side of his embrace. I watched as they disappeared into the house, and I willed myself to stay perfectly still as my body and mind filled with the memory of him, of us. I was shocked at my reaction. Although I believe no one ever truly gets over any relationship, I hadn't felt any romantic feelings for him in months, and yet something inside me was pushing me to him. I had to go downstairs to find my friends; surely they would talk some sense into me.

I ventured down the spiral staircase looking for a familiar face. I felt the panic rise up inside me. The last time I had felt like this was over a year ago, when I felt like I had no control over my thoughts and actions.

I realized that I wasn't looking for my friends. I was looking for him. For some inexplicable reason I had to talk to him. I felt like I was in *The Twilight Zone*. I had seen him enter the house no more than two minutes ago, and now he was nowhere to be found.

Frantically, I made my way outside. I had to get back into the fresh air, and I needed quiet so I could call him. Looking back, it was as though someone else's brain had taken over mine. This was not me, but I couldn't stop myself.

I watched as I scrolled down to the familiar number on my phone, albeit one that I hadn't dialed in a very long time. I brought the phone to my ear and began to walk. For some reason, the thought of standing still was impossible. I listened as it rang and rang, until finally an operator's voice spoke clearly on the other end, "The number you have dialed is no longer in service. Please hang up and try again." I was dumbfounded. Clearly there had been a mistake—this was his number, and it had been for two years. I tried again, and again, all to no avail. By this point, I couldn't tell if I wanted to talk to him anymore, or if I just wanted to prove to myself that the operator was wrong.

Out of pure frustration, I sat down on the stoop of a building. I had to gather my thoughts. I turned on my iPod, and Joni Mitchell's sweet, steady voice began to calm my anxiety. To my surprise, I felt tears streaming down my cheeks. I was all out of energy and excuses, and despite the fact that I was in public, I made no attempt to wipe my tears.

I buried my head in my lap for just a moment, and when I looked up, three boys were standing in front of me.

"Are you okay?" One of them cautiously asked, since I'm sure I looked like a mess.

"I'm fine," I lied.

"What are you listening to?"

"Joni Mitchell."

"Which album?"

"*Blue*."

He broke into a smile, "Well no matter what you're upset about, at least you have great taste in music." With that, he walked away, and the other two followed.

I should have been embarrassed but I just felt foolish. After all I had learned, I had let one silly moment push me back to ground zero, as if I hadn't spent the last year loving me for me.

It took the simple words of a stranger to help me remember that I was going to be absolutely fine, and that's the beauty of college. You never know who you're going to meet, and what wisdom they have to impart. So have no fear, you will be fine, and you just might learn a few things.

~Chase Bernstein

Closure

Courage is the power to let go of the familiar.
~Raymond Lindquist

I called my roommate as I was sitting in my car on the side of the highway. I had pulled over because I had a sudden urge to turn around and go back home. I couldn't decide if I should go to him, or go home.

"Go there," she said, "If you don't, you might regret it for the rest of your life. You have to know where this will take you, and if doesn't take you anywhere, at least you'll know for sure. And you can move on." She was right. After hanging up, I put the car in drive and started again in the direction of his house.

I pulled up to the house and took a minute to freshen up my make-up, adding a little lip gloss, just in case. I saw him open his front door and walk out towards my car as I got out. We both had smiles on our faces and halfway to the house we met, embracing.

"I missed you so much," he said while we hugged. I stopped and checked out the "New Eric."

"Wow, you look good," I said, flirtatiously.

"You look amazing," he complimented. We walked into his house and sat on the edge of his bed as he fumbled with my shirtsleeve. While we made small talk, I tried to ignore the memory of his choosing another girl over me last year. He told me all of the things I had wanted to hear for months, and it was nice to hear, but it didn't feel right. I chalked it up to nerves, until he pulled me into a kiss that caught me off guard. I didn't feel any sparks. Why didn't this feel right? He looked at me and smiled, "I've missed you for so long, it's almost unreal that you're here with me now."

Somehow, making out with him felt like kissing the back of my hand, and it started to worry me. I should love this! Why does it feel so plain? It wasn't the same. Something was different.

Then it hit me—I was different.

I lightly pushed him to lie beside me. I glanced at the clock. I had been there only thirty minutes and I hadn't even gotten to talk about the past and what had happened since we were dating.

"Eric, what's different with you?" I asked him, attempting to make things right before they got too serious. "You told me on the phone you had a lot to tell me. Talk to me for a bit."

"I missed you and I miss you. Come back and be with me. When we broke up, I did it because I didn't want to hold you back. You were well on your way to a new life, going out and having fun, but still keeping your head on straight. That's what's so cool about you." What he didn't know was that the whole time I was out looking like I was having a blast, I was really dying inside to be back here in his arms. But now I wasn't sure if I wanted to get serious with a man who had dropped me.

He curled up beside me and I held his hand. The room was quiet, but my mind was busy with thoughts and questions about all the pain he put me through when I was in my first year of college... wanting to be with me and then not, blowing me off, hurting me over and over again. Why should I go back to someone who controlled my every feeling for four years, cheated on me, and still managed to haunt me? I decided then I was ready to move on. This was exactly what I had needed—closure.

I took a deep breath. "Let's just call it what it is, and what it was, Eric. We both know that this wouldn't work out, even if we tried," I said without looking at him.

It must have taken a moment for the words to set in, and then he slowly let go of my hand and scooted away from me. "What? Why? I mean, if that's how you feel, then why did you come over to see me?" He looked so sad and angry at the same time.

"I wanted to see you. I missed you too; I wasn't lying about that, Eric. But seeing you is too strange for me. We can't jump into something that has changed so much. I just don't have it in me to try a round two."

He shook his head from side to side and then left the room, returning later with a drink in his hand. "I can't believe you," he said. "What does a guy need to do to prove he's changed?" But it didn't matter anymore. I couldn't force myself to feel anything for him. He sat on the edge of his bed with his back towards me.

"It's up to you. You know your way out of here, but if you go, you can't come back," he said quietly.

There it was—an ultimatum. It was now or never.

I stood there, contemplating the idea that he might just be sincere enough to have changed for me. But just as the happy memories from before came into mind, the bad quickly followed. Here he was, immature and upset, because I couldn't ignore the hurt he had given me for so long. Just because now he was ready didn't mean I was. After all, I had been waiting for a long time, and he didn't even give me a chance.

Giving him a light hug and a kiss on the shoulder, I got up and went for the door. This time after I walked out, I closed it behind me. I was finally closing the door on that chapter of my life. My roommate was right. This was exactly what I needed. I needed to see exactly what I wasn't missing.

I left there feeling refreshed. I guess after being hurt for so long, it made it easier to walk away. He had laid the cards on the table and made his bet, but I had chosen to quit the game forever. I didn't want to gamble with my heart anymore.

On the way home, he sent me a text:

Come back. Why are you doing this to me?

I looked at it and replied to his text:

I can't handle this anymore. I'm sorry.

That was it, my final goodbye. The drive home was smooth. I went back to my dorm and took a shower. I washed away any feeling of regret that lingered. Then I put on different clothes and got in bed. After turning out the lamp, sleep came rather easily that night. The next morning, I woke up emotionally ready to begin the first day of the rest of my life.

~Monica Sizemore

Campus Chronicles

Trying New Things

Anyone who has never made a mistake has never tried anything new.

~Albert Einstein

A Picture's Worth

The traveler sees what he sees. The tourist sees what he has come to see.
~G.K. Chesterton

When I went abroad, I chose Scotland seemingly at random, and St Andrews because it appeared to be the best of all possible options. There was an ocean, an entirely different culture, and a university full of traditions that had been around longer than my country.

I was sent an orientation guide full of things to keep in mind that ranged from the practical to the silly. For example, they made a big fuss about the fact that "I'll knock you up" means one thing in America, but in the UK it means "I'll knock on your door."

For the record, that has never come up in conversation during my time in the UK.

There were other things, like what a "quid" is (slang for a pound, the unit of currency, like "buck" refers to the dollar), warnings that only Americans or athletes wear white socks, and the all-mighty "what you'll need" list, including hiking boots (used them once), a backpack (used it but made myself look like a tourist in doing so), and a hidden passport pouch (don't get me started on this one).

Maybe all of that should have tipped me off, but part of me just didn't understand that when I got off that flight and opened exhausted eyes to the Scottish sun, I would be in an entirely different world.

To be fair, like many American Junior Year Abroad students at St Andrews, I didn't live a markedly different life from my one at my home college. Most of my friends had accents, that's true, and in my spare time I found myself in front of the Sacré-Coeur or the Tuscan hills. I was of a legal drinking age and found myself at pubs with my friends, but overall, nothing much had really changed when I look back on it. The scenery had switched and the people had rotated out, but I was still a college student living a college life.

I had this desperate need, as so many JYAs do, to take full advantage of this time in my life. Many of my peers thought this meant seeing as many countries as physically possible, and that was my first deviation. I knew I didn't want to fly past landmarks with my eyes hidden behind a camera, only pausing to absorb when I was back home and uploading the photos. I wanted to bask.

When I went to the Sacré-Coeur for the first time, I remember sitting on the steps in front of it with my breakfast, looking out over Paris as a light fog lifted. I took a few pictures, and then I put the camera away and I took a few deep breaths, not talking to the friend beside me. I got the sense then that there are pictures and there are moments, and your desire for the picture should never get in the way of the moment itself.

It was the beginning of a change.

I ended up transferring to St Andrews and finishing my degree there. For whatever the reason, I got the sense that I just was not finished with it yet. There was something that I hadn't felt yet, some immersion that just hadn't happened. There was a part of me yet to be fulfilled, a part of my home culture yet to be shed to fully dive into Scottish life.

I avidly pursued my degree, following my passion for writing in a way that wasn't encouraged in the States. My teachers and my family warned me that writing just wasn't a practical career; it wasn't likely to yield a sustainable income. In Scotland, for the first time, I felt like my passion was supported and encouraged; if I wanted to be a writer, what business did I have pursuing anything other than writing?

I continued to travel, and I stopped taking tours and started staying with friends, diving into a more genuine experience of a different location. I still took some amazing pictures, but those pictures were filled with laughter, with friends, with moments that I still look at and say, "No, wait, you have to hear the story behind that one!"

At the end of my senior year (fourth year, as they call it in Scotland), the days began stretching longer. Scotland is far enough north that the length of the day varies greatly based on the time of the year, and as June bloomed, the days seemed endless, as if they were accommodating the dwindling time I had left in the country.

My family arrived, early enough to do some traveling and make the best of their time abroad, and then we settled in for Graduation Week. My graduation ceremony itself was unlike anything I had seen, with traditions dating back hundreds of years. I remember the feeling of waiting in the wings, a faculty member straightening my robes and showing me how to hold my silk hood so that the University Principal could cast it over my shoulders and indicate that I was a proud graduate of the university.

I crossed the stage and knelt on a velvet step. The principal slapped me on the head with a piece of cloth (a piece of John Knox's pants, actually) and hooded me, and I rose a graduate.

The last event of Graduation Week was the Graduation Ball, and even that went far too quickly. It came to its bittersweet conclusion, and my friends and I looked to each other and knew it wasn't time to say goodbye just yet.

We went the only logical place to go. There is a beach beneath the ruins of St Andrews Castle, partially hidden from the cliffs above, and it was the site of countless memorable nights in St Andrews, the site of the infamous May Dip, a beautiful place that was as meaningful to students hundreds of years ago as it is today. I stood at the top of the cliff, about to go down to the beach, and I stopped.

It was almost 2 A.M., but the sun hadn't set completely. It was a small light in the corner of the sky, hiding just behind the ruins of the castle, just below the horizon but still casting a blue glow. The light refracted and set the tumultuous North Sea glittering, glowing, shining with unbelievable flecks of light blue against the velvet navy sky.

I couldn't move. I didn't reach for my camera. Tears began

welling in my eyes and my friend touched my arm and whispered, "I know."

People around us were trying to snap pictures, but their frustration was vocal and obvious; it just wasn't transferring into a photo. It was only appropriate, really. That moment could never be captured, could never be framed, could never be shared, and yet it will never be forgotten. Like all experiences that shape us and change us, it is right behind my eyes, ready to be called up, never far from my mind and my heart.

It wasn't just that I graduated. I had learned to live my life for the moments, and not for the pictures.

~AC Gaughen

Se Perde, Si Trova

Half the fun of the travel is the esthetic of lostness.
~Ray Bradbury

As I stepped onto the deck of the boat, with the sun shining on my back, I felt my heart begin to race. I closed my eyes and inhaled deeply, breathing in the sweet scent of the Adriatic Sea. I was about to set foot in a city that has left writers, painters, and philosophers baffled for centuries. I was about to spend a month in Venice.

If I could describe Venice in one word, it would be surreal. When you initially look at it, you can't help but pinch yourself, thinking its creators must have taken its design right out of childhood fairytales. It's as if you are about to enter a stunning castle surrounded by a majestic moat that is the Grand Canal. I knew as soon as stepped onto my first Venetian bridge that this was going to be a life-changing experience.

There are no cars in Venice, only boats, and it is a city of tight alleyways connected by several bridges, peppered with tiny shops and restaurants. It was clear to me that finding my way around was not going to be easy. But interestingly enough, the first thing the tour guide said to us was that in order to find our way, we were going to have to get lost. "*Se perde, si trova*," she would say. "If you get lost, you find yourself." I knew for a fact that this was going to happen, but for some reason, having always been horrible with directions, I had a feeling that this time around I was not going to mind it so much.

The first week flew by, as everyone on the trip began to get settled in and figure out what they were going to need for classes. On top of that, because we were still trying to get accustomed to our new surroundings and conquer the dreadful jet lag, everyone traveled together in groups. I didn't mind doing this, because I immediately found myself forming close friendships with several different people. We had something very significant in common; we were all trying to find our way. The second week was a little bit different, we traveled a lot more, especially to other parts of Italy, but I still hadn't gotten my much-anticipated opportunity to walk around the city by myself. I just wanted to be able to think and take in everything on a much deeper level than I had up until that point, and I knew if I was walking around with my friends this wasn't going to happen. Then, my last week in Venice, it did.

I had gotten out of class much earlier than usual and, coincidentally enough, had just finished reading a piece of work by George Sand, an author who spent much time in Venice trying to understand it and experience it to its fullest. One of the things she said was that all she wanted to do was walk around by herself, and this was the only way to really experience the city. I realized this was a perfect opportunity for me to do just that.

My aimless wandering around did not seem so aimless at first; it appeared I knew where I was going. But pretty soon, I was going down random alleyways unsure of where they would take me, and before I knew it, I was completely lost. I knew I'd stay lost until I found familiar landmarks — perhaps a restaurant I had visited, or a small shop.

Nervousness began to slowly consume me, because what seemed like only minutes of being lost quickly turned into what seemed like hours. And then out of nowhere I decided to take an unknown right turn. What I then came across was nothing less than what I've seen in Van Gogh paintings. I was in front of a railing, looking straight out into the Adriatic Sea, with what appeared to be a library on an island in the middle of it. Past the library was nothing but water.

It's difficult to explain what I felt at this moment. I took a seat on a bench and closed my eyes for a few moments. I ran every obstacle I had been faced with since being in college through my head over and over again, especially the past year and a half. It was like I could still harness the feelings of hopelessness if I tried hard enough. It gave me shivers thinking about it. And then, there I was, staring at this vast body of water that went on for miles. I was in what has been labeled the most mysterious and beautiful city in the world. I was on another continent.

It was honestly at that moment that I realized how many opportunities are available out there, and I knew I was meant to do something significant. Whether I end up applying my talents to singing, or decide to help people, I knew at that moment that from then on I had to focus on the things that make me happy, and not others. It was then that I knew something in me had shifted, and when it was time for me to go back to school, I would feel completely different.

The rest of the trip was amazing and filled with many classic times. But nothing compared to how I felt on that specific day, when so many different things began to make sense to me. It was as if that missing neuron in my brain finally clicked. I came back to school to find myself surrounded by much of the same trivial nonsense that I had left behind.

I am not sure if everyone was as changed as I was on this trip. After having experienced that moment on the bench, it made me realize just how very lost I was for so long. And to be honest, I still don't have all of the answers. But I guess it's not so bad getting lost, because in the end, you're really going to find your way. And more importantly, in the end, you're going to find yourself.

~Annmarie Sitar

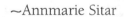

Taking a Break
from Spring Break

How wonderful it is that nobody need wait a single moment
before starting to improve the world.
~Anne Frank

A lot of people, when they think of college, think of endless parties, keg stands, and an even more endless supply of cute guys (or girls). And when it comes to Spring Break, they think of all of these things even more so, once they've gotten the cheapest flight to South Padre Island, Cabo San Lucas, or whatever the latest hip place is to go on a college budget.

I, too, was excited by all the prospects of a fun Spring Break location, especially this spring, during my senior year of college. Would I go to Texas... or maybe pay a bit more and go to Mexico or Jamaica? This being my last year of college, I wanted to make it good.

My friends all had various ideas, but I kept feeling that I wanted to do something different, with different people... but where, and with whom? Everyone but me was booking their airline tickets and hotels; time was about to run out.

Being at Marquette University, a Catholic school, I walked by the campus chapel and prayed for a sign. I looked around, but there were no signs in sight.

Toward the end of the day, I was running late between classes, so I detoured through the school Union, where I saw my sign — literally.

A poster board was on display in the middle of the foyer, "Looking for something different to do during Spring Break this year? Take an M.A.P. trip." (M.A.P. stands for "Marquette Action Program.")

As I read—about road-tripping to another state with a handful of other students, living in a low-income housing area, praying, making meals together—a girl came up and asked if I wanted to sign up. "I was just looking," I muttered. "We could use another person," she said. I thought about my friends' plans: sunbathing on the beach, staying out all night, meeting out-of-state guys... and decided right then and there that I could do the same thing—only, I would be in the snow, staying in all night with unknown classmates, and still meeting out-of-state guys in Rochester, NY. I had never been to New York, so I was intrigued.

Instead of spending money, I'd be saving it. Instead of spending time with people I knew, I'd be spending it with people I didn't. Instead of watching people try to use their fake IDs to get into bars, I'd be helping people who were recently released from behind bars of another kind.

When I told my friends, they were confused as to why I'd want to spend our last Spring Break away from them. I remember one saying, "So you'd rather pay to help the poor than pay to get a tan in Cabo?" "Yes," I said without hesitating. While my friends and apartment-mates packed bikinis and sunscreen, I packed my winter coat and gloves. While they put their plane tickets into their purses, I got into a university-sponsored van with four strangers for an eleven-hour drive from Milwaukee, WI, to Rochester, NY.

We finally arrived in Rochester, and our destination turned out to be a decrepit side street. I thought surely we must have been on the wrong street. We're sleeping here? In this neighborhood? And at a house with bars on the windows, one of them boarded up from what I could only imagine was a gunshot? And my friends are on the beach in Cabo San Lucas? Is it too late to get a ticket and join them? Maybe my mom could wire me the money. As I thought about all these things, a priest, Father Jim, came out and greeted us. He lived here and we'd be staying with him.

That first night, I didn't sleep. How could I, with all the visions of drive-by shootings I'd seen on the news? In no time at all, Father Jim was waking us up — at 6 A.M. Didn't Spring Break mean sleeping in? I bet my friends were doing that…. Father Jim explained that we had a lot of work to do. We'd start by volunteering at his parish, at a clothing drive. Then we'd go to a homeless shelter and play cards with people, as well as babysit some of their kids. Afterwards, we'd go to the local diner for lunch, a restaurant run by ex-inmates trying to turn their lives around. I imagined my friends ordering room service. Wasn't the point of Spring Break to take a break?

As the days went on, I thought less and less of my friends in Cabo and more and more about the people we were serving. There was Dolores, who became a regular at the homeless shelter after she became disabled, lost her job, and couldn't provide for her kids anymore on her own. She liked coming to the shelter for the camaraderie, limping from table to table, joining this game of bridge or that one; she was the reigning champ. There was Ted, a big, buff guy who worked at the diner as a waiter, who could have easily been a linebacker for the Packers in another place and time. He had been in jail for almost a decade, and was grateful to be anywhere but behind bars. There was Sheila, who hated for her kids to know how poor they were. She always tried to get to the church clothing drives first, to find the clothes with the fewest holes and things she could easily mend. When I looked at Sheila and her kids, I got tears in my eyes as I was reminded of going to church basement clothing sales as a child with my mother after her divorce.

At the end of the week, I didn't want to leave Rochester. As we drove away, I already missed everyone we'd met; I even missed the ducking down in Father Jim's house every time I heard a noise, something I had stopped doing by week's end.

When we got back to Milwaukee, I looked at my friends, hungover and sunburned from their Spring Breaks. They went on about the guys they had met — I went on about the ones I had met, too. I wondered if Dolores was still beating everyone at bridge. I thought about what Ted was serving as the dinner special tonight, curious as to when I would be a customer again. And I hoped that Sheila would continue to find the best secondhand clothes for her kids.

Even though my friends wanted me to spend Spring Break with them, I am glad I took a Spring Break of a different kind. After all, that's what college is all about: trying new things, even if that means spending Spring Break in the snow with a bunch of strangers.

~Natalia K. Lusinski

The Path
of a College
Entrepreneur

Success is a journey, not a destination. The doing is often more important than the outcome.
~Arthur Ashe

8:05 A.M. March 5, 2007: Washington, DC

Jumping down from the top bunk in my freshman dorm room, I feel a rush of excitement. Immediately I remember how early it is and that I should avoid waking my roommate. But there is so much to do! I need to call members of the team to confirm plans for today. I need to contact the farm and make sure all is organized for the truck to navigate through the narrow streets of Georgetown. Mark Toigo is personally driving the Toigo Orchards products down to supply our first delivery.

We have over eighty orders... not bad for the first day. Our group of eight should be able to handle those, right? But wait, Georgetown's off-campus deliveries might be harder. I'll call two friends to stand by as backups.

I need to brainstorm a solid marketing pitch for our service. When people see us carrying bags of fruit and ask, "What is Mission Three?" I need to be ready with the perfect explanation: "Mission Three is a fresh farm delivery service... and it's called Mission Three because our three values are Health, Environment, and Community." A month and a half ago, on the back of my pre-calculus notebook, I had drawn out ideas to create a partnership with local farmers and deliver their products to students. Now the concept is becoming reality.

10:07 A.M. August 3, 2007: Taipei, Taiwan

What on earth am I doing in Taiwan? It's so crazy to think that after six hours of work in the library, we wrote and submitted a fifty-page business plan to an international entrepreneurial contest. We are now presenting the company in our second foreign country this summer — the only American team here, and one of the youngest.

With a slight glance back, I think to myself that the Mission Three booth looks so much better after the improvements we made. In Panama it was decent, but nothing like this... custom banners showing our values, a quality image backdrop of Toigo Orchards, M3 canvas bags, the three of us in M3 shirts and even some Taiwanese fruit to show our efforts to always "keep it local."

I'm nervous about presenting the company to a panel of Taiwanese judges. I was told that our holistic approach might not jive with Asian sentiments. Nevertheless, I'll be content regardless of the outcome. I'm so glad that Julia, our head of philanthropy, is here to do the presentation with me. We can't go wrong when speaking from the heart about helping local farmers and offering affordable, healthy products to students.

9:56 P.M. November 16, 2007: Washington, DC

Running up the red brick staircase near the center of

campus, I feel overwhelmed. The thought of finishing my business stats homework for my 8 A.M. class doesn't faze me. Mission Three is what's really on my mind; especially the daunting thought of the meeting that I just left. I think about how well the Georgetown team has done since we moved to restructure the company, but how stressful the whole thing has been. We have maintained well over one hundred weekly subscribers to our service, but each team member has had a difficult time balancing challenging classes with coordinating a delivery service.

I think about how significant tonight's meeting was, for the simple reason that it adjourned with all of the team leaders' resignations. I had loaded them with too much work and too much responsibility. I had failed to spread out the workload down the chain.

I am concerned about next semester. What will we do? We have a great website. We have another location starting at Loyola. But this is our home base. We can't lose it. We can't throw in the towel. We have to make it work. I have to make it work.

I think back to a little over a month ago when a good friend from home passed away. I had to coordinate many people to fill the gap I left when I departed for the week. I remember how much I believe that a good leader should never ask of his workers what he would not do himself, but also that good leader should know how to delegate and teach others. I now realize the extent to which I have not done enough of the latter.

10:30 P.M. May 6, 2008: Washington, DC

Opening the grand doors of the McDonough School of Business boardroom, where Mission Three is now able to meet, optimism fills my mind as I see our team members gather around the table. I initiate a discussion about the new website for our newly branded delivery service. I think about the future of the service: our new Georgetown team, the one in Loyola, and my hopes to position the service so it can serve more students with more products.

Finally, I move to the last item on our agenda, the discussion of a new concept. After a few nights of passionate, philosophical conversations followed up by copious diagrams and charts to explain the idea, I try to present it simply: an ethical consulting service focused on the areas of Health, Environment, and Community. Looking around the room, I see mixed expressions—excitement, confusion, and apathy. I decide to explain a bit more: it's an ethical auditing service, whereby students are trained as consultants to analyze businesses and work with the business owners to set goals for improvements and create transparency for consumers. The expressions around the room are now a bit more relaxed and pleasant. I take that as a sign that perhaps it could work.

5:14 P.M. October 2, 2008: Viña Del Mar, Chile

Sipping a cup of coffee with my Chilean host family, I think about the multiple Skype calls I need to make tonight. I'm eager to get started on work now, yet I haven't been able to spend a lot of quality time with the family. Also, I could use more practice speaking Spanish, so I'll stick around at the table a little longer.

My excitement stems from the three services now under Mission Three, each at different stages, everything strongly moving forward. M3E Consulting now has fifteen team members and after receiving an award grant, it recently finished consulting its fifth client. We're launching a new college bike rental program called BorrowBike, and I am now at the drawing board with a new long-term concept: the establishment of a DC-based entrepreneurial incubation program that will offer an incredible learning experience to aspiring entrepreneurs.

Yeah sure, with these three endeavors I'm logging in more hours to Gmail and less to sleep, but that is to be expected. As far as studying in Chile for the semester, I have no regrets. The rich experience of being abroad is proving to be cultural and engaging. In fact, being out of the country, I'm finally learning the thing I never did quite well enough before: how to delegate. Our three services have depended on it and this truly has become the team endeavor that I always hoped for.

I feel a sense of accomplishment and joy, having had this experience at such an early age. However, at times it has been hard to backtrack and just be a student when I feel as though the entrepreneurial world is calling. Purely from a time management perspective, I have been challenged and stressed. At times, I have sacrificed my studies for my business interests. At times, this has left me desperate to find a way out and wishing that I had created a less complicated college life.

When I started Mission Three, I knew that this endeavor would provide me a remarkable hands-on learning experience; it definitely has. I have learned more about myself than I ever could have imagined. There were times along the way when my passion, commitment, and endurance were tested. Times when things looked bleak and when I considered giving up. I'm glad that I didn't.

I have come to realize that a college entrepreneur follows a path with many twists and turns. The most valuable results are not what lie at the end of that path; they lie in the journey it takes to get there.

~Arthur Woods

It's Not Just Sushi

Follow your passion, and success will follow you.
~Arthur Buddhold

Journalism—yes, in order to be a journalist you need to be able to write, but in order to be a broadcast journalist, you need to have some skills using the video camera as well. At my college, if your GPA is high enough you can opt to pursue a professional certificate through the university's School of Continuing and Professional Studies. All of the classes are non-credit and students participate in the program as an elective course of study. Being that I was studying broadcast journalism, I decided to get a certificate in digital filmmaking. I took some classes about lighting, sound and even interviewing, but the one that I learned the most from was most certainly a class called Digital Video Production I.

The class was held one day a week for eight hours each day over the summer. By the end of the class you were supposed to have finished your own short film. My professor began discussing potential topics we could pursue. He suggested doing something that had a personal meaning, but that would also appeal to a wider audience. I didn't even listen to the rest of the lecture because I knew exactly what my video was going to be about: sushi. I love sushi. Most people love sushi. I couldn't go wrong.

About a year before, I had given the Sushi Challenge at a local Japanese restaurant a shot. In order to complete the challenge, you have to eat thirty-two pieces of sushi (for a woman) or fifty-two pieces of sushi (for a man) in twenty minutes. Every time a contestant completes the challenge, the amount is raised by one. Considering I don't eat raw fish, doing the entire challenge with tomago (egg) and shrimp made it a little difficult and I lost by four pieces. As it turned out, the two worst parts about losing were paying for your sushi and leaving with a bit of a stomachache. I still thought it was worth it.

Soon after the professor approved my topic, *The Sushi Challenge* went into production. I found my actors, my equipment, and got the okay from the restaurant owner. In order to be able to film the entire thing by myself and still capture every moment and angle, I decided to have one of the actors fake the challenge. Basically, I paid for fifty-two pieces of sushi, had him pretend to stuff his face, and got myself dinner at the same time. I brought back my footage and spent the last month of class editing my material. On the last day of class I showed everyone my film. Their reaction astounded me. Not only were my production skills praised by the professor, but everyone in the class genuinely enjoyed my short.

I couldn't just let the film die with the class, so I decided to submit it to a few student filmmaking websites. On a whim, I also sent a copy to the New York International Independent Film & Video Festival. To my surprise, not only did I receive a call from a festival representative to tell me my film had been chosen, but I was also contacted by Yahoo.com. Someone at the website had seen my video on another website and wanted to feature it on their homepage for twenty-four hours. *The Sushi Challenge* went up and the phone calls started to pour in. I spoke to people I hadn't spoken to since my first years in high school. People I barely even knew sent me messages on Facebook just to tell me how much they enjoyed it. After the twenty-four-hour time period was up, over half a million people had seen my film. Their reactions were rather overwhelming.

The excitement didn't end there. November 11th rolled around—the day my film was being screened at the film festival. I was especially excited because my film was being shown in a theater that I often visit to see big, box office films. I arrived at the theater accompanied by my parents. Not only did my cousins come, as well as some close family friends, but a significant number of my sorority sisters too! You know that clichéd warm and fuzzy feeling that everyone talks about, but you don't think it's real? Well, it is. My film was screened and the reaction was more than anything I could have dreamed. I made people smile. I couldn't have asked for anything more.

I've since graduated from college, but have still left a legacy as the creator of *The Sushi Challenge*. And I'll never forget about the sushi craze I created.

~Perri Nemiroff

Backup Runner

There is no telling how many miles you will have to run while chasing a dream.
~Author Unknown

Sweat dripped from my face as I focused on my breathing. All I needed to do was pass the end line. As I passed through the town, it was just a blur; I seldom recognized anyone in the multitudes. When the water stops came, I grabbed the water, dumped it in my mouth, and took off. The fresh liquid flowed through my body and gave me strength to continue. There was a good chance of getting heat stroke from running in the sun, and if I collapsed I would not complete my objective. The steady beat of my shoes told me I was getting closer to the finish line. I had been running for one hour and forty-five minutes, when I started to think about what had happened that week. Something told me I was meant to have the great experience of running my first half marathon, since I never planned to run, and it had all happened out of the blue.

One of my friends at Masters College was going to run the Valencia Half Marathon, which is 13.1 miles, so he was training over the summer. Then, during a town clean up day, he was lifting a big tree stump and he pulled his back. Unable to run in the race, he asked a man from his dorm if he would like to run in his place. He agreed, and I was speed training with him the last two weeks before the half marathon. Unfortunately, he also got hurt. His ankle was fractured and he was put out of the race.

The pressure was on me since I was training with him. The last half of the week I ran seven miles, the farthest I had ever run at once. I took it easy on Friday and Saturday, and then I began the race at 7:00 A.M. on Sunday. It started out very quickly, and for the first four miles I was out of breath. But then I paced myself.

I had been running for two hours and was on the last mile. The sidelines were full of faces as I made my way to the end of the last turn. I could not think of anything except crossing the finish line. My pace quickened and I was giving all my body would offer. Never before had my fitness been tested so harshly. I was running the farthest I had ever run in my life. My heart was pounding and my stomach was cramping. I would not let it stop me. I rounded the turn and I saw the finish line and I bolted to the end. People were shouting and cheering, but it passed quickly. I was stopped at a large fence and funneled into a mass of people, where I was handed a gold medal because I finished.

I had completed the race. My legs had never been so sore, but I was thrilled. It was a breathtaking first experience I never expected I would have when I came to college. And I would do it again in a heartbeat.

~Taylor Sparks

More Mud, Please

Everyone has a "risk muscle." You keep it in shape by trying new things. If you don't, it atrophies. Make a point of using it at least once a day.
~Roger Von Oech

The stench in the room was almost unbearable, made worse by the skittish guinea pigs circling my feet and squealing as if they knew they would be dinner that evening. I tried to wipe the mud off my face, forgetting my hands were completely caked with the stuff. Giving up on cleanliness, I threw a big hunk of mud, full of hay, hair, and what looked an awful lot like feces, onto a brick. I glanced down—we had run out of mud.

"*Mas barro, por favor*," I said to the family. More mud, please.

Only a week ago I was on winter break in Connecticut, where my idea of filth had been the dust collecting on the top of my dresser. Now I was in the Andes with my college scholars group, building a clean burning stove for a Peruvian family who owned a lamb that was allowed to saunter through the kitchen whenever it pleased. The family (and the lamb) watched me as I worked, standing by the door with shovels, ready to bring me more mud the minute I ran out of the vile substance.

I tried to slap away a persistent fly buzzing in my ear and started hacking away at the wall of the kitchen with a pickaxe. The soot from the old stove caked on the adobe had made the wall crooked and not conducive to chimney building. Every time the pickaxe struck the hardened soot, the guinea pigs squealed, creating a strange cacophony of hand tool and rodent noises. I turned around to my stove-building partner and asked, for what felt like the hundredth time that week, "Are we really here right now?"

The minute we landed in Cusco after almost twenty-four hours of traveling, I felt my heart race from the thin Andean air and knew that my coddled existence was about to change. For a week and a half, I stayed with the Chihuantitos, my middle class host family of four. Marulyn, the mother, spoke only Spanish and I spoke only English, so our communication was based around my affinity for her food and her pitying looks as I walked through the front door covered head to toe in *barro*.

"Oh, Madeline," she'd sigh, with the look of a concerned mother that transcended any language barrier, and she'd gesture to the laundry basket, offering to wash my muddy clothes.

My outfit certainly wasn't the only dirty thing in Peru. A thin layer of grime seemed to cover everything in the city of Cusco, from the tables in the restaurants to the lukewarm shower in the Chihuantito's apartment. Up in the mountains in the town of Ancahuasi, the people we built stoves for often went barefoot down the dirt paths to their houses, leading the way to the stove-building site. The matriarch would walk ahead of me, her white top hat bobbing up and down with each step, her baby staring blankly from underneath folds of cloth on her back.

One of the last families I built a stove for lived very far from the meeting site we went to every morning. We trekked through hills and pastures and cornfields, holding out our arms to keep the corn stalks from whacking our sunburned faces. A cow looked menacingly at me as I passed it, standing by a stream of water, and I wondered briefly whether the hulking creature could shed the flimsy looking rope tied around its front hoof.

We came to a river with half a skinny tree trunk for a bridge. The Peruvian woman leading us charged fearlessly ahead, her gnarled feet stepping in a perfect line, one in front of the other. I stumbled across, breathing in sharp gasps as I looked at the rushing water below me.

Thinking I was almost done, we instead came to another, smaller river.

We stopped. I looked for a bridge. The woman, whose name I can't remember now but whose wrinkled, leathery face is etched in my memory, looked back at us, turned around, and threw herself across the river, grabbing the other side with her dirt-stained hands, grunting as she struggled up. She stood and looked at us, as if to say "Okay, your turn."

My partner jumped. I hesitated. Was I really being asked to jump across a river? The answer was absolutely yes. I made sure my backpack was secure, rolled up the sleeves of the dirty black shirt I'd been wearing for three days in a row, and launched myself across the river.

Needless to say, I made it.

When we returned to the United States, setting foot on American soil in the form of JFK airport, it felt like much more than ten days had passed. In my mud-stained backpack was a journal I'd written in to remember my time in Peru. The other day, I opened up the journal for the first time in months as a ticket to Machu Picchu, a postcard, and a map of Cusco tumbled out. I thumbed through the pages and found an entry about riding in the back of a pick-up truck, standing and breathing the Andean air while watching the mountains pass. It struck me in its simplicity and its ability to sum up my entire Peruvian experience. It read:

It was completely unsafe, terrifying, cold, hard, rough, dirty... and one of the most indescribably beautiful moments of my life.

Looking back, that's all there is to say about my trip to Peru. The only thing missing is this: I'll never forget it.

~Madeline Clapps

Pilgrimage

As I make my slow pilgrimage through the world,
a certain sense of beautiful mystery seems to gather and grow.
~·Arthur Christopher Benson

Near the end of my fall semester abroad in Valparaíso, Chile, I was at an *asado*—a Chilean barbecue—with my host family. It was Sunday of a long weekend for a religious holiday celebrating the end of the month of the Virgin Mary. Until 2008, Chile had three national holidays honoring the Virgin Mary. This one was the Day of the Immaculate Conception.

Every year the holiday is celebrated with a pilgrimage to Lo Vásquez, a religiously important church in the Central Valley between Santiago and the coast. To avoid the heat of summer, the pilgrims walk through the night. The authorities close down the relevant highways for the event. Thousands of people walk the thirty kilometers from the coast to Lo Vásquez. Others trickle in from other parts. A small number of dedicated people spend days walking from Santiago. When the highways reopen at 10 A.M. a flood of Chileans descends on the small church. Apparently, over the course of the three-day weekend 650,000 people make their way.

At the *asado*, several friends of my host mother were talking about the pilgrimage. I questioned them about it and they suggested I go. They knew a group of men who were planning on departing from a nearby church. I gave it a bit of thought and decided to do it.

They assured me the men would be perfectly welcoming even though I am completely non-religious.

At around 11 P.M., my host mom drove me to the church to meet the group. I had imagined a group of middle-aged men. Somehow I had expected them to be obviously religious. I probably wouldn't have been surprised if they had been wearing burlap monks' robes. Instead, I was introduced to a group of high school kids who looked pretty similar to my friends from home in Connecticut. There were eighteen of us. Before setting out we stood in a circle and prayed. One of the kids did most of the talking. He offered thanks to the Virgin Mary and said we were making the sacrifice of doing the pilgrimage for her. We started walking at 11:45.

A slow-moving herd of people covered the highway. To my surprise, the vast majority looked to be the age of my companions. A friendly, light-hearted atmosphere and a sense of camaraderie prevailed. Everyone seemed to be making the hike to Lo Vásquez with their closest friends. My group was close-knit too, and they were quick to bring me into the fold. As is typical of Chileans, many of my fellow pilgrims had nicknames and were eager to talk to the foreigner. Kiwi wanted to know about my host family. His friend, Palta (which means avocado), asked me about my university in the U.S. Gabriel talked to me about travel and practiced his English a bit.

While the majority of the pilgrims were quite young, there were people of all ages walking the highway. We passed one man with a clubfoot who was proceeding slowly with the help of two crutches. Later we passed a little old woman dressed in black supporting herself on the arm of a man who appeared to be her middle-aged son. There were a few families on the road who walked with babies in strollers.

All the pilgrims seemed to be devout Catholics. However, the reasons for undertaking the pilgrimage were diverse. For my new friends, it was a religious activity they took seriously, but they had a good time with it and it was a social outing, as well. For others, the walk through the night represented a genuine sacrifice. Some prayed that the sacrifice would bring health to a loved one. Others wanted to give thanks to the Virgin for having answered a prayer.

For anyone, the moonlit hike is a bit taxing. Even for me, a fit, 22-year-old, walking for seven hours while my body was accustomed to sleeping was difficult. By 5 A.M. my body was displeased with me and persistently lobbying for sleep. I closed my eyes to rest them. Shortly after, Gabriel tried to get my attention, "Mike... Mike!" I woke up from a dream and Gabe poked fun at me for sleepwalking while we hustled to catch up with the group that had gotten ahead of us.

Over the course of the walk there had been stands set up along-side the highway selling provisions to the pilgrims. As we got closer to Lo Vásquez, the stands were more frequent and elaborate. Some were full-fledged restaurants with large grills and wait service. Across the road, in the median, people had pitched tents to get a few hours rest before completing the last couple hours of walking. Others, who were less prepared, had simply passed out on the side of the road. Some of the naps might have been unplanned. The last few times my group stopped to rest, I fell asleep immediately to be awoken when it was time to continue.

Finally, we reached the crest of a ridge and could see the steeple of Lo Vásquez through the morning haze. An hour later we arrived. The highway near the church was packed with vendors selling every-thing from electronics to underwear. A bicycle repair stand was doing quite well as many pilgrims choose to bike the thirty kilometers. (According to the unwritten rules of the pilgrimage, pilgrims must arrive under their own power; so self-powered wheeled vehicles are acceptable. We saw three teenage boys on skateboards.)

After working our way through the market we regrouped near the church. The grounds had been turned into a densely populated, makeshift campground. We went straight to mass and managed to keep our eyes open throughout the service. About halfway through, an older woman fainted in the first row. A small team of volunteers whisked her away on a stretcher as the service continued. After mass, several of my companions went to confession. The group jokingly grumbled as Kiwi got in line, feigning concern that it would be a while.

Having successfully completed the pilgrimage, we moved towards a huge dirt parking lot where hundreds of small buses called *micros* awaited the business of exhausted pilgrims. Once our group had filled one of the *micros*, most of us fell asleep immediately.

My experience was memorable and it was the kind of experience that integrating into a foreign culture can afford you. Thinking about the pilgrimage later, I was struck by the fact that nothing like it would happen where I am from. It would be inconceivable for the Merritt Parkway to be closed down for a religious pilgrimage. Nevertheless, the people I did the pilgrimage with were not unlike the people who live near the Merritt. The different cultures just produce different customs. The group of close friends I walked with spent the night on a religious pilgrimage. My friends might spend a day together at a Dave Matthews concert. Although the events could hardly be more different, the social atmosphere and sense of camaraderie had a lot in common.

~Michael Damiano

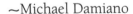

A Walkabout in Wisconsin

It's easy to make a buck. It's a lot tougher to make a difference.
~Tom Brokaw

While most of my colleagues interned their sophomore year at prestigious investment banks, I drove halfway across the country in my sputtering Toyota that summer to work with a Boys & Girls Club on Lac Courte Oreilles Indian Reservation in Wisconsin. Aside from praying that my car would not fall apart, I became more excited with every mile, as I anticipated this new opportunity to live and learn from the Ojibwa tribe. Princeton offered a special opportunity for students to improve our society through summer internships, and I jumped on the chance to do something that I might never have an option to do again.

Upon pulling into the driveway of the club, I realized that my challenge for the summer was not only building a cultural bridge between the staff at the Boys & Girls Club and the tribe members, but also tackling the crumbling state of both the program and the building. I spent my first hour on the job digging up some old clothes, leftover cans of paint, and plenty of sheets.

The listless group of ten-year-olds slumped on the front steps of the club didn't know what overcame them until they were outfitted in oversized rags and armed with paintbrushes. We were going to battle! The adversary was the color gray! A few paint cans later, I stopped to scan the tangled battleground. The faces of my soldiers were camouflaged with speckles of blue, red, green, and orange, cheeks ruddy from laughing, and their eyes held an eager sense of pride and accomplishment.

In just a few hours, a myriad of colors permeated the building and the walls were decorated with a hodgepodge of little handprints. From that day on, they understood that this club was no longer just a building where parents dumped children off for the free supervision and food, but rather a place they could call their own. Throughout the summer, we continued our crusade to renovate "our place" with boundless ideas, despite our limited supplies. The children became empowered as they observed their ideas turning the club into a vibrant, thriving place. It became their battle, and they won.

But there were many more battles to come. One night, I decided to host a camping night. I had visions of a few campers and me roasting marshmallows and telling ghost stories. The night before the big event, I only had three children signed up. While not really a success, it was a start. However, the night of the sleepover, word got out on the reservation about a free camping night (i.e. free babysitting) and children were dropped off in droves. One hundred children were dropped off with just two adults to supervise, and I almost had a heart attack.

To add to the madness, a surprise furry visitor smelled all of the food and decided to stop by for a snack. All I saw when the lumbering beast approached the crowd of children was the next morning's possible headlines, "Grizzly Bear Eats Native American Children and Jersey Girl." A call to the local ranger was made, and I decided this scene was better than the movie I had planned to show. Somehow, all of the children and the two adults made it through the night with only a few scrapes on knees and permanent wrinkles on brows.

Although every day I was met with frustrations and unanticipated disappointments, I went to bed every night knowing that I had learned more from this tribe about life than I had in my classes. Before long, the summer was over and I packed up my Toyota with treasures created by the children, my heart stuffed with memories that I would carry with me for a lifetime. You have your whole life to work in a suit and sit behind a desk, but in college you are given the rare gift of time—time to explore who you are through unusual opportunities that only the freedom of college allows. I have had a few "desk jobs" since graduating, yet the most memorable job I have ever had was my internship with the Ojibwa people at the Boys & Girls Club.

~Michelle Dette Gannon

26

Determining the Answer

I am not discouraged, because every wrong attempt discarded
is another step forward.
~Thomas Alva Edison

As a college student, I wondered how I was going to balance raising a family with pursuing a career. My female professors focused on the career part and ignored the raising the family part of my equation.

At the start of my junior year of college at the University of Virginia, I decided I wanted to be a part of a club for conservative-minded women, who wanted to both raise a family and pursue a career. I went directly to the club database at UVA to see if I could find a club for conservative college women.

There are more than 500 student clubs at UVA. Think of something you can do in a group and there most certainly is a club for it. There is an Archery Club, Belly Dance Club, Culinary Arts Club, Economics Club, Storm Chasing Club, and Fencing Club. The list goes on and on. But there were no clubs for conservative college women. I searched club databases at colleges throughout the country to see if they had clubs for conservative women. Again, nothing.

Why had a club for conservative college women not been created among the hundreds of clubs at UVA and thousands of college clubs throughout the nation? Two answers immediately dawned on me: either clubs for conservative college women had failed miserably or had never been tried. This was the unanswerable question.

A week after my initial database searches, I was walking home from class and saw a sign for the "Women's Center." Wow, I thought, this could be what I was looking for! I scheduled an appointment with one of the professors at the Women's Center. At the end of my visit, I asked the professor if the Women's Center would be willing to start a club for conservative college women. She looked at me like I was crazy, chuckled and replied, "Not here."

I grinned, said thanks, and decided to start a club for conservative college women on my own. I believed my idea would work and was determined to make it work after being laughed at by the professor at the Women's Center. Even more encouraging, I realized that the worst thing that could happen by starting this club was that no one would show up to the first meeting. But that was a risk I was willing to take!

I created the Network of enlightened Women (NeW) as a club for conservative college women. I structured NeW as a book club in which we would read about and discuss issues that are often unpopular on college campuses, such as the "hook-up" culture, balancing a career with motherhood, and the natural differences between the sexes. We wanted a club where we could critically discuss our beliefs in an open and intelligent manner. The club's aim since its inception has been to cultivate a community of conservative women. For the first meeting, we posted hot pink signs all over campus that asked:

Enjoy discussing the UVA "Hook-Up" culture?
Confused about politics?
Not sure how to balance work and family?
"Join the Network of enlightened Women!"

The hot pink fliers worked—the room was packed for our first meeting and word was spreading about NeW. At our second meeting, a professor who had published a book on the differences between the sexes spoke about how those sex differences should inform our decisions as young women and public policy more generally.

After this meeting, a liberal UVA newsmagazine placed a drawing of a young, pristine woman donning a perfectly pressed gingham dress on its cover. She had an apron on, and her hair was evenly curled. She was intently reading a book held in her left hand and mixing batter with her right. Nothing, however, could conceal a large device attached to her midsection that was popping out human babies: one, two, three... eleven. Eleven babies! She was a baby-making machine. This is how the liberal magazine portrayed NeW.

The cartoon confirmed the reason I started NeW—specifically that the campus political atmosphere needed to broaden its understanding of female issues. After having my efforts mocked by this cartoon, I didn't quit. Instead, I knew I was onto something.

Despite all the opposition, our membership grew quickly. Several times, our critics even came to our meetings to see what we were up to. Because we stood up against the politically correct campus orthodoxy, we were a threat.

With a growing membership, I was certain NeW had the potential to become a national organization. I believed in NeW's mission, so I began actively recruiting women to start chapters at their own universities. I have now helped women on fifteen different campuses throughout the country start NeW chapters. These women felt the same way I did and wanted a club in which they could discuss the difficult choices they will have to make in the future.

Four years after posting those pink fliers and fifteen chapters later, I am convinced that there was no club for conservative college women because it had not been tried. Rather than stopping at the question, I determined the answer.

~Karin L. Agness

Living among Greeks

The person who has lived the most is not the one who has lived the longest,
but the one with the richest experiences.
~Jean-Jacques Rousseau

When I was visiting colleges I had several important criteria: I wanted a small school at least a couple of hundred miles away from home, I wanted coed everything (I had been in an all-girls school for the last six years), and I wanted no math requirement. At the time, this seemed to cover all the important bases. Whether or not a school had a gazillion sports teams was of little importance to me. Greek life I could take or leave. In my book it was fine if they had it, just so long as I didn't have to do it.

Half the kids at the school I ended up attending were involved in Greek life. This was a lot, but since the other half of the student body was not Greek, I assumed I'd be fine.

In high school I had always been the shy kid and while I was determined to shed that image in college, I had never envisioned being part of a sorority. I wanted to be involved in campus social life, but not that involved. Not as involved as the girls in high school who had chosen their colleges and sororities in conjunction with one another. No, I was certainly not one of them. In fact, I had no specific knowledge of Greek life other than what I had seen in the movies, which wasn't particularly flattering.

Why I signed up for rush is still a mystery to me. Call it peer pressure if you like. During the first few weeks of school I had made a handful of friends I liked and respected. They talked me into it.

"It's a good way to meet upperclassmen," someone said.

"The rush parties are kind of fun," another noted.

"You don't have to pledge if you don't want to. Just see what happens."

Therefore, on some whim of oh-why-not-everybody's-doing-it, I went to the student center and filled out the rush form.

Me, in sorority rush. It was so absurd it had to be worth a try.

What I didn't know was that rush would be the single most ego-stroking social event I would ever participate in. The whole process was very formal and organized, with rushees sorted into groups with exact schedules and leaders who answered questions about the process and led our tours. In each house we were serenaded and welcomed by the active members, who feted us with cookies and juice. Without exception, the sorority girls were friendly and seemed genuinely interested in meeting us and telling us about their house.

I met lots of upperclassmen, as promised, and also made friends among my fellow rushees. Overall, it was everything it had been touted to be—a great way to meet lots of people. I had never felt so good, so in the middle of everything, in my whole life.

Subsequent rounds of parties cut things down a bit, but I was asked back to all my favorite houses. I remember being overjoyed and completely enamored with the whole experience. To a shy girl fresh from a high school career marked by relative obscurity, feeling so welcomed—so "in"—was simply beyond any expectation I had of college life. The sorority girls—in all the houses—were not like any stereotype I had ever known. They were just genuinely nice girls. From this side of the mirror I couldn't possibly see how it could be a bad thing to be included.

On pledge day, rushees were instructed to wear white and report to a cafeteria while the bids were distributed. We all knew we were in somewhere—those who had not received bids had been told ahead of time—but I can remember being overwhelmed and nervous as I sat there with my friends, waiting to see what my Greek fate would be. It is one of the defining moments of my college career. Like arriving on that first day, there was the sensation of being in a plane hurtling down the runway, not quite knowing whether the wings would support your weight. It's that moment between commitment and action, where you know you can still turn around, but to do so would be supremely bold. Like leaving your groom at the altar. Or walking away from a million-dollar job. And, of course, we didn't—none of us—although I suspect many of us had pause. I wondered if I was really doing the right thing for me.

With all the usual shrieking, jumping, hugging and fanfare, I became a Kappa Kappa Gamma that day. Kappa had been my first choice and I was thrilled. In my pledge photo, my face is round and red from smiling so hard for so long, and it was truly sincere. It was one of the happiest days of my life.

I think I was a good Kappa and I initiated with my pledge class the following January. The ceremony was moving and secret—an experience I will never forget. Admittedly, I also loved the party invitations I found shoved under my door like little Christmas presents all that first year. I became a sophomore, then a junior, making me a big sister to incoming pledges. I also participated in Kappa's philanthropic projects, and, as sisters, we encouraged each other and our new pledges to succeed academically.

It would be wrong to say that things went bad at some point. They didn't. It would also be wrong to imply that Kappa, and Greek life in general, are less than wonderful opportunities for college students. They are. However, even though I was proud to be a Kappa, the attachment never quite felt right. Many of my classmates became officers and progressively more involved, while I felt my own interests drifting elsewhere. As the months and years passed, I learned that the shy girl I had hidden under Greek letter sweatshirts and prodded to chapter meetings was still underneath. I had liked being her. I was still her, and she hadn't wanted to be part of all this. I began to wonder if maybe, after all, the shy girl was right. While Greek life was good, it wasn't me.

I left Kappa after rush my senior year. My friends told me I was crazy. Why leave just one year shy of graduation? But I was becoming jaded and it wasn't about them, it was about me. In three years I had learned a few things. I had been wrong about sororities, but right about myself. I learned that, in college and in life, so many things are good and worthwhile, but very few things are right for everyone. The tricky part is figuring out which ones are right for you and giving those everything you have. I am extremely thankful to Kappa for helping me learn who I am. I am also grateful for my Kappa sisters who understood my decision to go and supported me. Without them I would not have known that I had the confidence to be exactly who I am, and decide it was time to go it alone.

~Christina Kapp

28

Adventure for Two

An adventure is only an inconvenience rightly considered.
An inconvenience is only an adventure wrongly considered.
~G.K. Chesterton

My boyfriend Mike and I decided, after only three months of dating, that we wanted to spend our upcoming semester abroad together. It was a complicated decision and I was criticized by many of my friends for compromising the "real" purpose of studying abroad (apparently experiencing new things can only be done properly alone). However, by the time we were boarding our plane for Valparaíso, Chile, we were confident we had made the right choice and relieved that, after all our goodbyes to family and friends, we wouldn't have to say goodbye to each other.

One of the greatest benefits of our decision was that it gave us lots of opportunities to travel to exotic places together, something most couples our age never get to do. A few months into our trip, we planned a weeklong excursion to the Atacama Desert in the northern part of Chile. Though we knew we would spend most of our time in San Pedro (the tourist hub in the middle of the desert that offers accessibility to the most popular attractions), we wanted to cover a lot of ground and not have to depend on bus schedules, so we decided to rent a car and leave ourselves free to follow a map and explore wherever we pleased.

Mike and I spent a couple days of our trip traveling around the northernmost region of Chile and then decided to devote an afternoon and a good part of a night to making the 500-mile and 14-hour trip to San Pedro. We passed through the last town we would hit before San Pedro just as darkness set in. Now there was nothing left (not even pit stops or gas stations) but miles and miles of unfamiliar desert in the dark. We had heard the roads in the north weren't safe, and even that there were highway robbers in some areas, so we started to wonder if our late-night driving was such a good idea.

About half an hour after we had crossed into Región II (the region of Chile where San Pedro is) a large silver pick-up truck started tailing us aggressively, and then cut in front of us abruptly and recklessly. As soon as it was ahead of us it hit its brakes, forcing us to slam on our own. "What the hell?" Mike said out loud. My first thought was that it was a drunk driver, and it was obvious to both of us that we were better off avoiding the truck, so Mike passed back in front and sped off.

Immediately, however, the silver truck accelerated behind us and once it was tailing us again the passenger pulled out a flashlight and started shining it at our mirrors, flicking it around like he wanted us to pull over. Our next guess was that the truck wanted help, but we agreed it would be insane to pull over in the middle of the desert at what was now almost 1 A.M. for a complete stranger. However, despite all our obvious attempts to escape, the truck kept following us until it passed us again and slowed down ahead of us, still flicking the flashlight in our direction. Now every time Mike tried to pass the truck it would swerve to the middle of the road and block his attempts. It seemed it had trapped us.

I suddenly became very nervous. "DO NOT STOP FOR THEM," I pleaded, worried that Mike would give up. But we still couldn't get past. My heart rate sped up as I wracked my brain for an escape plan. Suddenly, Mike slammed on the brakes. "What are you doing?!" I yelled at him, panicked. The truck stopped too, just feet from us, and a tall Chilean man in a black jacket stepped out of the passenger side. I wondered what Mike was thinking, but I looked at his concentrated face and decided I trusted whatever plan he had. When the man was halfway towards us, Mike suddenly hit the gas and drove between the man and the truck. The truck slammed on the gas too and tried to block us, but Mike swerved around it.

We sped off in a confusion of headlights and screeching wheels. I watched in the rearview mirror as the truck slowed and allowed its passenger to scramble back in, but once he had, the truck sped up to follow us again. Luckily, we had a head start and we were going as fast as we could. I congratulated Mike on his stealthy escape but he was deeply concentrating and seemed convinced that we were far from safe. He put me in charge of looking backwards and keeping track of the headlights behind us, alerting him if any of them seemed to be moving particularly fast. But at the speed we were going I felt sure we had lost the truck quickly.

Just then a new thought occurred to me: what if it was customs? We had passed through what Mike thought was a weigh station when we entered Región II, but no one seemed to be there, and there were no indications that we should stop, so we had driven right through. What if it was a customs checkpoint and not a truck stop? I proposed this theory to Mike but he was unconvinced, mostly because of how recklessly the truck had been driving, and the fact that it was completely unmarked (in a country where outward appearance and formality are taken very seriously).

Mike continued to speed, since all signs indicated that our pursuers had bad intentions, and in the process we completely guzzled our gas. We realized this just as we were heading up into the mountains of the desert. Slowly, we registered the gravity of our situation: we were alone in the desert mountains, about to run out of gas, in the middle of the night, potentially with highway robbers following us.

Mike started driving especially slowly to conserve gas since all the driving was uphill. The gas tank arrow was down past empty, and I could tell that Mike had become the panicked one. I assured him that I had driven with the arrow past empty for a week without a problem, and he seemed relieved, but I silently reminded myself that the driving I did was infrequent and never up a steep mountain. We continued inching our way up and with such concentration that

I felt as though we were pushing the car on with our minds, willing it around every turn. At each corner we would pray we had found the top and were heading down, but instead we encountered more and more hill.

Just as we started to hear a sucking, bubbly noise that sounded like an indication of a completely drained tank, the peak of the mountain came into sight. We willed the car on as it crawled to it and, miraculously, began its descent. I had never been so relieved. We coasted down the rest of the mountain, braking as little as possible to conserve momentum, and rolled into a gas station at the bottom. Hallelujah. We survived our first (and hopefully last) desert car chase.

The next day, we related our story to several people in San Pedro, including a police officer, and everyone told us we must have been chased by highway robbers.

A few days later, on the way back to where we started our road trip, we passed through the mysterious truck stop again, and this time we were asked to stop and hand in our documentation. It was customs after all. As the woman behind the counter was stamping and signing things, Mike turned to me with an embarrassed but amused smile and mumbled, "Look behind you." I turned around, and there, in the parking lot sat the unmistakable silver truck.

Now we can only imagine how suspicious our very deliberate getaway must have looked, and we were extremely relieved that the woman behind the counter didn't have us arrested for evading Chilean authorities! But in this moment of relief, just like in the moments of panic, fear, exhilaration, and delight that had preceded it during our trip, I was reassured that Mike and I had made the right choice in going abroad together. Having someone you love along for the ride, I decided, makes any adventure much better.

~Emily Oot

Campus Chronicles

Good Friends... and Not

You can never forget the people who change your life.
You become a different person, and everything you do
is slightly altered by what they taught you.

~Ryanna Porter

29

Duerme con los Angeles

Walking with a friend in the dark is better than walking alone in the light.
~Helen Keller

A
ll summer, I waited apprehensively for the letter. Through the hot days in June and sticky days in July, I ran out to the mailbox and returned empty-handed and disappointed. After what felt like years, the crisp white envelope sealed with a blue Hofstra University crest finally arrived. No, this wasn't the letter declaring my acceptance or rejection to the University—that had come ages ago. This letter would reveal the name, address, and telephone number of the girl I'd be stuck with for the first year of my true adult life, and while I was anxious to find out who this stranger would be, I was not thrilled about having to share closer-than-close living quarters with a stranger.

In late July, the letter came. Ana Galdamez was her name, and she hailed from Flushing, Queens. I wasted no time, eager to learn whatever I could about her. I picked up the phone and dialed her number. After three rings, an answering machine clicked on, and a woman's voice streamed through the receiver.

"Hola, no nos encontramos en este momento, porfavor dejenos un mensaje y le devolveremos la llamada lo mas pronto possible...."

Spanish? The girl's answering machine recording was in Spanish? Of all of the horrors I feared (smelly feet, obnoxious habits, ugly bedding...), I never considered the possibility of being paired up with someone who might not even speak English. I slammed the phone down before the beep, my heart racing and my stomach churning. My knowledge of the Spanish language extended only as far as the Taco Bell commercials I had seen on TV. This was going to be worse than I thought.

In the next few weeks, I shopped, primped, and prepared for what I hoped would be the most exciting four years of my life. I stuffed my car with frilly pink bedding, sheer white curtains, sequined pillows, and all sorts of pretty trinkets. The impending stress of choosing a major, taking tests, and buying books wasn't really a concern; I was more excited to get to school as early as possible to claim the better bed, newer dresser, and bigger closet in my new room before my mystery roommate arrived.

On move-in morning, my family and I arrived before the suggested check-in time of 8:00 A.M., and I was surprised to see a line already forming outside my new dorm building. Despite all my efforts, a girl was already in my room—okay, our room—with some of her belongings unpacked, chatting cheerfully in Spanish with her own mother. She didn't seem to have a lot of things with her. I assumed they were still in the car.

Ana spoke before I could. "You must be Cassie! I'm so excited to meet you. I'm sorry we didn't get to talk this summer. I was away for most of it! Oh my gosh, you brought so much stuff! This is my mother. I saved the good furniture and the bigger closet for you; I don't really need the space!"

So she spoke English after all. Embarrassed about my assumption, I processed her words. She said she had saved the better set of furniture for me, and she wasn't kidding—I glanced around and noticed the furniture on my empty side of the room was made of polished wood, with a brand new plastic-wrapped mattress resting on top of my bed. Her furniture looked old and shabby, her mattress stained and torn and her closet significantly smaller than mine. A twinge of guilt passed through me.

I took a closer look at her now, feeling more at ease. She was pretty in a wholesome way, dressed in solid-colored clothes with no makeup or nail polish. I noticed a large, heavy-duty camouflage backpack next to her green bed.

"What's with the army bag?" I inquired.

"Oh, right. That. Well, I'm sort of in ROTC," she explained. "I wake up at four in the morning a few days a week. It's not a big deal."

Four in the morning? My stomach flipped. "Like, army training?" I knew my tone was offensive, but she didn't seem to notice. She smiled and nodded.

That evening, our parents left us to our own devices in our new half-earth-toned, half-frilled room. It took a great amount of effort for me not to grab my mother's ankles and beg her to take me back home with her. Sure, the girl seemed nice enough, but I still wasn't ready for this.

Surprisingly, we got right to talking. She was a hopeless romantic, her family was her life, and she had heaps upon heaps of exciting plans for herself and her future. As she talked, her eyes were bright, and each sentence she spoke rang with contentment and optimism. I had less to say, but was surprised to find myself wanting to learn more about her, even after we turned off the lights to go to sleep. I rested in my new bed, feeling guilty thinking of the time I wasted with my pretentious thoughts about her before we even met. I knew I had a lot to learn.

"*Duerme con los angeles*," Ana whispered, sounding like she was already half-asleep.

"Huh?" I mumbled.

"*Duerme con los angeles*. It means 'sleep with the angels,'" Ana explained, and her soothing voice wove itself into my dreams as I slept.

That year, without knowing it, Ana taught me invaluable lessons about patience and caring for others. Her own career and life goals rubbed off on me as I carefully chose a major and studied hard. She taught me to slow down, enjoy the coming years, and appreciate what I learned in my classes. Most importantly, she taught me not to give in to quick judgments as I always had before I met her.

We lived together—by choice—for the next two years. We grew and adjusted to our new home together, every day of college life bringing new challenges to each of us. No matter what changed, however, our nights ended the same way—with a whispered "*duerme con los angeles*," followed by a peaceful night's sleep.

~Cassie Goldberg

My Initiation

*The only people who are worth being friends with
are the people who like you as you are.*
~Charlotte Levy

She walked into our tiny room dragging a large green suit-case and carrying two shopping bags. She looked back at her parents and smiled —the kind of smile that makes you want to smile, the kind of smile that makes you want to share a secret with her. She was so beautiful that day, as she walked into our new dorm room at New York University.

Melissa drove a Jaguar in high school and hung out with rich and beautiful people. Her dad owned one of the biggest companies in the world, and basically, her life was perfect. The first day of fresh-men orientation, she wanted to take me to dinner. I didn't know what to wear, I didn't know what to say, I didn't know how to act. I was from Texas. I thought New York City would be a cool place to go to school. I had no idea how to deal with people like Melissa, let alone live with her.

I chose an unflattering blue dress with flat shoes. I immediately regretted not wearing heels like Melissa. She picked a Louis Vuitton clutch and threw on some platinum earrings. I liked Forever 21, and I still snuck into Claire's every once in a while to try on their bright pink hoops.

Melissa chose a restaurant in the West Village. It was the kind where the hostess pulled out the chair for you and handed you the menu as you sat down. I didn't know what kind of animal *ceviche* was, and I got my five-dollar scarf stuck under my chair. Melissa flawlessly ordered an appetizer and entree. I never got both—I always thought it was one or the other.

At the end of our meal, I couldn't bear to look at the check. Melissa coolly stuck out her credit card and said, "I've got this." I looked at her in awe. I thought I could never compete.

The next night, Melissa invited me to go out with her. "I love to party," she said as she curled her long, brown hair. "How much do you usually drink?" she looked at me and winked. I had never had alcohol before. My friends and I used to play board games for fun. "Oh, I don't know," I quietly laughed. "A lot, you know how it goes." She laughed along with me.

That night, she and I went to places I didn't know existed. She walked into bars and pushed through the crowds. When she got to the front, she would tell the bartenders to give her a vodka on the rocks, Grey Goose. The bartenders would lift their eyebrows a little, but I could tell they were interested. She looked back at me, "What do you want?" I calmly said, "The same of course." It tasted awful.

The next morning, I couldn't remember our night out. Melissa and I swapped stories, trying to piece together what happened. "Before you threw up, you were just yelling at everyone," she said. She almost couldn't breathe, she was laughing so hard. I had been accepted.

As the first day of class came closer, I got excited. I was the girl who liked to have different colored folders for each subject. I bought highlighters to match and college-ruled spirals. Melissa declared the first week of school, "Party week." She explained to me that it was the best time to miss classes. This was the time to drink and have fun because no one would be learning anything yet. I nodded and hid my bags of school supplies. "Yeah, let's go out," I replied.

It was one month later that she asked me whether I did drugs. She told me about her drug dealer back home, and how much cocaine she bought each week. "I love it," she said. "It's such a great high." I nodded and smiled. "Yeah, me too." She looked surprised for one second. But then she touched my arm and said, "Wow. I love you!" I had never been happier.

The next morning, my heart raced. I felt weak and restless at the same time. Melissa and I were lying on our beds watching trashy television. I tried to say something, but I felt too awful. "That was awesome," she muttered.

Melissa hadn't gone to class in three weeks. I had managed to roll out of bed and attend a few. I always felt guilty because all I wanted was to sit in bed and talk to Melissa. We partied five times a week. I spent more money than I thought possible. My parents started calling me more and more because they were concerned. I started answering the phone less and less because I didn't care.

Suddenly, one day, Melissa stopped talking to me. Just like that, in a matter of hours, there was silence. I would come home, and if she was there, it was a simple "Hey," and that was that. Other times, she would never come home. I started calling her obsessively, but she never answered anymore. I wondered what I had done wrong. I wondered what I would do without her. I felt insane.

I learned a few weeks later that Melissa had dropped out of school. She had missed so much class that she couldn't catch up. I learned that Melissa had a serious drug problem. I cried to no one in particular because, in a way, I hated myself. It was as if everything I had been working to become failed me. All of a sudden, the new life I thought was ideal had failed. I still wanted to talk to Melissa, to see if I could make anything better. I still thought maybe if I just apologized, she'd talk to me again. But I couldn't. And she wouldn't. It was over. But in reality, my life was just beginning.

~Reema

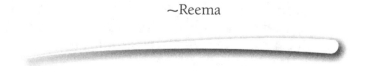

One Click

Life is partly what we make it,
and partly what it is made by the friends whom we choose.
~Tehyi Hsieh

Students of every color and rung on the socioeconomic ladder came together to receive a faith-based education at my high school. Many of my St. Ignatius classmates were the Spanish-speaking children of immigrant parents. We had a higher percentage of African Americans than any other private high school in Chicago, and our valedictorian lived in Chinatown with her grandparents, who barely spoke English. In addition, a large percentage of students were awarded full-tuition scholarships or substantial financial aid. I was happy to go to a school with a diverse community, and graduated with the belief that never again would I learn among students of such differing backgrounds.

My first year at Boston University forced me to reassess my definition of diversity. I realized with shock that I had never attended a school with a large Jewish population. In fact, my experience with the religion was limited to a two-week unit in high school religion and frequent ingestion of Jewish deli food. Somehow I doubted my affinity for potato latkes made me any more culturally adept.

During the chaos that is freshman year move-in, my dad, ever the chatterbox, discovered that one of my Claflin Hall floor-mates, Danielle Chelminsky, had spent the past year living in Israel, during which she voluntarily went through basic training for the Israeli army.

I had been a BU student for less than twenty-four hours, and already I couldn't believe that while I had been hanging candy canes on a Christmas tree, my future best friend was learning how to shoot an AK-47 in a Middle Eastern desert.

A few weeks into the year, Danielle introduced me to her friend Thalia Rybar, who, despite growing up in predominately Catholic Guatemala, was also Jewish. Although she speaks fluent English, her first language is Spanish. Grabbing dinner in the dining hall with Thalia, Danielle, and other "Latin Jews" at BU was always riveting. Perhaps my major, journalism, played a part in my intense curiosity—for the longest time, I took on the role of Dinner Interrogator. I wanted to know everything.

Thalia and her friends never ceased to entertain me with tales of growing up in developing countries. I learned that while there are a sizeable number of Latin Jews around the world, each country's individual community tends to stick together. The low cost of living means nearly all Latin Jews employ a full-time staff that includes maids, drivers, landscapers, and sometimes bodyguards. The maids, non-Jewish natives, must learn to prepare kosher meals. The bodyguards protect the families from kidnappers, who take wealthy members of the community for ransom. Sharon Malca, from Colombia, endured six months without her mother when she was taken hostage in the Colombian mountains.

Junior year, I moved into an apartment with Thalia, Danielle, and another friend, Pamela. By this time, aspects of Judaism that had once seemed foreign now felt commonplace. I learned the difference between Ashkenazi and Sephardic Jews, the proceedings of a Bar or Bat Mitzvah, countless Yiddish terms (*chutzpah* is a favorite), and the important role of Israel in the Jewish community. I attended Passover Seder at Danielle's house twice. Her family invited me to read the *haggadah*, or book containing the Passover story. Normally I would feel like an idiot stumbling over Hebrew words, but the overwhelming sense of encouragement I felt made me realize what an honor it was to be included in the tradition.

Thalia and her Latin friends often talked about their weekly get-togethers, which they call "Latin Shabbat." Shabbat, the Hebrew word for rest, takes place each Friday, and includes a special dinner. At Latin Shabbat, all the college-aged, Spanish-speaking Jews in Boston congregate for a huge meal. When Thalia invited me and Danielle, I had no clue what to expect—I had never been to any Shabbat dinner, much less a bilingual Shabbat.

If you think you've seen it all, work up an appetite for challah bread and attend Latin Shabbat. When I say I felt like a foreigner, I mean it. I was the only natural blonde, I don't speak Spanish, I didn't know the etiquette, the night's schedule, the words to the prayers, the lyrics to the songs, or even how to toast. I couldn't believe I was a mere hundred yards from my own apartment.

Hanging tentatively behind Thalia and Danielle, I entered the apartment. Immediately, the unfamiliar bombarded each of my senses: the strong scent of just-out-of-the-oven brisket mixed with red wine and expensive European perfumes and colognes. Loud, loud, Spanish, my *gringa* cheek being pressed against those of strangers in the customary Latin air kiss greeting. Thalia's stiletto-clad friends quickly maneuvered around folding chairs and tables to welcome me. What did I want to drink? Could they take my coat? My purse? I barely had time to respond before I was being ushered by five glamazons to meet David, the host.

Thalia, Sharon, and two other friends, Karina, and Sarah, spent the next ten minutes teaching me to salsa. I am admittedly a pathetic dancer—the type who bops to the right when everyone else is boogieing to the left—but I was a novelty to these girls, a project. We salsa-ed until we were all on the floor with tears in our eyes.

The dancing, the Spanglish banter, the delicious smells—I was having the time of my life, and for the first time in my life, I was the minority.

I left Latin Shabbat feeling exhilarated and full of energy, liberated at such newness. That night and many days after, I thought about what had been most special about that night, and why I had reacted so strongly. It took several days to realize that my amazement stemmed from the reverence and seriousness with which this group protected their religion, traditions, and culture.

Amidst the eating, the games, the goofing off, the drinking, and more eating, David stood at the head of the table. Instantly, the group silenced. In English, David earnestly thanked everyone for coming, specifically praising the girls, Thalia included, who had spent all day cooking the massive trays of brisket, potatoes, rice, chicken, salad, and desserts. I knew Thalia and her friends cooked for Shabbat every week, but I hadn't realized the extent of the meal. Like their mothers and grandmothers at home in Guatemala, Mexico, or Peru, and great-grandmothers in Eastern Europe and Israel, my friends were maintaining a tradition, and taking on a role. It was beautiful to see a group of modern, well-educated young women embrace their history.

Next, David read a prayer in Hebrew. It was flawless, not only in his delivery, but in his sincerity. I attended Catholic school for twelve years and had not once been to a gathering in which someone my age stood and recited a prayer. I can't even think of one friend who brought a Bible to school, let alone read from it on a regular basis. David's reading, and the subsequent explanation of its meaning, made me reassess the importance of organized religion. I have, at times, been skeptical of Catholicism. Suddenly, I felt compelled to embrace it.

Opening myself to the experience of another religion and culture has been the single greatest decision of my college experience. There is so much to learn, so much to absorb, so much to take away. Living with Thalia and Danielle was the result of a simple click on the housing website. That one click altered my worldview forever.

~Molly Fedick

Rushing

No person is your friend who demands your silence,
or denies your right to grow.
~Alice Walker

I felt so out of place.

Standing among the girls in my rush group, I stuck out. Freckles, glasses, wavy (read: unruly) red hair, and the freshman fifteen didn't exactly make me blend in with my fellow rushees who had flat-ironed straight blond or brown hair, flawless skin and fit figures.

I didn't even match the apparent dress code for rushing. As a practical dresser, I wore my big, red ski jacket and heavy-duty snow boots. It was technically spring semester, but still winter in Syracuse, New York. Other girls also dressed warmly, but a little more stylishly. Heeled leather boots. Tailored wool coats, short-waisted coats with fur trim, or the in-fashion puffy winter coats. I looked ready for hiking. They looked ready to go out.

Looking different I could handle — I came from an eclectic group of friends in high school. Feeling like an outsider, I could not. I felt uncomfortable. Girls chatted away with each other and friendships formed. I tried, but simply could not get a conversation going.

Maybe this wasn't for me.... But I was there. I figured I should at least give it a shot.

For the first round of rush, we toured all twelve sorority houses over the course of a few days.

After the first day of visiting, I realized that, like my rush group, I did not fit in at all. The sorority sisters were all very polite, but something didn't mesh.... I couldn't relate to most of these girls.

I grew up near Cape Cod in a small suburban town, raised as an outdoorsy girl. I camped. I fished. I played volleyball. I threw shot put and javelin. I spent all of fifteen minutes on hair and make-up in the morning. My friends and I leaned toward the dorky/nerdy side.

During the first round, sisters at each house interviewed us. These were casual conversations—at least in my view—about why we wanted to rush, our interests, our background, our families, etc. I answered matter-of-factly and honestly. Perhaps too honestly.

Why did I decide to rush? My best friend at school asked if I wanted to sign up with her. I did, figuring it would be a good experience, if nothing else. I don't think I won too many points with that answer.

I bombed nearly every single interview.

Yet, I was being myself. I figured the girls could accept me for how and who I was, or not. Whether it was socially naiveté or confidence, I don't know. Either way, I continued rush with this attitude.

For the second round of interviews, I got called back to two sororities—Alpha Gamma Delta and Pi Beta Phi. They seemed more my style, low-key and down-to-earth.

Both also called me back for the third, and final, round.

I didn't have to pledge a sorority. But I got caught up with the idea during the three rounds of rush, and decided I would.

I opted for Alpha Gamma Delta.

The sorority also opted for me. I fit in somewhere, apparently.

There was a buzz of excitement within my pledge group, and many of the sisters. I caught it too, at first. Mandatory study hours with my pledge sisters were fun because it typically led to more gabbing than working. Dinner at the house every once in a while was a nice break from the dining hall. Charity work was a great way to help and a better use of my time.

Yet a nagging feeling of not quite fitting stuck with me, while the excitement didn't.

Shortly after becoming a full-fledged sister, I started seeing my sorority duties as a burden.

Weekly Sunday night meetings became a hassle. They cut into my time to do homework, and I had to rush back for dinner with my friends. Dressing up one of the senior sisters in a crazy outfit for the annual bar crawl was a chore. Stopping by the house just to say hi to the sisters living there felt awkward—I didn't really know them.

At the same time, my circle of friends at school had grown. These sorority events took away time from them. I missed out on things. I had to rush back from the spring Block Party to get ready for the sorority's formal. Other times, I missed out on movies or game nights or general random fun times with everyone. I felt left out.

That's when I realized, Greek life is great for some people. Not me.

I already had a close-knit group of friends. And they didn't require interviews.

~Kristiana Glavin

Climbing the Tower of Babel

Friendship is genuine when two friends can enjoy each other's company without speaking a word to one another.

--George Ebers

During my four-hour wait on a bench at the Amerigo Vespucci Airport, I sipped my first legally purchased alcoholic beverage (a nice, cool Birra Moretti), shuffled through my Italian flashcards and wondered why America wasn't called Amerigo. It was the fall of my junior year and I had elected to spend the semester abroad, in a city that oozed paintings, sculpture and the vigor of the Renaissance from its every pore. It didn't hurt that Florence was also renowned for its culinary genius — a land of *cannoli*, homemade pasta, and mind-numbingly delicious gelato.

When my program's van finally arrived, I piled in with eight other Americans who, like me, were all enrolled in the Accademia Italiana of art and design. We made small talk in the back as our Italian driver navigated the narrow, alley-like streets of the city, coming this close to ramming into a moped or a car with every lane change or turn.

I was the first to be dropped off, since my apartment was located in the outskirts of the city. Massima, a Florentine girl who had accompanied us, unlocked an enormous gate and led me up four flights of spiraling, never-ending stairs. Just as I'd caught my breath, I lost it again when the door swung open, revealing soaring ceilings, wooden floorboards, and beautiful furniture—a far cry from the small, bare-bones apartment I'd envisioned!

"Two or three more will come, maybe soon," Massima said, referring to my future roommates, as she left to return to the idling van. I wandered around the stocked kitchen, the spacious living room and the two bedrooms, each with two twin beds. I was elated to discover a balcony, which overlooked courtyards and a school below.

Exhausted, I collapsed on one of the beds and slept until dark. When I awoke, I was ravenously hungry, but too fearful of going into the dark, foreign city alone to do anything about it.

The former brightness of my apartment had transformed into a stoic gloominess with the nightfall. With nowhere to go and no one to talk to, I was unsure of what to do with my jet-lagged self. I spent the night sleepless on my back, ignoring the growls of my stomach, and clapping my hands together left and right over buzzing mosquitoes.

At my program's orientation the following morning, I learned that everyone else had already met their roommates. All of the American students had been grouped together in twos, threes and fours in apartments all about the city. They'd all had their first meals in incredible *trattorias* or cheap cafés the night before. I soon discovered that this was because I—and I alone—had noted on my application that I preferred to live with international students.

My first roommate, Michela, didn't arrive until a few long days later. We cooked pasta together and I tried to apply all of my self-taught Italian to real-life conversation. Since Michela spoke almost no English, we made the Italian-English dictionary our third wheel, accompanying us everywhere we went. Surely, we thought, our other roommates would speak Italian or English and we'd soon be able to communicate more efficiently.

But the third arrived a few days later and, as it turned out, barely spoke English and could say only *grazie* and *ciao* in Italian. Benchawan (Ben, for short) was a thirty-six-year-old Thai masseuse, lover of meditation, and supreme fish sauce enthusiast. With every meal she prepared came a high-sodium, inescapable odor that filled every crack of our humid apartment! "You like to try?" she would say, hurtling a fork-full of rice and seafood toward our closed lips.

At times, seemingly out of nowhere, Ben would exclaim, "Welcome to Thailand!" by which, I came to realize, she meant that we should come visit her when our days in Florence together were bygones. Michela understood none of Ben's broken English and would merely look at me with a furrowed brow, click her tongue and mutter, "È pazza..." ("She's crazy...").

I held out hope that an English-speaking girl would soon fill the last bed in our incommunicative apartment. A week later, Diana, who was not American, Italian, or Thai, finally arrived. "Where are you from?" I eagerly asked. "Mexico," she replied, "Chihuahua." Once I came to understand that she was referring to a city—not to the breed of high-strung canine—I felt rather ignorant.

"A little," Diana said, when I asked if she spoke English. "Un poco," she said, when I asked if she spoke Italian. I didn't bother asking her about Thai.

During the first weeks, dictionaries littered the floors and tables of our apartment. We all became skilled gesticulators, piggy-backing off our limited vocabularies with elaborate gestures and props. Life began to resemble a non-stop game of charades and a successfully transmitted message was cause for great joy.

By the end of the first month, I no longer retained any desire to be living with my fellow Americans. I came to love surmounting the challenges of communication on the streets of Florence and also at home with my diverse roommates. I was grateful that my semester abroad was not only a foreign experience in terms of place, but also in terms of companionship. This was an opportunity for me to learn about aspects of myself and about others from around the world that I would take with me back to America, back to college in Ohio in the spring, and then continue to preserve in my mind, well beyond graduation.

The four of us overcame our real life "Tower of Babel." We defied our language barriers, divided cultural backgrounds, and age differences. We came together over consuming sickeningly large amounts of Nutella. We bonded over the hilarity of fish sauce, over our shared love for art, and over the inherent comedy in our disparities. That fall, we all learned a little bit of three new languages, became familiar with three new cultures, and realized that it's true what they say about laughter: it has no language, it knows no boundaries.

~Maya Silver

Holy Hayley

The right to do something does not mean that doing it is right.
~William Safire

Moving away to go to college was my first big taste of independence. Up until then, I'd been an unadventurous, quiet, content person. A writer, a computer nerd, and a bit shy, I knew that moving to a college across the state would give me the opportunity to find out who I was without the influence of friends and family.

I had attended my first year of college while living with my parents, so the transfer was a shock for many reasons. Even so, I was excited as I unpacked my things and waited for my roommate to arrive

Fresh from Nebraska, the hyper, free-spirited, energetic Hayley entered my life more like a Texas tornado. The college would have been hard pressed to find two people more opposite than us. The drinking, swearing, socialite Hayley seemed to find my calm, quiet ways a bit confusing at times. We made it work, though, and she was out of the room more often than not, so studying wasn't too hard.

I began to get the feeling that Hayley and I had a problem when I realized that our "cleaning schedule" wasn't working and I was doing all the cleaning. If I wanted a neat and tidy room, then I had to clean. The problem was that the mess was pretty much all hers.

For the first time in a long time, I stood up for myself. I decided that I was no one's maid and stopped cleaning up her things.

She didn't seem to care. Over the next few weeks, I discovered that Hayley owned more clothes than I had ever owned. She didn't care for hangers or even laundry baskets. Soon the entire floor, excluding the small area under my desk and chair, was covered in a layer of her clothing.

Then she began coming back to our dorm drunk. It was as if the mess of clothing had given her unspoken permission to get really down and dirty. And things only got worse from there. The only things she managed to keep clean were her dishes, which I think was more about the fact that she ate out a lot.

It was when she started kicking me out of our room so she could have some privacy with her male friends that I began to get truly depressed and unsure of what I could do. Thankfully, the girls in the room across the hall took pity on me and gave me a place to sleep on those nights. Refusal to leave would have gotten me nowhere, as Hayley had no problems with being an exhibitionist.

Despite all that, I think Hayley was able to sense something in me that I had not yet realized about myself. For all her bad habits, she was a soul truly in love with life, and that's something I lacked.

She got me to talk about what was going on in my life, cheered for me when I met the man who is now my husband, and even hugged me when I cried. There was a softer side in her that I glimpsed every now and then.

One night she discovered that I didn't wear make-up and rarely had. Despite my protests, she had me dress up in a combination of our best clothing, styled my hair, and then applied make-up.

It was like a scene from a movie. I felt fabulous, even pretty. She didn't leave it at that, though. She insisted that we go to the main part of campus so I could really show myself off.

And so we did.

The magic and good feelings of that night didn't last long enough, though, and as finals came, I found myself growing more and more frustrated with the drunken nights and the mess.

After finals, the night before we were both set to leave for Christmas break, she asked me to wake her up early so she could clean before leaving. I did as she asked the next morning, but she refused to get up. And when she finally did get up, she was overwhelmed by the mess.

I was more than happy to help, but her grandparents showed up. With a quick goodbye, she left me to clean up the whole mess.

I hit my breaking point then and began tossing all of her things—everything from her clothes to her toaster—in her closet. Books, CDs, and her coffee maker (with some grounds still in it, unfortunately) all went in. I couldn't believe she would just leave me with her mess. Her disrespect for me had gone too far and I wanted to pay it back in kind.

A few days before it was time to go back to college, I began to regret what I did. I felt bad for leaving things like that, but I figured I could fix everything with her somehow. Maybe I could buy her a cake or promise to thoroughly clean the whole room. But, as I opened the door to my room, I found Hayley's side empty. She had withdrawn from college.

She left me a nasty note that made me cry for days, but I gradually accepted that I couldn't change the past and now she was gone.

Later, in spring, I heard a familiar loud voice call my name. Hayley had come back from Nebraska to visit, and was staying with the girls across the hall. Later I had a laugh about the irony of it, but in that moment, I waited for her to bring up what I had done. I thought she would glare at me and try to pick a fight, but she smiled and laughed as if nothing had happened.

As we held each other's gaze for a moment, I think she felt sorry for pushing me past the line of anger and she knew I felt bad for what I had done.

And with that, we went our separate ways, accepting that some people just aren't meant to be friends.

~Jaime McDougall

Once Removed

What is a friend? A single soul dwelling in two bodies.
~Aristotle

I t was my first day of college at the University of South Carolina and I feared that my roommate wasn't coming.

"Don't worry," my mother comforted me, "I'm sure she'll be here."

But enough time passed that even she grew concerned. We wiped our perspiring brows and listened to the jarring sounds of the dormitory elevator doors and loud shrieks of the other girls as they lugged suitcases to their rooms and began discussing dinner plans. For weeks now, I had imagined how this experience might unfold: meet my roommate, decide on a color scheme for the room, venture to the cafeteria together to taste an unfamiliar meal, and begin the regular habit of saving seats for each other. The minutes ticked away.

Oh, God, I can't do this alone. She isn't coming!

Finally the heavy glass doors swung open. A young woman rushed in, petite and winded as she dragged her suitcase behind her. She had perfect cheekbones and the most enviable chocolate-brown hair, as rich and flowing as Julia Roberts's cascade of curls in *Pretty Woman.* Even after a lengthy car ride, this girl was stunning—amazing hair, tawny tan, and slender figure. I wanted to hate her.

"I'm so sorry I'm late." She smiled nervously, lowering her eyes so that a shyness was revealed, and her vulnerability disarmed me.

"I'm Candace," she said reaching out her hand for mine, and after some introductory chatter, we lugged our things up to our room.

We found our new home amid a crowded maze of darkened hallways, ill-prepared for how much it resembled a cheap motel. "So this is it," I announced, as we opened the door to what would become our cramped but cozy refuge. Opening the blinds allowed light in to reveal generic concrete walls, exposing the disappointing plainness of the room.

Candace was exotic to me because she was originally from California, a seemingly sharp contrast to my South Carolina roots. We sat Indian-style on our stiff beds and shared stories. She wanted to be a movie producer and planned to major in media arts. Her rhythmical voice was soothing and neutral, a contrast to my Southern drawl. Her belongings consisted of a fluffy black and white comforter, framed photos of her boyfriend, a large *Blues Brothers* poster, and an absurd number of troll dolls with bright shades of hair that flew in all directions when spun around. My decorations complemented her clutter: my complete stuffed dog collection to remind me of my beloved dog back home, a calendar displaying a calming photo of swimming tropical fish, and a boldly multi-colored bedspread. Our color schemes didn't match, and neither did our accents, but we learned we were very much alike. We talked straight through dinner, and stayed up all night, discussing the boyfriends we had left back home.

"Do you think you'll marry him?" she had asked, gesturing to my boyfriend's picture.

"Are you kidding?" I laughed. "I'm just getting started!"

All night the words and topics flowed easily—she thought she would marry her boyfriend, "... maybe not anytime soon... but someday." We discussed hairstyles and agreed that ponytails were an unflattering look for us both, reveled in our appreciation of retro fashion, and lamented over our less-than-desirable bra sizes.

"I have a great padded one," she giggled, unable to resist the urge to show it right there in the middle of the night, snapping on the lamp to pull it from a drawer. Squinting in the light, I reached out to feel its thickness, insisting we must go out the next day to buy one just like it for me!

And when talk turned to a shared habit of staying up too late on summer nights, we discovered an important, abiding connection: late-night sitcoms. We spent the rest of the night, back-and-forth, like a ping-pong game, spouting television trivia through muffled eruptions of laughter. We watched *Three's Company* together through a fuzzy picture on a bunny-eared television set, reciting Jack Tripper's lines of dialogue in unison, laughing until we cried. The next day we woke giddy and sleep-deprived, operating on solely the energy of newly-discovered friendship. We were tickled beyond belief at finding pieces of ourselves in one another.

Sixteen years later, Candace is still my best friend. There were times during these years that Candace and I lost touch, but we always made our way back to each other. We have always been this way. I was there for silent support when her father died during our sophomore year in college. I was a bridesmaid in her wedding, and helped her make the transition to life in New York City when she was accepted into graduate school at Columbia University. She helped me survive an ambulance ride to the emergency room when my knee dislocated during a college dance class. She was my maid of honor who put pink roses in my hair for my wedding, and helped me through each and every painful labor contraction before my daughter's birth.

In the hospital room, Candace stood apart, as if the moment of my daughter's first breath belonged only to my husband and me. Noticing this, I protested, "No, Candace, you come here too," reaching my hand out to her before the final push. Even though I was completely consumed by the miracle that was taking place, there was still the significance of Candace's presence in my life: the path from matching the right shade of heels for meaningless sorority parties until this moment, and I knew I wanted my friend by my side.

Candace has seen the best and the worst of me, and holds me in her memory like a safety deposit box. Her knowledge is more significant than any legal will or photographs would be for my daughter, and she fills in the details, the spaces between the puzzle pieces that complete me. Candace is me once removed, and for this I am filled with gratitude.

~Donna Buie Beall

Lucky Me

Praise the bridge that carried you over.
~George Colman

"Hi, welcome to Mertz third floor south, closest to heaven." Two guys approached as I heaved my luggage up the wide staircase.

"Um, hi," I panted. The brittle January weather had chilled my skin, which was finally starting to thaw from the effort of two flights of stairs. My heart, on the other hand, stayed colder than the coldest nights. I just didn't know it yet.

"You the exchange student from California?" asked the taller one with an impish smile, as he steered a remote control toy down the hall. "I'm Jim."

Great, I thought. College kids are just as immature here as back home.

The shorter, curly-haired boy took my suitcase and led the way. "I'm Dave. Lucky you. You're with Melissa in the big double at the end of the hall."

One by one, people stuck their heads out of their rooms as they heard the squeak of my suitcase wheels. All of them envied my luck and ogled at the girl from California.

The room was large—twice the size of every other on the floor. Lucky? Me lucky? I had come to this little Pennsylvania college for a fresh start, hoping to leave my nightmares behind.

No one here knew me. They didn't know my nickname. They couldn't pity my tragedy.

I couldn't wait for second semester classes to begin—something to keep my mind occupied—too busy to think about the past.

Jim turned out to be in my "Revolutions and Revolutionaries" history class. There were only a handful of students. The professor, who encouraged debate, kicked off the first class with a heated discussion. "Is there really any such thing as altruism?"

"Sure," Jim answered. "People do things for others all the time without getting or wanting anything in return."

"But they always get something in return," I countered. I was always up for a good argument—just another thing to beat back my reality. "Even if it's just a warm, fuzzy feeling from helping someone."

Despite the fact that he called me a cynic, we continued our exploration of the topic back in his room. Over the next few months, we had many conversations stemming from that class and elsewhere. I found myself working twice as hard on the papers for history—hoping to live up to Jim's high standards.

Yet, at the same time, he drove me crazy. I didn't know what it was that kept pulling me back to those debates. "He's always on my case," I complained to my roommate.

"Got any ideas for the next paper?" Jim asked me one evening.

I stared at him in bewilderment. "Me? None as good as yours."

"Oh, sure. Thought you could handle it." And he was gone. It drove me nuts.

Then there was the night—the ridiculous night—I sat by the phone in the common room, trying to decide whether to call my parents or not. I needed the connection, the hug across the wires. On the other hand, I did not want to upset them. Who else but me would be obsessed enough to calculate that on that day I had become older than my brother ever had the opportunity to be? Two and a half years before, at this exact age, his life was taken from him. Now, I was living to be older. It wasn't right. It wasn't fair. It should have been me.

Still stuck in the bargaining stage of recovery from the loss of my brother, I knew that my death wouldn't bring him back. However, it would have ended the *Monkey's Paw*-type nightmares. As I sat there, sobbing, I realized that the nightmares had become less frequent. Images of my new surroundings, new friends, and my history class swam before my eyes instead.

A few weeks later it was my birthday—a fact I kept well hidden. I just couldn't bear the thought of becoming nineteen when my older brother was frozen in time at eighteen. Perhaps this was part of getting away. Nobody here would recognize the event, and so I could somehow pretend that it hadn't happened.

Strolling back from the library, I paid little attention to the fact that Jim and Dave had opened the window in Dave's room and were singing "Happy Birthday" at the top of their lungs. Clearly, it was for somebody else.

It was naïve of me to think that someone else they knew at this small school shared my birthday. "Why didn't you tell anyone it was your birthday?" they demanded as I headed up the stairs.

"How'd you find out?" I asked, greeted by a common room full of people and large pizzas.

"Your grandmother called and left a message to wish you a happy birthday," Dave told me.

"Just my luck. No one was supposed to... I didn't want... what did you do all this for?" I stammered, realizing too late how ungrateful it must have sounded.

Jim rolled his eyes. "Oh yes, poor 'Deirdre of the sorrows' all wrapped up in her own self pity."

"That's not what I... could you just lay off for one second!"

At that moment our eyes met. It was the same impish smile from the first night, but suddenly different. Standing before me was a man who hadn't lost his joy and optimism, who still harbored faith in humankind and the belief in true altruism.

Always on my case. It suddenly occurred to me how wrong I was. Jim only did that every time I put myself down. I had become so self-deprecating, a sullen serious pessimist, constantly insulting myself before anyone else could. After all, it hurt less if I did it—or so I thought.

The door that stood between my life of depression and my future—the one Jim had been trying to help me to unlock all semester—had opened a crack. Smiling at Jim, I was able to stick my foot in that doorway to keep the bright light shining.

The semester was drawing to a close and it was time. I somehow had gotten what I'd come for—traveled three thousand miles to meet this altruistic person—a guy who returned my faith in humanity and in my own future.

I was scared to go, afraid the door would slam shut in my face back home in California. For the next year or so, Jim was always in my mind, like an angel on my shoulder, reminding me of the things he would have said. "You're so lucky," a classmate told me as I stepped forward to receive a special award on graduation day. I smiled at her. Luck had nothing to do with it.

~D.B. Zane

More than a Medical Kit

Luck can often mean simply taking advantage of a situation at the right moment. It is possible to "make" your luck by always being prepared.
~Michael Korda

"Anybody have a bandage?" a voice echoed down the dorm hallway.

It was our first week at college and we were all experiencing "forgot-it-itis." I had neglected to bring snacks for late-night munchies. Some poor girl on the wing had apparently forgotten bandages. We all felt a little displaced.

Several months before, I sat at my high school graduation party admiring my gifts and battling waves of post-high school sentimentality. The usual and beloved inspirational books were scattered around my feet, silently proclaiming the wealth of wisdom they wished to share. A small pile of personal checks lay nearby. Laundry items, desk supplies, sewing miscellany—all well-intentioned and well-received. They would demonstrate their givers' thoughtfulness over and over during my college career.

But one gift struck me as strange. I frowned when I opened it. Medicine? A small packet of pills and creams, ointments and lozenges lay within the wrappings. Who would give that as a gift?

"You'll need that once you're at school," Mom pointed out. "You won't have to chase down the campus nurse for every cough."

Good point.

Not long after, in August, I packed my life into a borrowed truck and slipped the bag of medicine in with my toiletries. I barely thought about it once I reached campus, caught in the whirlwind of unpacking, book-buying, scheduling and meeting new friends.

When "anybody have a bandage?" rang out in the dormitory hall that day, I remembered my little medicinal package.

I swallowed self-consciously. "Actually," I gave a little wave, "I have one."

"Great," my new wing-mate chimed.

As I dug out the kit, we began to chat.

Soon, many of the other girls on the wing heard of my little kit and paid me a visit. One had bug bites—anti-itch cream popped out of my supply. The wing-mate with the headache nearly kissed my hands when I passed her simple painkillers. As cold season approached, many needed cough drops. Each girl stayed to chat for a few moments.

The little gift I had questioned now led me toward new friendships. As it broke fevers, it also broke the ice, allowing me to meet and befriend many on the wing.

Gradually, the others purchased their own supplies and my kit rarely left the closet.

Eventually, I graduated and threw the dangerously outdated bottles into the garbage, along with stacks of papers and trash—all items now unnecessary. I began my adult life, forgetting the simple medical kit and how it helped me befriend others.

Then one day, I received a party invitation. A young friend was graduating from high school. "Come celebrate with Sarah!" read the cheerful type. Memories of my own party rushed back to me, and I smiled at the opportunity presenting itself.

As I drove to the pharmacy, I knew exactly what gift I would give her. The chance to be a friend.

~Jaclyn S. Miller

Less than Perfect Strangers

How far we travel in life matters far less than who we meet along the way.
~Anonymous

Moving away from home and settling into my residence hall at an Ivy League college was exciting, but now I was anxious to meet my roommate—the girl I would live with during my first year at Cornell University in Ithaca, New York. A clatter of trunks and suitcases and electrical appliances and sound equipment exploded through the door and landed at my feet. LuAnne had arrived.

Like everything from Texas, LuAnne was larger than life. I don't mean that she was overweight. She was petite and pretty enough to lasso the interest of campus cowboys. It was more like she filled up all the available psychological space in our small room. Every nook and cranny of the room reverberated with her energy. Even the ivy-covered walls of the sedate university halls seemed to tremble as LuAnne walked across campus.

One wall of our room now sported LuAnne's large confederate flag. Her high-powered amp blasted waves of rock music down the hall. And though first year students were not supposed to have vehicles on campus, LuAnne managed to smuggle her chrome motorbike up the back elevator and store it in our room. In a few months, we would also have an energetic black Labrador sharing our space. No, pets were not allowed either, but what could our resident advisor say when she kept a floppy-eared rabbit in her own room?

LuAnne quickly settled into her own unique nine-day cycle. For three days she would party with friends. They gathered in our room and formed a rock band. Rehearsals ended with a trip to a local bar. The next three days were quiet as LuAnne slept off the effects of her wild parties. When her headache abated, she would suddenly realize that she had missed six days of classes, and thus the last three days of the cycle were devoted to all-night study sessions as she caught up on all her class assignments. And when she caught up? Well, the cycle began again.

During those first weeks I was in a state of shock. After all, I came from a home full of books and quiet board games. My family might turn on the stereo to listen to classical music or Broadway tunes. Chores and homework were priorities. Had LuAnne moved into our home, she would likely have needed a defibrillator to recover from the contrast to her own lifestyle.

It wasn't that the university hadn't tried to match up roommates with care. My guess is that they figured with me being from California and LuAnne being from Texas, we would both be far from home. We'd share a love for wide-open spaces and all things western. We were both listed as attending the same church denomination too, though I never saw LuAnne step inside a church during our time together. Too bad the university staff didn't know I was originally from Massachusetts and descended from dry, austere, old New England stock.

Gradually, LuAnne and I adjusted to living in close proximity. She couldn't understand my routine any more than I could understand hers, but she came to accept my studious habits. I would never live a wild life like LuAnne, but I began to take steps beyond my comfort zone. When a friend invited me to go skydiving, I went along and jumped out of a plane.

Some months later, several agricultural students tossed a greased piglet in the elevator of our residence hall. They pushed a random button on the control panel, and the elevator doors confined the panicked pig in a few square feet. When the doors opened on our floor, the pig escaped and its squeals rivaled any smoke alarm.

Soon girls all over the floor were squealing too. "A pig! A pig! Get it out of here!"

Girls in underwear climbed up on their desks. One hid in her closet. The more people that joined in the chase, the more frantic the creature became. It ran up and down the halls searching for an escape.

Suddenly the noise stopped. As quickly as the chaos began, it died down.

LuAnne walked in the door of our room holding a squirming piglet under the crook of her arm. She grinned. "Did I ever tell you that I won greased pig contests in Texas?"

LuAnne and I began as less than perfect strangers, but, as room-mates, together we were learning a lot more about life than what was taught in our college textbooks.

~Emily Parke Chase

More than Luck

In prosperity, our friends know us; in adversity, we know our friends.
~John Churton Collins

"**C**ome to the party! Come, I miss you guys!" Ben screamed over what sounded like hundreds of people.

I put my hand over the mouthpiece of the phone and whispered to my friends: "Should we go?"

"It's not like we have anything better to do," Morgan, my room-mate, responded. "We haven't seen Ben since last semester; let's just go for a little."

"Ben," I screamed into the phone. "Ben, where did you say the party was?"

• • •

We trekked three blocks and found ourselves staring at a huge house, bouncing with the booming bass. Ben was already outside waiting for us, sweating through his tight jeans and sweater vest. He was always well-dressed; I wouldn't be surprised if he became a model. He was talking to a group of people I knew were some of his really good friends, holding his cell in his left hand, and a Keystone in his right.

After the usual hugging and chatter that comes with reuniting after a three-month-long summer vacation, Ben's friends bid him farewell. "Take care of him!" they said, and I smiled, knowing that wouldn't be a problem. He led us inside, where a thick fog and darkness immediately engulfed us. When Ben offered me his beer, spilling it on my new dress, I knew that he was drunker than I'd ever seen him before.

The party was like any other party, except it included more hugging because it was the first weekend of the semester. Ben knew so many people. He kept disappearing, but he always made time to come back and steal me away from whomever I was telling about my summer as a cashier at Bed Bath & Beyond in order to drag me to the dance floor.

We ran into Hannah, my friend who lives down the hall, and we all briefly remembered how good it felt to be back at college.

An hour and another beer later, Hannah found me and said she was tired. Morgan and others had already left, and now it was time for us to leave too.

I looked around for Ben, but he wasn't there. I finally found him chatting up some girls, and told him that it was time to go. We all held hands as we walked toward the door, a chain of friendship that would be hard to break. It made me smile, but as I stepped out of the house, Ben let go.

"You know what Jen?" he said. "I'm going to stay—I ran into some people I haven't seen in a while."

"Ben," I said. "Are you sure you'll be okay?"

"Of course, go home! Don't worry about me, I'll be fine!"

As Hannah and I walked down the driveway, I was having second thoughts. "Should I go back in and get him?" I asked. Hannah told me to stop acting like a mother, that he was in good hands, blah blah blah.

We were halfway back to the dorm when I heard a girl clomping in her heels behind us.

"Oh my GOD!" she cried. "Oh my God, someone's been hit by a car!"

Everyone on the sidewalk stopped walking and turned around, and sure enough, there was a crowd of people in the middle of the street, hovering over something, someone. I felt a pit in my stomach, and the girl who announced the news threw up all over herself.

Hannah and I didn't know what to do or where to go. We stood there for a few minutes, praying silently under our breaths that whoever it was would be okay. An ambulance came a few seconds later, and cops started shining flashlights on the sidewalk.

"Everyone go home," they shouted. "There's nothing to see here, move along."

I texted Ben a simple "Are you alright?" just to reassure myself of his safety, but he didn't answer—even though he's always glued to his phone.

We were silent the remaining block back to our dorm, not knowing what to say, and the second we got home we relayed the news to Morgan.

"Oh God," she whispered. "I hope he or she is alright."

"Me too," I said. "Me too."

• • •

I woke up at eleven the next morning to a text from Ben, a simple "Yes." I laughed. Of course he would respond to my frantic text the morning after I sent it.

At breakfast, we were all laughing at the grossness of the dining hall food that we hadn't missed over summer, when Morgan got a call from an unknown number.

"Hello? Oh, hi! I'm good, how are you? WHAT? Oh my God," we heard her say, as she got up and walked over to a corner, pacing back and forth.

"Jeez, I hope everything's okay," someone said.

"I wonder who that could be," I said as I ate my cereal. "Sounded serious."

Ten minutes later, Morgan returned, her eyes puffy and wet. "Ben got hit by a car last night," she whispered. "The kid everyone was talking about, that was him." I dropped the spoon, milk splattered, and before I knew it, my face was drowning in tears.

···

"It's all my fault," I whispered as we waited in the entrance of the hospital lobby, three days after the accident. I was clutching a homemade get-well card, looking at the ground. "I should have forced him to come back with me."

"It's not your fault," Morgan said, stroking my back. "It's the drunk driver's fault, and nobody else's."

We walked up to the fourth floor, intensive care, and took a deep breath before walking towards Ben's room. From a distance, he looked so small. He was curled up on a cot, and I could see the purple bruises on his face from a distance. We walked closer—his arm was in a cast and his leg was wrapped up.

That's when he started crying. His mom, who had come from home as soon as she heard the news, was standing over him, petting his hair, and a doctor came running in. Ben was moaning, and I wondered if it was as painful for him as it was painful to hear.

Doctors came from everywhere and told us we had to leave. We stood against a wall as Ben was wheeled down the hallway, screaming, and crying, not looking at all like the well-dressed, happy Ben we all knew.

The screams finally faded, and the silence cut me like a sword

···

Every day, he got progressively better. I jumped every time the phone rang, waiting for updates. He survived with all limbs intact, minor scrapes and bruises, a few missing teeth, no permanent damage, and a strong will.

When I finally saw Ben a week after the accident, he smiled wide. He was looking great under the circumstances, and he asked just one question:

"Where is my vest?"

The doctors said it was luck, but I know it was more than that.

And I'm certain it's going to take much more than a drunk driver to break our chain of friendship.

~Jennifer Alberts

The Gift of the Magi

Wherever there is a human being, there is an opportunity for a kindness.
~Seneca

My head was pounding. I willed myself to focus on my reading: *The Fall of the House of Habsburg.* I didn't think my mind could actually expand enough to hold all the information I was expected to spew forth in the coming days. Finals loomed like a dark thunderhead ready to break. I tried to rub the fatigue from my eyes and my temples, but to no avail. So I stood and stretched and looked through my blinds to watch the first snow of the season.

As I stared out the window, images of my freshman fall semester seemed to twirl earthward with the falling snow. Memories of the maps I had drawn on sticky notes and then attached to my notebooks to help me navigate my way between classes — in the vain attempt to hide my freshman ignorance. (I'm sure I hadn't succeeded.) My astonishment at finding out that I had enrolled in an upper division class: 300-level Honors Austrian History. (No one had informed me that the numbers in front of a class actually meant something.) The date my friends had set up for me with the guy I was head-over-heels in love with. The too many 7:00 A.M. classes that I had slept through. (I swore never to take a class at that time again.) Indeed, going off to college was more than just taking more challenging courses. It was learning a whole new way of living.

I sat back down at my desk and tried to focus on my studies. In just seven more days, finals would be over and all the students in my freshman college dorm would be leaving to go home—except for me. I would be moving temporarily to another dorm for the Christmas break. Instead of feasting on homemade pies and chewy cookies, roasted turkey and buttery rolls, I would be choking down cafeteria food. Not a prospect I looked forward to.

I had no choice. I was a student from Pennsylvania attending college in Utah and my family of ten couldn't afford to pay for my ticket home. The only reason I was even able to attend college at all was because of the several scholarships I had received.

I stared back at the white fluff dancing through the air. This would be my first Christmas away from home. I was already so homesick I could weep. I tried to block out the Christmas music that filled my dorm floor with its merriness. I tried not to watch my neighbors as they trimmed their doorways with silvery garland and lush red holly berries. I tried instead to think about Austrian history. No luck. My heart and head were filled with too many other things—happy things turned sad. Stockings hung in a long row down our wooden banister. My younger brothers and sisters waking me up much too early with their giggles and excitement. Mountains of wrapping paper Dad would carefully sift through to be sure no gift was accidentally thrown away. Only there would be less wrapping paper in that mountain this year. I swallowed down the ache that was rising in my throat.

My wallowing in pity was interrupted by the ringing of the phone. I reached over and picked it up.

"Hello?"

"Hi, Teddi. This is Elsie." What was my boss from my high school grocery job calling me for? "All the full-time workers here heard that you weren't able to make it home this year, so we all pitched in and bought you a ticket. You're coming home!"

I screamed.

Fifteen minutes later I was off the phone and jumping up and down for joy. Neighbors came over to see what the ruckus was all about.

"I'm going home for Christmas! I'm going home for Christmas! My friends at my high school job chipped in and bought me a ticket! I'm going home!"

My friend Ruth started belting out, "I'll Be Home for Christmas." The rest of those who had gathered and I joined in, "You can count on me!"

Christmas morning, I was awoken too early by giggles and shrieks of joy. But the smell of roasting turkey and buttery rolls baking while the mounds of wrapping paper grew higher and higher filled me with gratitude and love. The kindness of some special friends helped me, a lonely freshman, to have the best Christmas ever.

~Teddi Eberly Martin

Campus Chronicles

Campus Antics

You can lead a boy to college but you can't make him think.

—Elbert Hubbard

Pegged with Eggs

Women do most delight in revenge.
~Sir Thomas Browne

I usually end up dreading the things that most people find fun. I do my best not to let on—my friends and family mostly think I'm a pretty social guy, but I only pretend to be enthused at parties and family reunions. So it was a dumb decision for me to accept an invitation from a pretty college friend named Melissa to attend her sorority's fall formal. It was going to be held in an old warehouse in Knoxville that had been turned into a nightclub, and I was going to have to dress up. It was a wallflower's nightmare, but she was pretty, I got caught up in the moment, and now I was obligated.

I met Melissa in her dorm room the night of the formal and spent half an hour watching her finish fixing her hair. I could tell that she spent a lot of money and effort trying to look good for the night—her dress was red-carpet worthy, her nails were French manicured. She did look good, and it softened my mood a little.

She opened up her mini fridge and tossed me a beer. "We're taking busses over to the club," she said. "So feel free to drink." I asked her whether everyone else was going to be drunk at the formal. "Oh no," she said. "No one's going to be drunk. Our sorority is known around campus as the really classy one."

What happened while we waited for the bus suggested otherwise. One of the girls in Melissa's sorority was stumbling back and forth across the Wendy's parking lot where the bus was supposed to meet us. She fell backwards into her date's arms, and her left shoulder strap somehow got too low. She covered up quickly, but the damage was already done.

Something even more unexpected happened as the group of us stood in the parking lot that night. I hadn't known that the rivalry between sororities was so fierce. Girls walked by us in everyday attire, rolling their eyes and shaking their heads. Some of them muttered insults as they passed.

It wasn't until I felt the first egg hit my chest that I understood the degree of this contention.

A blue Ford Mustang peeled around the corner with a girl leaning out the passenger window, yelling obscenities and giving us the finger. Then the eggs were upon us. Melissa was hit in the stomach and the guy beside me took one in the ear. The girl who was overexposed earlier felt like she needed to regain her dignity, I guess, so she lunged in front of a number of us like a soldier diving on a grenade, and was immediately pummeled with grade As. Those who weren't hit directly were blasted with ricochet.

When the car screeched out of sight, we were left to pick up the pieces. Melissa had fallen to her knees and was sobbing quietly, whispering something about her dress. Courageous boob girl lay on the pavement, covered in egg and motionless. A few of the men in the group tried to chase after the Mustang, but it was useless. We had been utterly defeated by a surprise attack from a rival sorority. Girls on the pavement swore revenge. I looked down at the yellow tie I had picked to match Melissa's dress. Ruined.

Soon the busses came, and most of the sorority and their dates piled in with heavy hearts. Before I could step on, Melissa grabbed my arm and pulled me away. "We're going after the eggers," she said. She was looking down at her cell phone. "I sent a text alert out for the blue Mustang all over Knoxville, and I should get a response in a second." No sooner had she finished her sentence than her phone rang.

Minutes later, I found myself in Melissa's car, barreling down the road. The radio was off and she wasn't talking—the girl wasn't happy.

She was leaning real far over the steering wheel and breathing heavily. Egg dripped down her cleavage.

The blue Mustang had been spotted outside a McDonald's. "When we get there, what exactly are we planning to do?" I finally asked. "Do you think we should maybe just leave it alone?"

Melissa slammed on the brakes and turned to me. "Do you know how much this dress cost?" she growled. "Do you know much these shoes cost? I got my hair done at four this afternoon. Do you know how much that cost? I have yolk underneath my manicured nails. This girl disrespected my sorority, my clothing, and my date. Do you really think I'm going to let her get away with it?"

I shook my head. "Good," she muttered.

We pulled into the McDonald's moments later. Melissa reached over and took off my ruined tie, and then told me to take off my jacket. "I want you to go in there and order two large Cokes," she said. "The girls won't recognize you." I nodded and got out of the car.

"What do I do after I get the drinks?" I asked, before shutting the door.

"I'll be in there in a minute," she said. "You'll know what do."

I walked into the McDonald's and slowly made my way towards the counter, spotting the eggers on the way. I bought the drinks and turned around just in time to watch Melissa walk through the door. She was wearing a T-shirt and shorts—she always kept dirty clothes in the back of her car. Her hair was still up. The eggers didn't seem to find anything out of place, though, because Melissa walked right up to them and began a smile-filled conversation. She stood at the side of their table, and I approached from behind, unnoticed.

"What sorority are you girls in?" Melissa asked, beaming. The girls responded with the name of the rival sorority. Melissa grinned and I inched closer.

"Did you guys hear about what happened?" Melissa asked. "Someone threw a ton of eggs at a formal group. All their clothes were ruined!" Melissa laughed and the girls followed suit. During their laughter, she shot a glance at me and nodded. I knew what she wanted me to do, but I hesitated. What could this possibly solve? I would only be promoting more sorority warfare and wasting delicious beverages.

But then I thought about boob girl. I thought about her sacrifice for the group. I thought about her laying face down on the pavement, motionless and covered in eggs that had been targeted at others. And for that split second, I have to admit, I was filled with sorority pride.

The girls were stunned for a few seconds after the drinks drenched their heads, so Melissa slid their burgers into their laps. They screamed and shot out of their chairs but Melissa grabbed their shoulders and shoved them back down. Melissa took her hands off of them when they began to cry. They just sat there and mumbled words between sobs that I couldn't understand. The McDonald's employees began shouting at us to leave.

Although I hated every second of that night, I was still glad it happened. I quickly stopped feeling sorry for the girls I dumped drinks on—they had it coming.

~Michael Wassmer

Tree of Knowledge

Never regret. If it's good, it's wonderful. If it's bad, it's experience.
~Victoria Holt

I hefted my backpack onto my shoulder, locked my dorm room, and headed for the stairwell. Outside, I looked around for my bicycle, but couldn't see it anywhere. Then I glanced up and saw the bike — nestled high in a cluster of tree branches, completely out of my reach.

I experienced many an excruciating moment during my first, and only, quarter away at college. But this had to be the most excruciating of all. My cheeks burned with humiliation. Who had done this? Did I know the person? Had I angered someone? Or was it just some random and unkind act? It took all my strength not to fall to the concrete in a sobbing heap.

Unfortunately, this was only the latest in a series of incidents that led me to a huge decision. I'd had it. I withdrew from the University of California at Davis only a few weeks later.

I'd decided to attend Davis for one and only one reason — my friend, Karin, was going there. "It's close enough for us to come home when we want, but just far enough away so that it feels like a true college experience," Karin maintained. But she and I ended up living across campus from each other. I was left adrift on a raucous, coed floor (I'd asked for a same-sex, "quiet" floor). I grew lonely and depressed, homesick beyond words. I began restricting my food intake, the only area of my life I felt I could control. If it weren't for my no-holds-barred weekends of eating back at home, I might have easily succumbed to anorexia or bulimia.

One afternoon, I found out that the boys on the floor had rated each of us girls on a scale from 1 to 10. I scored second from the bottom, with a paltry three. I'd never felt so undesirable. How would I ever find a boyfriend?

It didn't help that the one boy I danced with, at the one get-together I attended, didn't talk to me afterwards and ignored me when we passed in the hallways. My self-esteem was suddenly at an all-time low.

Meanwhile, my roommate viewed dorm life as the ideal chance to break away from her conservative upbringing. She began experimenting with drinking, partying, and sex. Because her college experience was at the opposite end of the spectrum from mine, she couldn't sympathize with my unhappiness. And Karin was busy making new friends. She loved the dorms and the socializing. She also couldn't understand my plight. It seemed like no one could.

The story had a happy ending, however. I graduated three years later from UC Berkeley (a university I was able to attend while living at home) a much happier woman. I was wiser, too, for I had learned an invaluable lesson about myself. I was not a typical college student.

Our society places a high premium on going to college, and views the social opportunities to be just as important as the educational ones. Living in the dorms is considered an important and desirable rite of passage. But not everyone is made for college, nor is everyone made for a college dorm. I had a miserable time at Davis, but I learned something important—I wasn't like everyone else. I needed a lot of alone time and privacy, and it took me awhile to warm up to people. I didn't like staying up all night, and preferred reading to partying. And all of that was okay. That was just me.

No textbook or teacher could have taught me a better lesson, and for that reason I don't regret my brief foray into college life. Well, maybe I do regret parking my bike so close to that tree.

~Carol E. Ayer

Blind Instinct

*Good instincts usually tell you what to do long before
your head has figured it out.*
~Michael Burke

"**I** got your name from the college babysitting service," the
man on the phone said. "My wife and I were wondering if
you could watch our two boys next Saturday night."

"Sure." I leaned against the modular desk in my dorm room as
we went over the particulars.

Babysitting wasn't my idea of a glam college job, but I thought
it might be a fun change of pace. That was the best part of college—getting to try new things. I'd done pretty well on that score
in three years at the university, except when it came to dating. With
only a handful of dates to my credit, I still lacked the self-confidence
I sought in those social one-on-ones: what to say, where to sit, how
to act. Everyone said to trust your instincts, but how did you when
you didn't have a clue what your instincts were?

So that Saturday night, while some of my friends primped for
their dates and others hunkered down in their sweats to study, I
pulled on my lime green cutoffs and a T-shirt for my night romping
with two preschoolers. Promptly at seven the phone rang.

"Ivers here. I'm in the lobby."

I grabbed my bag and skipped down the stairs.

"Susan?" A clean-cut man dressed in a sporty knit shirt and tan
chinos approached me, extending his hand. "I'm Tom."

We shook hands. He seemed young to be the father of two but what did I know?

We walked around the horseshoe drive and he stopped at a dark Mustang. A bit ritzy for a grad student's wheels but who was I to judge? He opened the door for me and we settled in.

"I'm new in town. I was hoping you might have some ideas for tonight." He picked the campus paper from the back seat and handed it to me.

"Okay." I rubbed the fringe of my cutoffs between my thumb and forefinger: strange how he wanted advice from the babysitter on where to go with his wife. Midwestern courtesy won out, though, and I pointed to the ads and the weekend calendar. "There are some great movies playing this weekend and there's a concert at the auditorium."

As we talked more about the possibilities, I began to wonder about this guy. His conversation, his demeanor, seemed more like he was on a date while I was definitely on my way to babysit. Or was I? I had to speak up, but what should I say? I went over the possibilities in my head. Everything sounded so dumb. This was worse than a date. He put his keys in the ignition. I couldn't wait any longer.

In desperation I blurted out, "How old are your kids?"

He almost jumped out of his bucket seat.

"KIDS? I don't have any kids."

Guess that was the right question, but not the answer I'd hoped for. My heart pounded. I wished I could turn back the clock and start down the stairs from my dorm room once again—anything to avoid this moment, to see this conversation through to its painful conclusion. But I drew up my courage and continued.

"A-aren't you T-Thomas Ivers?"

"NO!" His voice rose to a question. "You're not Susan Lieberman?"

I knew the name, but it wasn't mine. I shook my head.

We sprinted back to the dorm, racing to be the first one to the lobby.

Skinny Mr. Ivers stood at the phone bank, looking exactly like a frazzled grad student and father of two in his plain white shirt and dull brown pants with his dark hair in need of a trim. Susan Lieberman was there too, dressed much more for a date than I was. Off she went on her blind date and off I went on my blind babysitting job. Guess I didn't need a date to learn how to trust my instincts.

~Susan Rothrock Deo

Showdown on Bedford Park Boulevard

A squirrel is just a rat with a cuter outfit.
~Sarah Jessica Parker

It was a crisp fall morning in the Bronx, a bit cold but still nice enough to have the windows open before we left for school. I was living off campus in a three-story brownstone, starting my first year at Fordham University. My roommates had already headed out and I was about to sit down to a quick breakfast. I went back to my bedroom for a moment to get a book. By the time I returned, a squirrel had planted himself squarely in the middle of the kitchen table. He must have climbed the fire escape and entered the open window. Judging from the puddle on the table, he had either sampled my orange juice or marked his newfound territory in a most vulgar manner. Now he was eating my toast.

It was probably just as well my roommates weren't there, since they were city girls and not up to dealing with wild animals. Still, it was just a fluffy squirrel and they might have thought it was cute as it nibbled away at my breakfast.

"Shoo!" I commanded. The squirrel ignored me and continued stuffing rye bread in his cheeks.

"Shoo!" I repeated, this time waving my hands and approaching a bit closer.

He stopped rather deliberately, looking a bit peeved, and swiveled his head slowly to peer at the interruption to his repast. In all my country years of squirrel interaction, I'd never actually looked one in the eye. They usually scurried away rather meekly, fearful of a big, mighty human. But this squirrel's stare was as cold as his tail was fluffy. I was suddenly reminded I was no longer in the country, but rather nose-to-nose with a New York City rodent. A rat in the 'hood.

"Shoo!" I said again, not sure what else to say. I did not speak squirrel, especially city-squirrel.

Without losing eye contact, he tossed the toast to the side and turned methodically, squaring his body to face me. I sensed a showdown.

In our back woods, my dad once cut down a tree that a squirrel was residing in. The squirrel leaped from the falling tree and ran for what he thought was another tree. It was my dad's leg. He got about hip high before he realized trees don't usually wear jeans, gave my dad the squirrel equivalent of the "Oh my god!" look, and leaped again. Happy ending—my dad lived, the squirrel relocated, and the balance of power between Man and Mini-fur-things was maintained.

In the city, however, Darwin's pecking order had mutated. With his cheeks full of bread, the urban squirrel waddled toward me, swinging his hips like a gunslinger. He stopped at the edge of the table, still glaring, and made a weird chirping sound. It sounded something like, "Bring it on."

No way, I thought, am I getting dissed by an arrogant metrorodent. I laughed and said, "You are SO out of your league, treefreak." I know he understood because he tapped his chest twice and chirped again. Then he drew in a deep breath, as deep as he could take with a mouth full of stolen rye.

Suddenly, he leapt from the table and ran straight at me, chirping nonstop at the top of his little lungs, spewing bits of toast everywhere. Surprised and stumbling, I backpedaled into the hallway as fast as I could. He was inches from me when I slammed the bathroom door in his face, knocking still more bread bits from his cheek. He scratched viciously at the door, calling me all sorts of bad names in squirrel-talk.

Finally the chattering stopped. I waited a few more minutes, looking about for a weapon with which to defend myself. I thought about tossing a towel over him. Not my towel, of course. That could be risky if he escaped, so I passed on the idea. I grabbed my roommate's toothbrush to defend myself and peeked out the door.

The fur-pig was scarfing down the rest of my breakfast. He glowered back at me, trying to chirp, but was too full to say much. Instead, in a gesture of squirrelly rebellion, he pushed over my glass of juice, as if to say, "Let this be a warning."

I thought I could slink down the hallway to my room, get my keys, and leave. He saw me try to escape and jumped to the floor again, running toward me, amazingly quick for a chubby chunk of fur. I was forced to retreat back into the bathroom.

This went on for nearly forty minutes. That corpulent rodent held rule over my house, keeping me trapped in the bathroom, while he trashed the kitchen. I was now quite late for class. Finally, he was gone.

The first facet of an event is the experience itself. The rest, the sizzle to the steak as it were, is in the telling. I suppose I could have lied to my teacher, invented a believable story to explain my tardiness. In hindsight that would have served me better than the peals of laughter that met my truth.

And to the person who left the stuffed squirrel in my seat in class the next day—I WILL find you.

~Annie Mannix

Live Together, Pee Together

My roommate says, "I'm going to take a shower and shave,
does anyone need to use the bathroom?"
It's like some weird quiz where he reveals the answer first.
~Mitch Hedberg

I thought I was ready for dorm life. I had five other family members, plus a dog, so I was used to noise and being around people all the time. Furthermore, I had spent three summers in an academic program on a college campus. I knew how to set boundaries with roommates, raise and lower an extra-long bed, and I knew to bring snacks for late-night cravings.

But there was one element of my college that I was not prepared for. I discovered it on the first day, when my parents were helping me unpack my things, and Mom returned to my tiny single two seconds after she'd left for the bathroom, her cheeks pink. "The bathroom on your floor is for boys."

"Oh good!" said Dad, rather insensitively. "I have to go." But he, too, returned sooner than he should have. "I'll just go when we get out of here," he muttered.

The bathroom was coed.

And not just that bathroom, as I discovered after drinking way too much iced tea at the Welcome Freshmen Picnic. Every bathroom in my building was gender-free.

It wasn't exactly the gravest dilemma in the world. It was just a little jarring to walk into the bathroom and pass that guy with the mohawk, who I'd seen at the picnic, brushing his teeth. Should I say hi? Or should I just head to the stall? And what if I had, you know, a little more substantial business to do? Was I supposed to just let loose with him standing two feet away from me? What if he brought it up later? I could see it now, saying hey to him on the quad, followed by his reply: "That was a huge dump you took last night, huh?"

What would I say? "Yeah, man, that chili was killer."

I settled for a nod as I walked into the stall, and waited to hear his footsteps trail off before proceeding further.

Our bathroom was located between two hallways, so the quickest way to get to the next hallway was to walk through the bathroom. In other words, the bathroom was like an extension of the hallway, and thus, rarely vacant. It was routine to hear snippets of conversation as people passed through while you were showering.

"So last night Jared told me he wanted to open up the relationship."

"He did not!"

I wanted to run out of the shower and scream at them, "Please let me shower in peace! I'm around people all the time! Can't I at least have a quiet shower?" But I couldn't, because I was naked.

Or worse, I would look down and see the hairy feet of the guy showering in the stall next to mine and realize, ew, he was not wearing shower shoes, or have him call out, "Hey, is that you, Eve? This is Chris!" and expect me to carry on a conversation, or the very worst, seeing two pairs of feet in the stall next to mine. Why couldn't they be considerate and at least wait until they had access to a private bathroom?

The older students, it seemed, had fully adjusted to our private business taking place in a public space. On my third week of school, I found a manila folder taped to the inside wall of a stall with a pamphlet sitting inside. It was titled *Read While You Poop*, and contained student-written essays, poetry, and comics. Another day, I entered an upperclassman hallway to find several students of both genders crouching conspiratorially in front of the bathroom door. They motioned for me to halt and stay quiet.

"Matt's showering," one of them whispered. "When Lauren gives the signal, we're going to run in and pelt him with water balloons!"

I began to see that there were two approaches I could take to the bathroom situation. I could continue to cringe every time I had to go, to whine about privacy and loathe anyone who complicated my bathroom experience, or I could make like my upperclassman friends and find the humor. After all, it wasn't the shower-interrupters or male toothbrushers' fault that the building was designed this way. The best I could do was to go about my business and let them go about theirs. And with the exception of the occasional drunk guy who forgot to close the door to his stall (which was just gross), the whole coed bathroom-hallway setup was, after all, pretty comical.

By the end of the year, when I saw Chris in the hallway with his bathrobe and shampoo caddy, I said, "Hey Chris! Showering, huh? Hold on, I need to do that too." I ran to my room to don my own gear, and flip-flopped my way over to the shower stall next to the occupied one. I closed the door, and heard the water start next to me, removed my bathrobe, and turned on my water.

"So," I said, reaching for my shampoo. "Have you started the Psych paper yet?"

~Eve Legato

Goldie

Until one has loved an animal, a part of one's soul remains unawakened.
~Anatole France

I never had a pet. My mother did not want one, but I grew up—in spite of that deprivation—reasonably sane and secure, graduated from high school, and went away to college.

My roommate and I hit it off immediately. We giggled uncontrollably, like idiots, through an entire orientation session, and a bond was created that still exists today. We set up our room and loved every second of it. A place to call our own.

One night we hitched a ride to the local Woolworth's for supplies, and there was Goldie, swimming around with a hundred of her friends and family in a huge tank. I knew right away I had to have her. I bought the fish, the bowl, a net, food, and home to the dorm we went.

I watched her swim and thought she was the most amazing creature in the world, living her graceful, carefree, sparkling life under the sea, so to speak. She waited for me each evening to sprinkle those precious flakes into the water and up she'd come, lips puckered and ready.

The first time I noticed how dirty the water was, I hesitated about the commitment, but only for a second. It became a monthly ritual carrying the bowl into the common bathroom, plugging the sink, standing guard so nobody inadvertently sent her to an early watery grave. I cleaned and scrubbed that bowl, returned her to the water and she would swim around happily once more for everyone to see. No acclimation time — what did I know? Goldie never seemed to mind. She was a hearty, healthy goldfish.

She was there for me whenever I needed her. Tough paper to write? She inspired me from her sparkling depths. Exams to cram for? She stayed up all night keeping me company, never dozing off. She watched as I foolishly let a nursing student pierce my ears. She was the first thing I saw when they revived me from my faint.

Boyfriends came and went, and Goldie listened patiently to my tales of woe and heartbreak. She was a constant in my life, and in my roommate's life too — our personal mascot. Everyone checked in on her when they visited our room and she entertained them obligingly. Most of them had real pets to tell stories about, loyal cats and dogs, but I only had Goldie.

Winter break came. I didn't even think twice. She would have to make the trip home with me. I couldn't leave her with anyone else or abandon her either, so home she came, on my lap in her bowl, for a four-hour car ride. It was tricky, leaning into the bumps and turns to hold her steady, but she survived unscathed.

My mother made no comment, but my father was quite taken with her. He came into my room and visited her, joked often about eating her for dessert, all in good fun. At the end of winter break, I let a little water out of the bowl, and back on my lap she went for the long drive to our home away from home.

Once, a show-off science major boyfriend suggested that I was buying new Goldies to replace old Goldies as they perished, in disbelief that an ordinary goldfish could enjoy such longevity. That was the end of him.

Goldie traveled back and forth to school with me every year, and then, before I knew it, graduation day was near. The usual frantic paper writing, marathon study sessions, and endless parties ensued. In the end, my roommate and I made it to the big day. My parents came down, sisters, brothers, a big event about to unfold.

After the ceremonies we returned to my room to load up the million more possessions I had now accumulated.

I found my father leaning intently over Goldie's bowl.

"Anne, I think your fish is in trouble," he said.

"Funny Dad," I responded.

He was silent. Then, "Anne, I really think you better take a look."

I reluctantly approached the bowl. There she was, floating on her side, dead. I couldn't believe it. I blamed myself... had I forgotten to feed her in the graduation rush? Had I neglected her in some way? I was devastated.

I took Goldie into the bathroom where I had so carefully cleaned her bowl while she swam peacefully in the sink, remembering the good times we had shared, and then I closed my eyes and flushed her down the toilet. I shed a few tears, but somehow it seemed right and made perfect sense. She had stuck with me through it all and now, at the end of this leg in the journey of my life, she was gracefully bowing out, our time together over.

Whenever I think of my college days I remember Goldie. A philosophy professor once told me that people and pets enter our lives at different times for different reasons and sometimes it's best not to wonder why, just to love them while you have them because you never know. He must have had a pet goldfish in college too.

~Anne S. Cook

Last Minute

Life is never fair, and perhaps it is a good thing for most of us that it is not.
~Oscar Wilde

It was my junior year of college and I was taking Comparative Family Systems, a General Education course, but one I actually found interesting. I was a pretty good student in this class: I got to class on time, I wasn't late with my assignments, and I generally paid attention.

One day, my teacher was getting ready to start the class and he told us we could place our papers on his desk.

Papers?! I frantically flipped to my syllabus. Sure enough, we had a paper due that day. I had completely forgotten about the assignment! It wasn't just that I had put it off and didn't finish it — I hadn't even remembered we had to do it! It was supposed to be on the structure of our families and the roles each person played. I didn't want to turn the paper in late, so I had to come up with something... fast.

Luckily, I brought my laptop with me to class that day. While I sat "listening" to the lecture, I typed out my paper. I figured it probably had to be about two or three pages. Since I was in class, it was normal for me to have my textbook out and to be typing. I finished my paper and quickly e-mailed it to myself (thank God for wireless internet!). Then I slipped out of the classroom as if I were going to the bathroom. I quickly went around the building to the library, got on a computer, printed out the paper I had just e-mailed to myself, stapled it together, and headed back to class. I slipped back in, doing my best to hide the neatly rolled-up paper, and slid back into my seat. When class was over, I placed my paper in the stack with everyone else's.

At the next class session we got our papers back. I got an A!

In the same class, we had an assignment to write about the qualities we wanted in a spouse. I was excited about this project and worked on it for a couple of days, really putting thought into what qualities I wanted my future husband to possess. I turned it in (on time) and waited for my grade.

As the teacher passed them back, I felt happy knowing that this paper I had worked so diligently on and put a lot of thought into was surely going to get me another A. If I could write a paper last minute during class and get an A, I could definitely get an A on a paper that was basically my opinion.

The teacher walked by and dropped my paper off. I turned it over.

I had gotten a B.

Sometimes, things like that just happen.

~Genellyn Driver

Lost Cause

The rate at which a person can mature is directly proportional to the embarrassment he can tolerate.
~Douglas Engelbart

It all started so innocently. During my last year of grad school at the University of Wisconsin, an instructor I ardently admired, Professor Gooden, asked me to apply for an administrative position with the renowned Professor Smithson. But I told her I couldn't handle a full-time job in addition to my classes.

She explained that I shouldn't worry, because I was a woman, and Smithson always hired men. I couldn't see the point, but Gooden insisted I would gain valuable experience by using the interview as practice since I would be job-hunting when the school term ended. I reluctantly agreed.

On the day of the interview I learned I was the first candidate to be interviewed and therefore needed to make a strong impression on the professor. I certainly fulfilled that requirement.

I arrived with my combination book bag/purse, stuffed but organized, including cough lozenges and a small packet of tissues. I had recently been knocked out by a nasty cold and still had trouble with occasional symptoms, but I was ready.

Professor Smithson asked me to sit down in the only chair in the room. It was deeply cushioned and featured such a backward cant that it was impossible to sit upright, much less gracefully. I had to wrap my legs around the modular base to keep from sinking out of eye contact with Smithson, all the while keeping my skirt in the appropriate position. I usually wore pants, so the skirt was, as it turned out, an ill-fated nod to the seriousness of a job interview.

As the professor droned on about the job duties, I realized my grip on the chair was slipping and my skirt had bunched itself up much too far. I fumbled hastily with the fabric, trying to right the situation while at the same time keeping balance.

My nervousness must have triggered my latent cold symptoms because I started coughing. No problem; I reached for the cough lozenges in my book bag. Unfortunately, because of my awkward position, I knocked the bag on the floor and the entire contents skittered across the room.

As my nervousness rapidly accelerated, my cough became so pronounced that I began gagging. I tried not to panic, but had to find water immediately. Professor Smithson was oblivious to my predicament and asked me to kindly pick up my things while I pantomimed that I would be back in a short time. At least that was my intention; who knows what he thought my hand gestures meant.

It's not easy to find water quickly in an unfamiliar building, but I located a bathroom and hastily slurped water until my throat settled down. It was the men's room, but no one else was there. The only hitch was that there was no mirror so while I could dab my eyes and nose, I couldn't see my make-up. Only later was it apparent that black mascara and eyeliner had drifted south. Fortunately, since I used make-up lightly, it looked more sloppy than Goth-gone-wrong.

I returned to the professor, who gave me a long look and again asked me to pick up my belongings, which, I realized, included a confetti of receipts and wallet-sized cards. In order to retrieve things from their myriad landing sites, I would have to get down on my hands and knees, which would only have made the interview more uncomfortable.

So I sat there trying to continue the interview until he bellowed, "Pick up your things!" At first I tried scooping with my foot, which proved useless, so I confess I crawled across his office floor on my hands and knees retrieving most, but not all, of my possessions.

Anxiety threatened to highjack my common sense as I obsessed about not leaving anything I would have to come back for.

Worse, my nose started running again and my tissues were missing. The "moisture" was accumulating on my upper lip and there was nothing in sight that could act as an absorbent. Since there was no choice, I decided to leave. My best friend, Rita, told me later, "Honey, it was the only thing a reasonable person would do."

I grabbed what I had salvaged of my belongings and started for the door as I squeaked, "Thank you for your time." But fate wasn't done with me yet. The professor, perhaps feeling awkward for shouting at me, began expounding on his contributions, which were many, to "Ye Olde University" by launching into a description of every successful project he had overseen. Much as I tried to appear interested, my main concern was leaving as quickly as possible.

My upper lip was now full and I had mere seconds before the spillage cascaded downward. As the professor sing-songed without sign of letup, I did the only thing I could; I had to lessen the eventuality of simple physics. I slid my right hand under my nose, wiped furtively, and attempted to flee. But as I turned to leave, Professor Smithson grabbed the same hand to shake it in a farewell gesture.

When he slowly released my hand—how should I say this?—there was a persistent, silvery, dangling bridge of m-u-c-o-u-s between us.

Neither of us made a sound or a movement. He didn't flinch in the slightest. I couldn't tell you what his face looked like because looking at him was more than I could manage. Finally, I staggered to the door and left without a word. What could I possibly have said?

I called my friend Rita and after much consoling on her part she convinced me there was nothing I could do to remedy the situation. "Honey," she moaned, "you have sailed on the Ship of Lost Causes... without a crew. Remember this: 'Forward.' That's the Wisconsin state motto and it sounds like as good a plan as any."

But the next morning, at 5:45 A.M., my phone rang. I thought it might be an emergency and was frightened about my family's welfare.

Unbelievably, it was Professor Smithson. All he said was, "I thought you should know you didn't get the job."

Even though I am not at my best, or even functioning, that early in the morning, instead of making a regrettable comment, I followed the path of maximum restraint and quietly said, "You're kidding. I am so surprised."

He did not say another word. My graduation day did not arrive a moment too soon. And the student Professor Smithson hired didn't even last one semester.

~Kathleen McNamara

Stealth Santa

Never forget that it is the spirit with which you endow your work
that makes it useful or futile.
~Adelaide Hasse

It was December and my first year at college. As it should happen, I was patrolling the campus dressed as Santa Claus, and what a fine embodiment of Santa Claus I represented. I was the Saint Nicholas to stand above all Saint Nicholases. When I spoke, my voice boomed from one block to another. My "HO HO HO" rumbled through my entire body, exploding from my bushy beard in a voice that could defy thunder. And when I called for the reindeer, people two dormitories over would look to the sky expecting a flight of hoofed caribou to cascade down to Earth. Naturally, it only took me about thirty minutes before I was intercepted by the police.

I was heading south on Indiana Street. The police car was coming north. It passed me, slowed down, and stopped. An overwhelming sensation of doom came over me.

I can only imagine what the officer had called in on his radio. "Man in giant red suit with oversize beard; looks like he stuffed a turkey under his outfit."

I thought about offering him a candy cane from the satchel I was carrying, but was concerned that would be grounds for him to draw his gun on me. These are things you have to consider when dressed as Santa.

Instead I simply greeted him with one of my ground-rumbling "HO HO HOs" followed by "Merry Christmas."

He ignored the greeting and asked what I was doing.

I felt that "Pretending to be Santa" was overstating the obvious, but I'm not sure what else he was looking for. I went for safe ground: "Trying to spread a little holiday cheer and Christmas spirit around campus," I told him in a voice that would have caused a tyrannosaurus to tremble. "Would you like a candy cane?" I asked, pulling one out. I decided to take my chances with the gun.

The man did not tremble. Nor did he warm to my offering of treats. He shrugged off the peppermint crook with a dismissive hand gesture. "Are you a student here?" he asked instead.

I didn't have a good Santa response for this one. "I am," I said simply. The words stuck like dried cotton to the air in front of me.

"Can I see your student ID?"

Sadly, my pants were without pockets, but I had thought ahead to wear a pair of workout shorts underneath them and had stashed my ID in these. My reason for doing so was because the ID was needed to get into buildings on campus, not so much because I expected someone to question Santa's authenticity. The picture did not match the beard, potbelly, or the abundance of red I had donned, but he seemed to accept it. He looked up the name on a computer in his car and then traced it in a large binder he had on the passenger seat before returning it.

He seemed satisfied and thanked me. I wished him a "happy holidays," but it felt stilted. Apparently his black book did not say to shoot me on sight. Nor did it say to give me metal bracelets for Christmas. It's good to know Santa is respected by the law.

I watched the policeman drive off while overhead clouds moved slowly across the sky and the moon waned peacefully in its solitude. I shivered. It was cold and my suit only provided limited insulation.

About an hour later I had managed to edge my way onto the third floor of a college dorm, joining a holiday party in progress. I had been there for perhaps fifteen minutes when someone tapped me on my arm. "I think there are some people here for you," the tapper said. Had some female shown up dressed as an elf? A sexy elf? The messenger seemed a little too grave in his delivery for it to be a sexy elf, but who else would be requesting Santa's presence?

I turned around and found the police officer from earlier that night standing by the stairs. He was accompanied by a second officer. They were pretty far removed from being sexy elves. Both of them were somber, and when the first officer saw me looking at them, he motioned me over with a gloved index finger.

Unless I wanted to try my luck at jumping through a window, I was probably going to be having a second conversation with the police. "We've been getting calls," the second officer explained. "People are concerned because they've seen a figure dressed as Santa walking around campus."

"They think you might try and mug someone," the first officer continued. "The problem is primarily with your face being covered."

My heart shattered. Where is the heart and soul of Santa? Does it reside in the potbelly that bulges and shakes? Does it come from his black boots with golden buckles? Is it in his white-gloved hands? No. The spirit is in the snow-white beard, the large red hat, the smile and curl of the mustache. There are thousands of greeting cards with only Santa's face depicted on them, laughing gaily. I don't think I've seen a single Hallmark card featuring Santa's torso.

"Perhaps I should call it a night," I told them in a cool voice. I did not put any of my former mirth into it.

"That'd probably be a good idea," the first officer told me.

Dejected, I left, pulling the beard and hat from my face as I went. The two police officers followed. I don't know if they made sure I returned to my own dormitory or not. I didn't pay much attention. Now I was just some kid dressed up in a red suit.

I got back to my room and stripped off the costume and hung it up. I could have let this end my holiday career. I could have accepted the wave of dejection and finished the holidays as a studious, reserved college kid.

But I didn't.

The police may not have known it, but they had broken a

crusading Santa of mirth and warmth and let rise from the ashes a Santa of stealth. From then on, late in the evening without expecting it, students across campus might hear the loud echo of my laugh, or my declaration of good tidings. But by the time any law enforcement showed up I'd be gone, spreading my cheer at another location. I was Santa and neither the law nor the skeptical campus denizens could change that. They could provide deterrents, but ultimately my spirit, and my faith in spreading that spirit, were unbreakable.

~Rob Snyder

Chapter
6

Campus Chronicles

Difficulties and Obstacles

Adversity is like a strong wind. It tears away from us all but the things that cannot be torn, so that we see ourselves as we really are.

~*Arthur Golden*, Memoirs of a Geisha

Diabetes 101

If you can find a path with no obstacles, it probably doesn't lead anywhere.
~Frank A. Clark

Brushing the sand off my Reefs and throwing my beach bag in the trunk of the car, it dawned on me that there were only a few weekends left in the summer. Slamming the trunk shut, I thought about my life a few summers ago, getting ready to move off to college for the first time.

After discussing my diabetes management with the dean, it was decided that my diabetes supplies were to be kept in my dorm room in a lockable container, alleviating any fear of people stumbling across my syringes and lancets. It was the oddest back-to-school shopping trip I had ever experienced. Of course, there were the standard clothing purchases and restocking of school supplies, but I was the only college newbie who made the hardware store an integral part of her preparation. My mom and I purchased the biggest red tackle box we could find and a padlock to go with it. It safely housed all of my supplies.

In addition to this tackle box, I also had a Tupperware container filled with low blood sugar reaction supplies. Fruit Roll-Ups, juice boxes, raisins, tubes of Insta-Glucose, peanut butter crackers... it was a potluck of fast-acting, just-in-case carbs. And there were cake gel tubes to treat lows stashed everywhere. I had one in every purse, in my testing kit, the bedside table, the bathroom. I looked like I had a bakery fetish.

Aside from my cache of snacks, there were a few other tricks up my sleeve. Tucked inside my wallet, right beside my license, was a medic alert card that read, "My name is Kerri Morrone. I have Type 1 diabetes. If I appear disoriented or intoxicated, please allow me to test my blood sugar, as I may need sugar." I also had my trusty diabetes medic alert bracelet circling my wrist. Emergency contact numbers were pasted to my computer tower.

All of my diabetes accoutrements were in order. All I needed to do was start disclosing my condition to my new roommate and my new friends.

Growing up, everyone around me had always just known. They knew me growing up, before I was diagnosed, and they learned about the disease as I did. Diagnosed as a little kid, my mom took care of explaining everything to my friends' parents. "Kerri has diabetes. She tests her blood sugar and takes insulin. I brought some sugar-free peanut butter cups for when the other kids have dessert. If she looks a little lost, she might need some juice. Oh, and she talks incessantly. That has nothing to do with diabetes." There was no need for me to give a big explanation, as my mother made sure she took care of it.

But now there was this whole college thing. Whole different story. Here I was, thrust into an enormous state university where I didn't know my roommate or anyone who lived in my 300-person dorm, for that matter.

I barely knew this girl's name... how was I going to tell her that I had diabetes? How would she react to my red tackle box filled with syringes? Would she think it was weird to see my little army of white insulin boxes standing at attention in our dorm room fridge? What if my blood sugar plummeted and I needed her to help me? I panicked. How was I going to do this?

When I received my roommate's contact information a few weeks before college started, I called her and introduced myself. We talked about where we were from, what bands we were listening to, and what we were majoring in. She told me she played the cello and would be practicing in the room sometimes. I told her I had diabetes and would be shooting up in the bathroom.

She laughed.

"Really? You take needles?"

"Yeah. I've had diabetes since I was a little kid. It's not a huge deal. All the needles and stuff will be locked up in a tackle box, so you'll probably never see them."

"That's cool."

The conversation gently shifted back to her music career and her life in upstate NY. I told her about my aspirations to be a writer. I breathed easier.

The summer ended and my first day as a college freshman drew near. After a full day of moving all my stuff into the university dorms, my parents kissed me on the cheek and the door clicked shut behind them as they left. Me, a college freshman. I shook my head in disbelief as I started to unpack. Clothes in the closet. Tackle box on the bed. Books spilled out across my desk.

The door opened and my new roommate walked in, suitcases in hand.

She smiled. "I'm Julie." She paused and took note of the red tackle box on the bed.

"I'm ready to go fishing whenever you are."

~Kerri Morrone Sparling

51

A Dangerous Comfort

*It does not matter how deep you fall,
what matters is how high you bounce back.*

~Unknown

"I t's not like you're going to eat any of the cake anyway," said my mother, cutting huge slices of a cold and creamy cheesecake with a chocolate cookie-crumbed bottom, for the guests at my high school graduation party. In just a month I was going off to a prestigious college in a big city to study acting.

"Well, I dunno," I said, confused. I walked away, feeling bad about even having been tempted by the cake. But the desire to have permission to eat it seemed stronger than ever. Well, why can't I? I found myself thinking. All my teen years, as a competitive figure skater and aspiring actress, watching my weight was an obsession in my life. But now that I was entering a new phase in life, I seemed to want to rebel against that restraint.

At the party, I told myself I could only eat the vegetables and focused on smiling at my guests as they congratulated me for being accepted to university and making my professional theatre debut in the months before I went. But inside I was teeming with anxiety. What if I couldn't live up to everything?

Later that night, feeling empty and uncertain, I wandered past the kitchen freezer and found the rest of the cake inside. Everyone in my house had gone to bed. I quietly swiped my finger into the rich creaminess and tasted. Then, as if one bite sparked an uncontrollable craving for more, I ate the rest of the pie and threw it up.

Thus began a five-year battle with bulimia.

A few weeks later, in college, resorting to this behavior quickly became a very viable option for escaping the difficulty of adjusting to city life. From the very first week of school, I found myself bombarded with feelings I could not identify, new responsibilities, and a desire to stand out and make a splash. Deep down, I had trouble trusting that my emotions were valid. I was very good at covering up my anxiety, presenting a golden girl image. I wanted to get it right, to please, to go above and beyond teachers' expectations.

In studying acting more thoroughly, tapping into deeper reservoirs became necessary. Sometimes after scene work classes I felt vulnerable and wanted someone to just hold me, but I was afraid to let down my guard and ask. Instead, late at night, anxious about the next day's work, or writing a paper or reading a difficult text, the most self-reliant thing I could think of was to visit the plethora of food shops.

I have to be thin, I have to be thin. What am I doing?! Those were my thoughts after I grabbed the food. I began to spin out of control. There would be restriction in calories, fad diets (all protein, detox teas, raw foods) followed by binges, vomiting, and a lapse back into the never-ending cycle. Soon, I was engaging in the bulimia a few times a week, then a few times a day.

I was afraid my vomit would clog the toilets so I started using plastic containers or jars. In that, there was also a perverse pleasure in seeing how much I had thrown up. As a result of my behavior, I often felt depressed, drained, listless, angry, and numbed.

Then, during an acting exercise in my last year of college, an intuitive voice teacher looked me in the eye and said, "You have to embrace your inner dragon." At first, I dismissed it as new age mumbo jumbo, but now I see that this wise woman's words were right on target. Recovering from bulimia is about learning to take care of yourself, about knowing your needs, which, if ignored, will otherwise erupt like a dragon's fire.

In the fourth year of struggling to deal with my problem, I finally started seeing a psychotherapist, who helped me look at the underlying tensions in my life. I started saying no to things that triggered the feelings of conflict, powerlessness, and anxiety that were manifested in bulimia.

For example, in my struggle to make money as a young artist in the city, I had been hired a few times as a masseuse at a "guy's night poker party." At the third and last party, as I walked around massaging the stranger's shoulders while they blew cigar smoke in my face with a feigned virility, I felt repulsed by both them and myself. "I don't need to do this!" I realized. The next time they called I said no. There was better work out there.

I started being smarter about my relationships with men in general. I decided to take things slower. In therapy, I discovered a great parallel between my relationship with men and that with food. Jumping into things sexually right away seemed to be my instinctual response when I met someone, but it always ended up being too much to digest, so the romance would quickly be over—just like my overeating followed by the need to purge.

Recovery has been a slow, frustrating process. Relapses were frequent for a long time. But then I started cutting myself some slack. I am the one in charge of my life and decisions. I don't have to be perfect. I don't have to put on a show. I don't have to eat like a health-nut all the time. Stopping the vomiting was a key step, and the toughest part at first was not vomiting after a binge. Soon, things began to regulate themselves naturally. I find it is still very important to constantly stay in touch with my feelings and have a lot of patience.

What I hope to spread to other people struggling with this serious problem is this piece of advice: try to understand yourself. What is it about wanting to eat? What do you really want? For me, it was often a longing for someone else to take care of me, a seeking of comfort from the harsh world. Every day more and more, I realize it is ME who has to be that caretaker.

~Meredith Marie

52

Chicken Soup for the Soul

My Chair
of Perseverance

When you come to the end of your rope, tie a knot and hang on.
~Franklin D. Roosevelt

O utwardly, I joined in the crazy giggles that marked the moments I spent with my girlfriends. We blurted out expectations of college life and teased each other about the guys we'd meet. But inside, my heart ached. Not even my best friend knew the burden I had tucked inside.

Five years earlier, I'd sat in the chair at the ophthalmologist's office, face propped on the chin rest, with a bright light shining on my dilated pupils. Moments later, the doctor turned to my parents. "She does show signs of the disease."

"There's got to be a cure," my mom anguished.

The doctor shook his head. "Everyone's retina reacts differently. We know the disease is hereditary, but the exact prognosis is unknown. She may lose her sight, but when, no one really knows."

But I knew, all too quickly. Night blindness, the first symptom, had come on like a dark monster. Its effect changed my teen years from fun with friends to moments of fear and insecurity.

Exploding with excitement, my friends and I had dashed to our first high school freshman dance. My heart thumped when the star soccer player, gorgeous as can be, asked me to dance. Even when nervousness stiffened my dance moves, the Cinderella syndrome bubbled in me. But the glass slippers didn't fit. To my horror, unable to see in the dim lighting, I ended up with my back to him until he eventually walked away. Crushed, I shuffled toward my friends, my face burning with embarrassment.

I carried that agonizing moment through high school. But now, college bound, independence lured me, but tormenting thoughts about my night blindness dampened my expectations.

Once at the campus, we pulled into the dorm's parking lot with the car stereo blaring our favorite song. Guys tossed a football outside a frat house. Muscles and flirty looks resulted in more excitement.

We unloaded the car, turning our dorm room into crowded quarters of piled boxes and clothes. Once settled in, the afternoon sun filtered through the sparse curtains covering the small window. I looped my long, black hair into a ponytail, slipped into my flip-flops and headed out with my friends. Exploring the campus was our top priority, but for me, another priority dominated my thoughts—finish the walk before dusk. Should night catch me outside, I'd never make it back to the dorm without assistance. The thought of being a burden and imposing on my girlfriends to lead me around turned my stomach. I'd do anything to avoid that humiliating first impression. Hours later, I was relieved to be back in the dorm before dusk.

Unpacking, we giggled and talked into the evening. Lights went on as the blackness of night peered in from the window. My roommate turned from her make-up mirror toward me. "Hey, aren't you coming tonight?"

"Nah, kind of tired," I said. "Think I'll stay in. Besides, I'm not into that kind of music."

What a lie. I would've loved to be with my friends and potentially meet new ones. But the thought of running into someone, falling down steps, or having to hang onto my friends to walk in the dark areas of campus wiped out any longing to venture out.

"Honey, not being able to see at night isn't the end of the world. You'll be fine," Mom had said. But I wasn't fine. I was miserable, angry and lonely. Mom had noticed my "accidents" before when I ran into people, furniture or even walls when the lighting was too dim—dim for me, but not for the rest of the world.

Only a couple of weeks went by and the dreaded possibility happened. A guy in my Humanities class asked me out. My palms grew sweaty, but I gave him a smile and with gentle words, turned him down. The next week he asked again. Finally, out of nowhere, the truth came out. Maybe I thought telling him the real reason would dissuade him. But, to my shock, he shrugged his shoulders and said, "No big deal. If you have trouble seeing, just hold on to me."

Hold on to him? I didn't even know him, but the possibility provided a glimpse of hope. If not, my dating would have to be limited to daytime hours—a ridiculous thought.

Everything changed weeks later. As I strode down the hall toward the cafeteria, I spotted a student in a wheelchair. Unable to use his hands, he moved down the hall while pushing his wheelchair backwards with his foot. With awkward movements, he turned the corner and his books slipped out from his bag. I rushed to pick them up, placed them in the bag and patted his thin, crooked hand. "No problem, they're all back where they should be."

The hint of a smile that shone through the sharp movements of his head planted reality in me. He didn't seem to mind his appearance or the gawky way he maneuvered through campus. I took that image with me to my room that day. In my insecurity, I'd built walls that kept opportunities out and instead, locked myself in my grief. The following week, the same guy who'd asked me out earlier, asked again and I accepted.

With that date, a whirlwind of dating began. Each person provided just enough assistance to navigate through places with dim lighting. Though I never ventured out alone at night, I sensed freedom when I accepted other's assistance. But what shone brighter yet was letting go of my secret.

During my senior year in college, I met the love of my life. But eventually, my vision diminished, robbing even my daytime sight. Devastated, I rewound the scene of the student in his wheelchair who pressed on. And even when complete blindness eventually dropped a black curtain into my world, I remembered how he pushed his chair backwards with determination to move forward. I also used my resolve and drive to face my obstacles and learned new ways to navigate through life. And rather than be impaired by self-pity, I learned to navigate through life by pushing my own wheelchair of perseverance.

~Janet Perez Eckles

53

A Dream of Green Grass

The only thing that overcomes hard luck is hard work.
~Harry Golden

I was born in one of the poorest neighborhoods of Caracas, Venezuela. My dad was a truck driver and my mom was working in a mayonnaise factory when they met. Both had moved from the countryside looking for better opportunities, and in a way they found them. At least they had electricity in their new house.

Neither Mom nor Dad went to school, but Dad was an avid reader and encouraged us to be like him, and they went to great lengths to make sure we did what they could not. I studied hard to make them proud. I was always number one in my class, teachers loved me and I loved learning new things every day.

By the time I was fifteen, we had discussed what I wanted to do when I grew up. Dad dreamed of me being a lawyer, but he was afraid corruption was too powerful in our country so he never insisted. He supported me when I decided to become a journalist.

Mom was very excited about my future too. One day she came home with a brochure from one of the most prestigious colleges in the country, which happened to be located fairly close to our neighborhood. She was so happy—they had a journalism school and the tests were just a few months away. We had to get ready!

I looked at her dumbfounded. She couldn't be serious. That was one of the most expensive colleges in the country, and sometimes we barely had money to take the bus. I didn't say so though; I just told her I didn't want to study with some snobbish kids who surely had no idea what real life was like. I wanted to go to a state college, where the people were more like me.

The only problem with that option was that the constant riots and strikes made it almost impossible to finish a degree there. People would study eight years instead of the five it was supposed to take because of all the time they lost during the never-ending political protests. We knew I needed to graduate quickly, so I could find a job and help out financially at home.

I tried to tell her it was impossible for me to be accepted. True, I had great grades, but journalism was the most sought-after degree, and there were thousands of people fighting for each place.

Mom said there was only one way to find out: by taking the admissions test. I fell back on my last argument — money. I explained what had been obvious to me since the beginning of the conversation. We could not afford it. At that point she smiled triumphantly and opened the brochure she had been holding.

Among the descriptions of the courses and facilities and other information was a very small paragraph indicating that there was a scholarship program. I decided to let her dream a little bit longer, and I agreed to submit my application. I didn't pay attention to the subject until the day of the admittance test. I have to confess I took the exam to humor my mom.

The first surprise came when I saw my name on the list. I was accepted! Only one other kid from my high school was accepted that year.

My dad, who is usually the most pessimistic person in the universe, was terrified. How were we going to pay the tuition? My mom used one of her typical answers, "I don't know, but we will. Even if we have to work day and night, our daughter is going to that college." Her determination was so strong we didn't dare say anything. It wasn't only my dad, though — my whole family thought we were just plain crazy. It was a college for rich people—how did we even think it was possible?

By this time, I was allowing myself to get excited by the idea. I knew a degree from that college would open doors that I never dreamed of, but I was still too afraid to get my hopes up. We filed the papers for the scholarship and for weeks we waited, wavering between eagerness and panic about what the answer might mean to us.

Finally I received the news. I got a scholarship that would cover eighty-five percent of the tuition for three years, and if I earned good grades they would give me a soft loan for the remaining two years that I could pay back once I got a job. What had seemed impossible only a couple of months ago was really happening. I was going to attend one of the most exclusive colleges in Venezuela.

I won't say college was easy. I did feel out of place most of the time. I had to borrow material and books because we could barely find the money to pay the fifteen percent the scholarship didn't cover, much less for other things like books or photocopies. I had only one pair of jeans and two tops.

I did not go on vacation to Miami or Europe, but I still got good grades and met the best friends I could ever imagine. We would sit on the grass, which was always so green and fresh, and talk and laugh and study.

The day I graduated, I gave my mom the medal. We walked by the campus, with everyone smiling at us, my mom beaming. She was so proud. I remember telling her that if it weren't for her, I would have never even tried. In her characteristic nonchalant way she said, "Don't worry about it, baby. Even before you were born I would pass in front of this university every day on my way to work at the factory. And from the window of the bus I would see the mowed lawns and the students lying on the grass, and I would think: one day a daughter of mine is going to study there. You see? I just knew you would. I dreamed of this green grass too many times; it had to come true."

I found a good job after college, paid off my loan, and won another scholarship for a master's degree. I now work for an international company. I've traveled around the world. I'm moving to New

York, and the time when I didn't have money for the bus seems really far away. But I never forget that it was my mom's dream that made me do what everyone thought was impossible.

~Moraima Garcia

Waiting in Line

A hug is the shortest distance between friends.
—Author Unknown

I tried not to cringe when Maggie told me the first thing she does every morning is take ten different pills. Then she has a cup of tea—coffee contains too much caffeine for her heart to handle. She then heats up some breakfast, but she takes careful note not to stand in front of the microwave. Exposing her chest to radiation waves could make her pass out.

Maggie and I were in a linguistics class during my first semester at Syracuse. We sat and giggled together at our white-bearded professor, who mumbled to himself in a lecture hall of 500-plus students and told his assistant to scram. Maggie seemed amicable enough, and I'd been having trouble making friends, so I finally summoned the courage to ask her to grab some lunch one day after class. She seemed thrilled beyond belief.

As we walked around the quad, Maggie revealed to me that she didn't have many friends at Syracuse. Real friends, that is—ones who would support her, regardless of her condition. I looked her in the eye. Condition? Did she mean being a transfer student from Oklahoma? Maggie sighed. She asked for my confidentiality, and we made an awkward pinky-swear on the sidewalk.

She told me about that fateful day during her high school chemistry class when she first blacked out. The muscles in her heart had hardened, preventing the chambers from properly filling with blood.

Over the course of the year, she had sensed slight arrhythmic imperfections with her breathing.

It wasn't until six months later that Maggie was diagnosed with restrictive cardiomyopathy at the Mayo Clinic in Flagstaff, Arizona. Her heart was a normal size, but it could not expand or contract between heartbeats. We had just begun our fourth lap around the quad—well past lunchtime—when Maggie started tearing up. If I hugged her, would it seem like I just felt bad for her? I wanted to empathize, not sympathize, but I had no idea how.

"It was so traumatic for my family, especially for my dad," Maggie told me. Her dad had been diagnosed with restrictive cardiomyopathy eight years ago, when he was forty-one, and has been living with a heart transplant for six years. But since the condition is much rarer in young adults and females, Maggie told me, her likelihood of receiving a heart transplant in the near future was grim. I could only think back to my own family traumas. They paled in comparison.

"My condition is progressive, so every day it gets worse," Maggie said. She lifted her blouse and pointed to her heart, where an artificial pacemaker regulated her heart rate. "But everyone's dying anyway, right?"

I winced as she spit out the stats like they were a list of lunch specials. The growth of the waiting list for a heart transplant outpaces the number of donors, she said, and each year fewer than one-third of the people who need organs get them. Doctors want you on your deathbed before you are eligible to move to the top of the list. Sporadically, she'd receive voicemail updates regarding her priority on the waiting list.

My mind was frantic. You can't die, Maggie. You have too much to live for! Keep fighting! I had only shared two classes a week with this girl, but it was as though she could read my mind. "The hardest part is broaching the 'I'm dying' subject when meeting new people," she said. She recalled telling some friends in high school, but they backed away and stopped calling. Her boyfriend of several years had just broken up with her because her condition had gotten too intense for him.

I asked her if she resented the doctors and nurses who had put her on that dreadful waiting list, who had prescribed the dozens of pills she'd be taking for the rest of her life. "We act like the only solution is transplants," Maggie said. She told me about her dream—a career in preemptive health to make things better for others. "Modern technology allows so much, and I want to be a part of that." She smiled as she wiped away the tears that had gathered in the corners of her eyes.

It was our seventh lap around the quad, and I couldn't help noticing all my carefree colleagues playing Frisbee and basking in the sun (a phenomenon in snowy Syracuse). They had no idea about Maggie's restrictions, or her struggle just to make it up a flight of stairs. For a moment, I hated all of them, so naïve about the harsh world out there. But Maggie stopped me. "Life isn't about keeping score," she said simply. "God doesn't give us more than he knows we can handle."

That afternoon on the quad, I learned from Maggie. Everyone you meet is fighting a harder battle. I held out my arms and asked her if she needed a hug. Indeed, she did. And so did I.

~Megan Hess

Caleb, Maybe

Trouble and perplexity drive me to prayer
and prayer drives away perplexity and trouble.
~Philip Melanchthen

I t was the dawn of a new day to most people, but I had yet to get a wink of sleep. I watched the rain all night. This particular morning was murky, cold, and misty. My alarm went off at six.

Dressed in a T-shirt and jeans, I sat nervously waiting. I bit my nails with my eyes on the clock. The telephone rang and I jumped. I grabbed my coat and my keys as I made my way to the telephone. "Hello," I answered. It was my friend.

She squeakily said, "Hey, you ready?"

I gravely responded, "Yeah, I'll be down in a minute."

We met in front of our dorm and as we made our way to the parking lot, I reflected on our years of friendship. I remembered talks we had in middle school about what we wanted to do after graduating from high school, at what age we wanted to get married and start a family, and how many kids we wanted to have. She wanted to go to college, get married in her mid- to late-twenties, and have one child, a boy. Curious about her choice of name, I asked her what she had in mind. "Caleb, maybe," she responded.

That was nearly six years ago. She had blossomed into a beautiful, outgoing, and dignified young woman. In high school she was a member of the National Honors Society, an exceptional soccer player, a counselor at our local Boys & Girls Club, and a dedicated volunteer in our community. She had a boyfriend whom she dated through high school. She knew how to balance family, friends, school, and a relationship. I looked up to her.

It was going to be a long trip. We stopped at a nearby McDonald's. She only ordered a hash brown and a small orange juice, since she was not supposed to eat anything too heavy. We hit the road. No radio, no conversation, just the sounds of the engine and the wheels against the road. It was the longest, most silent eighty miles, perhaps for the both of us.

As I drove into the patient parking lot of the National Women's Health Organization, I parked beside a silver C-Class Mercedes Benz. I looked at my friend with concerned eyes. I saw the uncertainty and took her hand. "We're here. Do you still want to do this?" She didn't answer. She unbuckled her seatbelt and headed into the clinic. Turning off the car, I sighed.

We sat in the waiting room. All types of women were here—young women who looked to be of high school and college age, middle-aged women who looked as if they already had a few kids, and then there was a particular woman who looked as if she had a very successful career. Some of these women had the support of husbands, some of boyfriends, some of friends, and then some were alone like the businesswoman.

We waited until my friend's name was called for the pre-counseling session. She asked me to go with her. We entered the counseling room. The drab little room contained a round table cluttered with paperwork. I frowned at the unkempt appearance of the facility. I left the counseling room when the session was over and found my way back to the waiting room. My friend was taken to the room where they would do the procedure.

The dismal atmosphere of the overcrowded waiting room was not alleviated despite efforts to decorate it warmly with vivid bouquets of flowers and lively abstract paintings. I decided to wait in the car. Upon exiting the clinic, I witnessed what I had only seen in movies and on the news. Before me, about thirty feet away, were anti-abortion protesters. There were nine protesters. One man held a seven-foot crucifix made of wood. Two girls were holding an over-sized poster reading, "I got an abortion, and I regret it every day." All the protesters were saying a prayer. "God, bless the sinners, for they know not what they do…" is all I heard as I made my way to the car with a heavy heart.

I reclined my seat and attempted to adjust myself to take a nap before the trip back to school, but I never found comfort. Apprehension clouded my mind, sorrow robbed my soul, and desolation permeated my heart. I felt myself breaking down. It had been a difficult struggle. I was her friend and she had called upon me to fulfill the obligation that true friends share. I couldn't hold back any longer. I let my tears go and did the only other thing I knew how to do. I prayed. I held on to the thought that she might walk out of the clinic untouched; however, that was not what I prayed for. I prayed that God would give her what she needed: a clear mind and the strength to persevere. Her life was going to be different either way. That day would always remain with her, invading her thoughts and manifesting itself in unsolicited dreams. The decision she faced, and what she felt that day, would become all too familiar, and if she remained haunted, I prayed that I would be there, comforting her.

As I wiped my tear-stained face, I pulled down the visor to protect my eyes from the sun. A 4"x 6" piece of glossy white paper fell into my lap. I had stumbled upon a picture of an ultrasound. I held the picture close to my heart, and said to myself, "Caleb, maybe."

~Jestena Hinton

Katrina University

A bend in the road is not the end of the road
unless you fail to make the turn.
~Author Unknown

New Orleans. New Orleans isn't just a city; it's a state of mind, a way of living, an understanding among people, a sign of hope, a place of faith, and uniqueness and creativity at its finest. When New Orleans first entered my life, it was just the place where I would attend college for the next four years. I knew it would be my home away from home, but I didn't realize it would steal my heart.

My first three days of college at Loyola University New Orleans were normal. Attending freshmen orientation activities, meeting new people, signing up for classes and adjusting to the glories of dorm life. The fourth day was a little different. None of my friends from home got a wake-up call similar to mine.

My suitemate woke me and delivered the news that would alter my future dramatically: "There is a hurricane heading our way, and we have to evacuate... now." I hopped on a Greyhound bus with my roommate to go visit a friend for the weekend at the University of Alabama. I figured that it would just be a three-day journey away from my new life, but after my twentieth hour on the bus, I had a feeling I might not be returning for quite some time. After missing connecting buses, taking cabs, sleeping in hotel rooms and never actually making it to my original destination due to hurricane traffic, my parents eventually convinced me to take a flight home.

When I finally returned to Connecticut to find out that a Category 5 hurricane was headed right for my new city, reality hit. I prayed and hoped that somehow the laws of nature would spare New Orleans. Then the levees broke.

New Orleans went into a complete state of chaos. My eyes were fixed to the television as I saw suffering and devastation. People being lifted from their houses, weak and scared. Whole communities washed away, only the rooftops still visible from a bird's eye view. I saw the mayhem and kept asking myself, "Is this America?" It was hard for me to comprehend that what I was seeing on television was the United States and not some unruly third world country.

I sat miserably on my couch for days with my eyes glued to CNN. I couldn't even imagine what the next step would be. After a week went by, it was obvious we would not be returning that semester... maybe never. Loyola's communication system was down, and we were left confused and lost, with no direction from the school on what to do next.

We eventually found out that other Jesuit schools were opening their doors to hurricane students, so my fellow New Orleanians and I took a trip up to Boston College. When we got to Boston, we were anything but excited. The admissions people were taking us on tours, introducing us to deans and priests, showing us their course selection, and bragging about their facilities. Even if they had had castles as dorms and swimming pools as classrooms, I would not be content, simply because Boston was not New Orleans. When I went to receive my Boston College ID, I think I scared the photographer with my death stare. I couldn't wait to get out of there, but even more, I dreaded my return in three days.

I went home to prepare for entering a new college... again. But I didn't even have anything to pack. As a girl, in her freshman year of college, it is safe to say I took everything I owned to New Orleans. I evacuated with a pair of jeans, a shirt or two, and oddly enough, my comforter from my bed because I thought I would be sleeping on the floor in my friend's dorm. I had nothing else. I packed up all of the old, out-of-style clothes that I had planned on never wearing again. I rummaged through my mom's and sister's closets to see if I could find anything that fit, but my mission was unsuccessful. I attempted to go shopping, but for the first time, shopping was not fun. I had no motivation to get anything; I didn't even know where to start.

I made the same trip to Bed Bath & Beyond that I had made a week prior in New Orleans. I purchased the same bright blue and green towels, the same shoe rack, the same fold-up laundry bag, and the same 300-thread-count Egyptian sheets. On that Sunday, my parents packed up the car, since I had no willingness to do it myself, and I began my journey up to Beantown.

When I arrived, my parents were "ooing and awing" as we pulled up to the cathedral style buildings, enormous stone walls, perfectly manicured football stadium, and aligned, full oak trees. We were directed to my dorm, otherwise known as the old seminary. It was a beautiful stone building up on a grass hill across from campus. When I arrived, it was the first time in days I felt relief as I saw other students miserably unloading their belongings and fighting with their parents; I knew I wasn't alone.

While some of my peers grew up during their first year of college, I was forced to grow up in my first week. Boston College was very accommodating to us, but my first semester of college was a tough journey. I had to completely change my plans and my state of mind, and think quickly on my feet. After the semester was over, we had to decide if we wanted to go back to New Orleans or make other plans. There was no doubt in my mind; I wanted to return to where I was originally supposed to be.

I can't pinpoint what made me come back after the hurricane. I'm not sure if it was my long, painful Greyhound bus ride out of the city that made me think that, after all the effort, I had to go back. I'm not sure if it was the intense passion I felt while watching the eye of a Category 5 hurricane head straight for my bowl of a city, or seeing the first signs of hope and life emerging in the French Quarter. It might have been the loyalty I saw coming from the people who stayed behind and stood strong. It could have been those three days I spent there that drew me back. Then again, it could be all of those reasons. All I know is that I saw something in this city. I felt a feeling that I had never felt before; it was a deep, soul-burning passion that pulled me in like quicksand and pulled me back once again.

~Cristina Catanzaro

Impossible Is Nothing

I ask not for a lighter burden, but for broader shoulders.
~Jewish Proverb

I was a very athletic college student; so athletic, in fact, that I ran the Boston Marathon the first three years of college, and had every intention of running it for a final time my senior year. I would have run it every year I was in college.

I was just beginning my last year of college in Worcester, MA, which was very much a college town, and times were near perfect. I had a full-time academic career, a part-time job, and a very smart and beautiful full-time girlfriend.

My best pal Ben had just visited me. Our friendship had survived a lot: fights, girls, summers, and living states away made it difficult to maintain a friendship, but we did. Tonight, another friend, from home, was coming out to my school to check out my campus life, and then the rest of the weekend would be devoted to the young woman who had stolen my heart a little over a year before, Jenna.

I had recently celebrated my twenty-first birthday with a campfire in my backyard and a few friends back in the beginning of July, and I was excited about the proximity of my college dorm to all the local Worcester bars. I could walk the half-mile to the bars with my friends and not have to worry about a designated driver. But we were going to be walking from party to party, rather than bar to bar, tonight because my friend from home was still a few months away from his twenty-first birthday. In my rush to get the night started, I locked my keys in my dorm room. A few hours (and parties) later, when we were intoxicated, we noticed that we couldn't get into my room. I, being the daredevil, just thought to myself "Okay, this is not a big deal. I'll just climb from the hallway window to the big tree branch and into my room window." An easy enough stunt, and I'd be able to show off for my fellow dorm residents who had begun to form an audience.

I climbed out the window a few minutes after it began to rain. I got from the hallway window to the tree branch without any problem, but as I attempted to climb from the branch to my window I felt the slippery bark begin to lose its traction....

That's it. That's all I remember from that point on for a few months. That night I was declared brain dead. My parents received "that call," the telephone call that says your son has been in an accident under the influence of alcohol, and that you should come to the hospital as fast as you can. Upon my folks' arrival at the hospital, I was confirmed legally brain dead. My parents refused to accept that I was gone. They pushed, prayed, and pleaded for surgeons to attempt an emergency neurosurgery. They did, and the surgery was miraculously successful despite the surgeon's caveat that a successful surgery at best would mean a life in a vegetative state. What ensued was twenty-three days in a coma, four months in the hospital, and two years as an outpatient at numerous rehabilitation hospitals.

• • •

Now, for the good news—in less than three short years I have gone from being a marathon runner, to a label six on the coma scale (which is the point at which the hospital calls the coroner) to a college graduate, to a motivational speaker whose aim is to educate students about the consequences of the decisions that anyone can make under the influence of alcohol.

I awoke from the coma, the victim of a TBI (Traumatic Brain

Injury), unable to speak, walk, talk, or even breathe on my own. I went through an unsuccessful surgery to amputate my right leg due to internal bleeding and what is known in the medical community as "tone" and "compartment syndrome."

On April 16th, two years later, I proved a motto that I now live by to be true. I overcame the impossible. Doctors said it had only been done once, to their knowledge.

What happened on April 16th, you may ask? I ran the Boston Marathon for a fourth and (I think) final time. The year after the accident, I was in a wheelchair. The next year, I could hobble no more than a few steps. As soon as I was able, I attempted and completed the marathon in seven hours and fifty-one minutes flat.

The motto I live by?

Impossible is nothing.

~Scott Maloney

58

One Too Many Times

Nobody can make you feel inferior without your consent.
~Eleanor Roosevelt

"**D**on't go in there!" my roommate Suzy whispered seconds before I was about to open my bedroom door.

"Not again?" Exasperated, I whispered to Suzy who was sitting on the couch. "It's two in the afternoon!"

Suzy giggled, "I guess Rachel doesn't care what time it is."

"I need my portfolio case; it's in my bedroom," I said with a sigh, and joined Suzy on the couch.

"Knock on the door."

"No! Who's in there anyway? Jack? Rob? Mike?"

"It's Mike."

Suzy, Lauren, and I were high school friends. The three of us met Rachel at a party. She seemed nice enough, and we needed one more person to share the rent for a two-bedroom apartment. The four of us happily signed a one-year lease. Excited to be "roomies," Rachel and I shared a room and Suzy and Lauren shared the other. Our apartment was perfect, close to the university, nicely furnished, and we even had a laundry room next door.

"This is ridiculous; my room has turned into Rachel's brothel," I told Suzy. I went into the kitchen to gather my feelings.

I yanked open the refrigerator door. Pickles, ketchup, and mayonnaise rattled as my anger began to grow. Should I keep giving up my room? No! I shouldn't have to keep giving up my room! I pay rent! I slammed the peanut butter and jelly down on the counter.

It all started the first time I said "Yes" to Rachel's request. A few months back, when I came home after studying in the library, Rachel was making spaghetti for a guy I had never seen before. They were drinking and laughing.

Rachel quickly ran over to me and whispered in my ear, "Do you mind sleeping on the couch tonight?"

My first thought was, yes, I did mind sleeping on the couch! But then, I thought I'm in college now. College life is notorious for this, when you have a roommate. I wanted to be cool, not a prude. After all, it was only one night.

"Sure," I said.

I opened the peanut butter jar and tried to stay focused on making lunch. I dug some out with my knife. Smearing it on, I accidentally tore a big hole in the bread.

"Great," I said, dipping the knife into the jelly.

Another galling thought. It was the night when I beat Rachel home after a party. I raced to my bed and felt immense satisfaction. If she brought home a guy tonight, they would have to sleep on the couch, not me. Early the next morning, I made my way to the bathroom and accidentally glanced at the couch. Hanging off of the couch was a bare-bottom rump. And it wasn't Rachel's. It belonged to some guy she met at a party. He had his leg swung over hers. The faded worn blanket they shared didn't cover much of their skin. A creepy quiver came over me and I felt sick to my stomach. Oh my gosh, it was so gross—our nice apartment had turned into Rachel's male playground. Unbelievable.

Deep in thought, I added too much jelly to the slice of bread and it slid off the crust. I had a sandwich disaster that I would have to clean up.

While I grabbed for the sponge, another moment replayed in my mind. It happened on a rainy day when I came home early from class. I didn't think anyone was home until I heard a duet of giggles and manly laughter from the bathroom. As the shower ran, their voices got louder and louder. Before I knew it, they came frolicking out wrapped in towels, chasing each other into my room. I was speechless.

Rachel just giggled some more when she saw me and said, "Oh, I didn't know you were home, Ande."

All I could say was, "Yeah."

I was fed up that my other roommates weren't taking some of the brunt of Rachel's monkey business.

The next time I heard, "Ande, don't go in your room, Rachel's brought home another guy," I said, "One of you sleep on the couch instead of me!"

Suzy gave up her bed, but sleeping on her used sheets didn't feel right to me. All I wanted was my own room and my own bed — that I paid rent for.

Rachel's seemingly innocent request months ago, "Do you mind sleeping on the couch?" was a pile of you-know-what. One night turned into another and another. One boyfriend wasn't enough for Rachel. Once a week, she brought home a new guy and made him dinner or drinks. The weeks added up, and before long she had a different guy for breakfast, lunch, and dinner. How she managed to keep them straight in her mind was a mystery, not to mention they never knew about the others.

My appetite was gone. I scooped up my sloppy peanut butter and jelly sandwich into a squishy ball. With sticky fingers I threw it into the trash. Washing my hands, I thought of all the things I was going to tell Rachel. Enough was enough. No longer would I be a pushover to her skuzzy ways. My other roommates weren't going to say a peep, that was obvious. It was all up to me. I was an adult and in college now, and if I didn't speak up, no one else would.

After Rachel's "man of the day" left, I met up with her in our bedroom.

"Rachel?"

"Yeah."

"You know this is my room too?"

"Yeah, so?"

My anger boiled, I blurted, "So... I am sleeping in my bed from now on. If you want to sleep around with lots of guys you better go somewhere else." After I spoke, I surprised myself.

She let out a huff and looked away. Then she said, "No worries. All you had to do was tell me."

"Good." My uneasy heart pounded. Finally, after many nights on the couch—why had I waited so long? On second thought, was it really a waste of time? Speaking up for myself was a lesson that I never learned in class. After my frustration and fury had subsided I realized I had been taught a valuable life lesson. Being Rachel's room-mate made me grow personally. Spending one too many times in shock over Rachel's actions had helped me learn to speak my mind. I would never be the same again.

~Ande Cantini

59

Roommate Wars

I don't need to pay a therapist to give me crap.
I have a roommate that does it for free.
~Ally McBeal

"Eww! Gross!" When Maddi's drunk boyfriend started
to hurl, my four roommates cleared out in a hurry.
Including Maddi, who scrambled for her room, saying, "I can't deal with this."

This naturally left me to clean up yet another mess. Ever since
I'd moved into this apartment at the beginning of my junior year,
my dreams of escaping dorm life—and a string of awful roommates—had turned into a nightmare.

Freshman year, I'd started with Party Girl, who went out just
about every night, since her late class schedule let her sleep till the
afternoon. She'd bump into the corner of my bed at 2 A.M. and throw
on the lights. Her boyfriend came up for days at a time, giving me a
choice between sleeping on someone else's floor or being treated to
a live sex show.

Next, I lived with the Prison Matron. At first, I was thrilled to be
with someone who kept regular hours. Soon, I was receiving the glare
and a loud sigh when I spoke softly on the phone with my mom at
9 P.M., or didn't turn the lights and my computer off by 10. She was
better than an alarm clock in the morning, too, since she popped out
of the hay with the roosters while it was still dark out.

I got used to stepping over other people's mess. I got used to listening to twenty-four-hour show tunes. I got used to other girls' hair in the sink and shower drain. But slowly, dorm living had been driving me insane.

Now, I'd discovered apartment life was no better. I shared a tiny room with two other girls. One had had sex in my bed while I was away. Another set a hot iron on the carpet and burned a hole we all ended up paying for. The special food I'd put aside was cooked and eaten, and my scorched pots were left in the sink to grow miniature rain forests of mold. The others threw drinking parties that could have gotten us arrested. They routinely left the doors unlocked and the windows open when the apartment was empty or we slept at night. My lamp was knocked over and broken.

But Maddi was the flat-out worst in a very competitive field. Raised to be her parents' princess, she simply didn't understand any other way of being in the world. At first, I thought we could compromise on the sorest points, including having her boyfriend living practically rent-free in our very crowded apartment. I was sick of having to "cover up" just to grab a drink from the fridge, or be confined to my cramped three-girl bedroom because every single night Maddi and Tim were using the living room that my rent was paying for. I wanted to cry when I walked into the kitchen, just in time to see them fixing two triple-egg omelets, using the last six of my eggs!

So finally I approached her with the gentle suggestion that she and Tim go to his apartment a couple of evenings a week. She gave me a blank look, clearly puzzled. "But I don't want to." She said the words slowly, so I could understand her.

Soon, things got worse. Every time her toilet clogged—a regular event—she called on me to attack it with the plunger. She never washed a dish, never carried out trash, never picked up. I tried "roommate meetings," complete with doughnuts for good will. She'd promise to vacuum, which was the least "icky" of the chores, but then not follow through. Even my other roommates grew just as frustrated with her as I was.

When she took a dislike to another girl in the building—whom she didn't even know—she dropped food off our balcony onto the girl's car. Not only was this a mean thing to do, but any idiot could figure out pretty quick just which apartment to check for the perpetrator.

When I was talking to any of our other roommates, Maddi listened in, always sure we were talking about her. In all honesty, a lot of times we were. With Tim always there, we had no privacy, and our living situation was becoming intolerable. I couldn't get anywhere trying to reason with her, so I basically started ignoring her.

Then she called her mother and cried, because her roommates didn't like her. Next thing I knew, her mother had driven six hours to hold court in our living room, screaming at Maddi's bedroom-mate and flinging obscenities at her, threatening to have her kicked out of college and her parents' home taken away.

As a music major, I needed to go play a concert, but I was actually afraid to walk through my own living room. I called my mother in a husky whisper, sounding — I'm sure — like a war correspondent. "Mom, I'm trapped in my bedroom!"

Mom suggested I just leave quietly, and smile and be polite if confronted. When I did this, Maddi's mother whirled on me. "What are you smiling at, b*tch?! You're going to get what's coming to you!"

Things escalated after that, with Maddi's father, an attorney, repeatedly calling my mother at home at 10 P.M., threatening lawsuits if I didn't start treating his daughter better. Mostly, he talked about how we'd made her cry because we didn't include her in things. Mom tried to calm him down, but finally he announced his daughter had been forced to move out because I had subjected Maddi to anti-Semitic abuse! He told Mom he was filing a lawsuit and also asking the administration to expel me. Mom tried to tell him that my grandfather was Jewish and we had many Jewish relatives, but he hung up before she could get the words out.

In the following weeks, my orchestra conductor spoke to me. He'd received a complaint from Maddi and her family, and asked if I had any trouble with staying in orchestra because of her. I told him of course not, and he smiled and that was that. Fortunately, he knew me better than they did.

The middle of senior year, I moved into a single room in a shared house. I had to carry my own toilet paper with me or it all disappeared. And the kitchen overflowed with trash, skuzzy dishes and scummy water. My neighbor on the other side of my thin bedroom wall played finger cymbals night and day. And the illegal sublet in the back part of the house flipped out one night over the way his mail had been handled, and stabbed a note into the wall with a kitchen knife to express his anger before he was finally reported to the police and evicted.

Now I'm in grad school. Roommates? No thanks!

~Marcela Dario Fuentes

60

Still Here

If you're going through hell, keep going.
~Winston Churchill

He is wearing the same knit beanie cap they described on CNN. His face, emotionless, scans the audience at random, pausing when he detects his next target. I am sitting there, in that poorly lit auditorium, in the same chair where I always sat during that same class two years ago, surveying his every evil motion. He moves with a sort of order and ease, as if he has been planning this attack since birth. He looks at me, and I at him. His steely gaze holds me for a moment, as I realize I am looking into the eyes of Satan himself.

And then I wake up. Unbearably cold, yet ironically sweaty, I sit up in bed and adjust my eyes to the darkness around me. He is gone, along with the hard metal rows of seats and the sheer panic and disorder of the classroom.

• • •

I was hoping for roses. Two hours away from my boyfriend, on love's biggest holiday, I was secretly wishing for a bouquet of flowers. It was as if he had read my mind when I heard a knock that Thursday afternoon. I had just come back from campus, and was watching a stupid talk show because nothing else was on. The delivery guy wished me a happy Valentine's Day as he handed me a large package that I knew to be flowers, and I wished him the same as I smiled back.

The arrival of the twelve red roses marked my last ten minutes of normalcy and security as a twenty-two-year-old girl. I wish I had used those ten minutes differently. I should have gone walking and absorbed the beauty around me, as I often did when I was a child. I never suspected that the beauty would disappear for me in just a matter of minutes, nor did I imagine that it would take so long to come back to me. I should've captured that world before it lost its innocence.

I was thanking my boyfriend for the thoughtful flowers when my call waiting beeped. My roommate was calling while she waited for the bus after her last class. I clicked over, excited to tell her that I skipped my last class to come home early in hope of flowers. I never got the chance to mention the roses. She was out of breath and panicky as she told me of a shooting in Cole Hall. She knew nothing else, only that a teacher had told them to stay in their building because someone said something about a gunman.

I went online to find a yellow alert on the school's webpage. "Possible gunman on campus," it read. "Get to a safe area and take precautions." My mind reeling, I wondered what a safe area consisted of. Was my apartment, five minutes from campus, a "safe area?" Was a crazed maniac with a gun on the loose, seeking shelter from the police in any apartment he could find? I checked all my windows to make sure they were locked.

In a panic, I tried to call my father, only to find my phone had stopped working. I dialed again, and again, and yet again... still my numerous attempts at reaching the outside world floundered. Now, in a full-fledged panic, I found myself cursing Verizon Wireless. My thought process and reason delayed, it finally occurred to me to turn the television station to the news. And there it was—my school! There were all of my buildings on national news; all of my former safe places were now a scene of sheer chaos and panic. I did not cry. I did not move. I sat in front of the screen that had moments before displayed smut entertainment and watched as my school fell apart at the hands of brutality. What had once been Columbine and Virginia Tech was now Northern Illinois University.

After I discovered that no cell phones were working, I realized that Verizon Wireless had not failed me after all. The hardest realization, however, and perhaps the most frightening, was that my school had not failed me, either. I could not point a finger at NIU officials or our police officers or our professors. There was no blame to be placed on my fellow students or my friends or my family. For the first time in my seemingly short life, I could not hold anyone accountable for my gut-wrenching pain. The only person I could blame for creating this living hell was Steven Kazmierczak, who, in killing himself and five amazing individuals, also murdered my sense of safety and security.

More than two weeks later, away from the quiet rage and hurt we were all experiencing on our beloved campus, I sat in a dark movie theater and tried to focus on some dumb comedy my boyfriend had convinced me to see. He nudged me throughout the film, asking why I wasn't laughing. Didn't I find the movie funny? How could I explain to him, to everyone so far removed from February 14th, that I couldn't see the humor in the movie because I was too busy looking at the audience. Did anyone seem out of place? Could someone have brought a gun into the theater? Could I die tonight? I calculated which exit I would crawl to if the situation arose. A friend later asked me if the movie was worth seeing. I had no idea.

In class the other day, a counselor brought up symptoms of grief and depression. She grabbed my attention when she brought up the term "survivor's guilt." Was it possible that I felt guilty for not being in that classroom on Thursday? This idea seemed preposterous to me. Of course I did not feel guilt... did I?

Alone with my unbearable thoughts, I now know what that counselor was talking about. I don't know if guilt is quite the right word, but I am experiencing something very similar. For some unknown reason, Steven Kazmierczak did not select my particular classrooms that day. He could have. He very well could have. Had he woken up earlier in the morning, was there a chance he would have picked the building next to Cole—the building where I sat bored and inatten-tive, oblivious to what would unfold just hours later? Did I see him that afternoon? Was he parking his car as I was leaving campus? The questions will not stop, and although I am fully aware I will never find answers, my mind will not sit still. We will never know why it was Cole Hall, but indeed it was, and I am still here. I cannot make any sense of this.

My roses died that night—fittingly, it may seem. They must've realized the joy they momentarily brought was over, and their deep red color made me cringe. It was the same red that soaked the dirty snow outside Cole Hall—the same red that seeped from the wounds of my fellow, fallen Huskies.

• • •

I put on my brown, furry snow boots, kick at the snow, and wait for the bus. It eventually arrives and I take my seat with the other stu-dents as we head off to campus—tired, deprived of dreamless sleep, and eerily quiet. We look at each other, though. For once in my four years at this school, we actually really look at each other. And we feel the pain, and we bear the hurt, and we share the agony of that day. We wear our red and black ribbons over our shattered hearts, and we keep going. The bus drives on and we look out the windows, hopeful that one day it will take us back to the harmlessness of yesterday. For a moment, as we pass untouched snow and aged oak trees, it seems almost possible. I close my eyes and take it all in.

The brakes of the Huskie Bus signal our stop, and I open my eyes. We are stopped in front of Cole Hall.

~Stefanie Smith

Graduation and Liberation

Strength does not come from physical capacity.
It comes from an indomitable will.
~Mahatma Gandhi

Graduation day is a peculiar one. After spending four years completely immersed in the lives of your friends, you abruptly shift your attention to family and future. For weeks you've been in survival mode—papers and finals and late-night pizza and parties—and then suddenly there you are, on the day where you formally and finally exit this world that has been your... everything.

I remember that sunny day in May well. My roommates and I were living off-campus in a building filled with upperclassmen. After spending two years in a dorm room the size of a walk-in closet, this three-room apartment was heaven. It was an old building, but that only lent charm to our autonomy—wood floors, sculpted moldings, high ceilings, and tall windows letting in lots of light.

On the morning of our graduation, the apartment was abuzz with preparations—hair, gowns, caps, and families arriving for the traditional brunch before the ceremony. My parents were recently divorced, so the day had been neatly split in two: the more affordable breakfast with Mom and my stepfather, followed by the expensive dinner with my dad and his girlfriend. My younger sister Robin would ride up with my mother to bridge the divide—attending both the celebrations. Everyone would be at the graduation, of course, in separate seating.

My roommate Margie's parents arrived first, and then Annie's. Everyone lingered, waiting for my family. Before they left, Margie asked if I wanted to join them. She was in high spirits. Annie's family stayed on, growing concerned. "Are you sure you don't want to come to breakfast with us, Kelly?" they pressed. I wasn't worried at all and practically had to force them out of the apartment. My family had a longer drive than theirs, close to two hours if there was traffic, and I would rather have a rushed breakfast with them than a leisurely one without them.

Just as the apartment emptied, the phone rang. It was my sister Robin on the other end, and she was sobbing. They weren't running late, they weren't stuck in traffic, and they hadn't had an accident. They hadn't left yet, and they weren't coming— at all. My mother was drunk.

The apartment grew larger and emptier and quieter, and I grew more alone. How would I face my roommates and their families with this news? I couldn't inflict this on their day too.

"Why?" I wondered through tears I tried to stave off. "Why today? Why me?"

It made sense to me when my mother drank because her life was lonely and empty with my father working all the time, or when she drank because of troubles in her new marriage, but it didn't make sense now. I had been her friend, her ally, and her confidante all these years. Why would she be drunk on my graduation day, and so early in the morning at that?

After suggesting my sister quickly call my father to salvage a ride for herself, I hung up the phone and felt a chilled emptiness replace the excitement inside me. I considered lying to my roommates and their families. I considered not going to graduation at all. I considered not existing at all.

I didn't want to be in this messed up family. I didn't want this story to be mine. I had grown up in a "good" family where my mom kept the house clean and made cookies for Christmas. She was always there—after school, whenever I called, no matter what I asked for. What kind of graduation gift was this?

I let out a deep exhale of grief, and then sucked in determination. This is MY graduation day, I told myself. This is the day that celebrates my last four years of studying and learning. I am graduating Magna Cum Laude! This is MY day. This is about ME.

I draped my robe and cap over my shoulder and began walking the thirteen city blocks to campus. I continued walking past the college until I got to Cavanaughs on City Line, our hangout. My roommates and I joked that we had purchased their new ceiling with all the dollars we spent there. Opening the heavy door, I moved out of the sun and into the cool, dank darkness. There, even though it was morning and graduation day at that, I found another classmate having a beer. I hopped up on a barstool and joined him. There were even pastries laid out instead of the classic relish tray of hot peppers, horseradish, and spicy mustard. In a booth alongside us, another friend sat with his family. I regained my sense of place, and a bittersweet feeling of belonging. With a beer and a pastry for breakfast, I reclaimed this day as mine and headed to my graduation ceremony.

There's not much more I remember from that day. Most of my friends were in the Business College so I sat among relative strangers in the college of Arts and Sciences—without having to explain my morning. There's a photo of me with the sun in my face as I received my diploma. Afterwards, I hugged friends goodbye and we all rejoined our families. My father took me to my favorite upscale Italian place on City Line. Though it seeped from my pores, there was no talk about my mother and what happened that morning, especially in the presence of our future stepmother. My sister and I smiled at each other from across the table with weary eyes and bruised hearts.

My mother's drinking got worse that summer and instead of joining the "real world," I left it, backpacking through Europe in the fall while classmates embarked on careers. The following year, I fell in love with the man who became my best friend and partner.

My mother "hit bottom" the week of our wedding and arrived

drunk with matted hair. We had two ushers escort her down the aisle. In the face of community pity, I was thankful she made it at all. We both wore the same shoes—hers in cream, mine in white. We had picked them out together. Her dress hung on her emaciated form.

While away on my honeymoon, she went into rehab, and then spent the next ten years sober. She apologized for my graduation and my wedding. I just smiled and told her it was okay. I loved her too much to feel all the anger and betrayal and sadness. I didn't want to threaten her precious fragility.

My mother was diagnosed with lung cancer during my last trimester and died two weeks following the birth of my son. Her beautiful photo sits beside my computer as I write. Sometimes I yell at her, and sometimes I cry tears of anguish and abandonment. But mostly, I smile, grateful for her and for knowing who I am apart from it all.

My graduation morning stands out as a defining moment in my life's story. Sharing it now drains what hold it still claims on my heart and spirit, revealing a strength of character and purpose that I'm proud to call my own

~Kelly Salasin

Chapter
7

Campus Chronicles

Lessons Learned

Remember, there are no mistakes, only lessons.
Love yourself, trust your choices, and everything is possible

~Cherie Carter-Scott

Learning to Pay Our Way

When on the brink of complete discouragement, success is discerning that...
the line between failure and success is so fine that often a single extra effort
is all that is needed to bring victory out of defeat.
~Elbert Hubbard

I t was in our junior year that my brother Larry and I ran into money problems. When we first started college, we were at a state school where tuition was cheap. But after transferring to a smaller private school, the tuition skyrocketed. Trying to figure out how to pay for college for the two of us turned out to be a lesson in itself.

At first, we managed with student loans, grants from the government, and work study. Work study was part-time work we did on campus, in this case working at the university library. It helped to defray part of our college costs, and being among all those wonderful books was a fringe benefit of the job. We juggled this financial cascade for the first two years with no problem. Then came the summer of our junior year.

Usually during the summer we worked full time and didn't take any classes. Our work study program provided enough hours for us to save for the coming fall semester. It was a formula that worked very well, provided we scrimped and saved. Luxuries were not part of the program. Still, we felt ourselves pretty lucky to have a job that allowed us to help pay for school.

But the third year that we walked into the business office ready to sign our work contracts for another summer, we were told that the rules had changed. Unless we were enrolled for classes during the summer we couldn't work for the college. But because we didn't have the funds for summer school we couldn't enroll, and that meant we couldn't work during the summer to save money for the following fall.

We tried to argue our way past this Catch-22, but the reply was always the same: rules were rules. Besides, according to the new rules, even if we were offered summer jobs at the library they'd be at greatly reduced hours. The chances of finding outside jobs this late in the summer were pretty slim and it looked like our chances of staying enrolled in school through to the next semester were about to fall apart.

Then our supervisor offered us a slim chance. She said there was something that the campus needed done, a project that they had lost money on and were looking to recoup their losses. We were led to a large auditorium in the science building. Inside this gigantic lecture hall we were confronted with a mountain of junk. The junk was the disassembled and broken pieces of office modules; fragments of walls, desks, and cabinets used to create new office spaces.

"Here's the deal," our supervisor told us. "This was a bad buy for the campus. Our engineering team tells us there's nothing we can do with it. We bought it to provide offices and departments with desks, workspaces, and the like. Right now it's a total loss. If you want, I'll give you the summer to find a way to turn this junk into something we can use. You'll be independent contractors. Find a way to do that and I'll pay you for a summer's work."

"And if we can't do it?" I asked.

"Then you don't get paid. That's the best offer I can give you."

My brother and I looked at each other. "What have we got to lose?" he told me.

"We'll do it," I told our supervisor. "You've got yourself a couple of fix-it men."

Our first big hurdle was where to start. It took us a week to separate the huge roomful of junk into smaller piles of walls, cabinets, hinges, and bits of plastic and metal that we couldn't put a name to. There were no blueprints, no instructions to follow. We looked at our collection of bits and pieces and began scratching our heads.

Next we scouted out the departments and offices that had requested tables, desks, and workspaces, measuring and taking notes. Some offices needed new desks. Other departments needed cabinets. The campus library, the department we couldn't work for during the summer, needed a ton of shelves for new books. We sat on the floor of the auditorium and sketched out what needed to go where. There was no way the pieces would go together as they originally had. Some we'd have to saw and hammer back into shape. We'd have to design our own tables, desks, and shelves and figure out how to put them together.

We went down to the wood shop; the basement where the props and backgrounds were made by the drama department for plays produced on campus. We commandeered electric saws, hammers and nails, everything we'd need to do the job. By the time we'd set everything up in the auditorium, we had a game plan.

For the next three months, we measured and sawed and hammered and screwed and bolted those pieces of junk together. Bits of plastic and metal that had been consigned to the junkyard slowly turned into desks, tables, cabinets, shelves, workspaces, and everything else we could imagine and put together. We built dozens of shelves for the library. Each day, we carried heavy metal, wood, and plastic pieces from one end of the campus to the other. We worked harder that summer than we'd ever worked before. By the time we were finished, the only things left that we hadn't found a use for were a few nuts and bolts and a handful of plastic.

We took our supervisor on a tour of the campus, going from department to department, office to office, showing her the things we had created from that massive pile of junk. She looked everything over, tested its strength and use, and watched as people used the things my brother and I had built together.

"Well," she finally said, smiling at us. "Looks like I owe the two of you for a full summer's work."

My brother Larry and I sat in the empty auditorium on the last day of summer, remembering the mountain of junk that had first greeted us here. When fall came around and we were able to pay for our tuition, we knew we'd learned something here at college that we hadn't anticipated learning. We'd learned our own worth, through the creativity we'd brought to the job, the belief that we could do it, and the sweat that we'd poured into it. That summer was a summer of learning that served us well through the rest of our college careers and beyond.

~John P. Buentello

Wednesdays

It's not who you are that holds you back, it's who you think you're not.
~Author Unknown

In my high school, one of the most popular cliques was a group of ten or so preppy, sporty, attractive girls who splatter-painted white Juicy Couture jumpsuits that said "Seniors '08" in their senior year and wore them around school every other Friday. They were dubbed "The Jumps" at graduation. When I heard this I almost died with laughter, and then practically dissolved into tears. "Oh no," I thought, "I had a stereotypical high school experience. With clique names and everything. Oh the shame."

I was under the impression that traditions like this would be replaced in college by "real" groups of friends who enjoyed each other's company and bonded in healthy friendship and happiness forever and ever.

My first week at Northwestern University was a whirlwind of sleepless "New Student Week" excitement. I made good friends with my peer advisor, a girl named Jane. I was drawn to her awesome theatrical resume, and since theatre was my major, I decided to interview her about it. Apparently, she was the most accomplished sophomore in the theatre program, having worked on thirteen theatrical productions in her freshman year on the production and management end of things. I stared wide-eyed as she explained her achievements and all the opportunities she had been exposed to and taken advantage of in the theatre culture on campus. She had a ton of hilarious and cool friends. She got great grades. She knew what classes to take. I had gone to Northwestern to be her. She was my college role model, the big sister I never had.

I decided right then and there, the first day of New Student Week, to become Jane Williams as soon as humanly possible. I developed a plan. I would study her brilliance with precision and subtle persistence, never letting on that my desire was to become just like her, but instead flattering her enough and being "cool" enough that she would think I was the logical choice for a mentee/apprentice.

One night, Jane introduced me to her friend Steven who was producing a show with a student theatre group that I wanted to join. We talked about the show he was producing and how interested I was in participating. Jane bragged about me, "This girl is the next big thing—she's awesome."

Later that night, I received an e-mail from Steven asking me to assistant produce the show. I had six heart attacks and screamed and woke my roommate. I couldn't believe it! Me? Getting to assistant produce as a freshman in my first few weeks of school? I could hardly breathe. Things were starting for me. I'd make connections in the student theatre network and do more productions and then I'd be on my way to being just like Jane Williams. I patted myself on the back.

I was on a cloud for another couple of days until one night I received a text from Jane: "What r u up 2 tonite?"

My heart skipped. Could she actually be asking me to hang out with her? Impossible. She had older friends. They wouldn't actually want to hang out with me.

"Come over 2 my apartment at 10."

Oh my God. Oh my God. Oh my God. I knew that Jane was going to be my mentor but I couldn't imagine that she was going to be my friend, too. I was going to be in her group of friends! She was my "in" to social success, as well as academic success. I couldn't believe my skill. I felt like I'd pulled in the big fish and now it was taking me for a joy ride around the water.

I spent about thirty minutes choosing what to wear. I tried to look casual and put-together at the same time. I left twenty minutes early so I wouldn't get lost. I rehearsed a few things to say and a few jokes. I smiled in my pocket mirror. I did breathing exercises to calm my heart. I felt three years younger than I actually was, so unprepared and unqualified.

I knocked on the apartment door and they let me in excitedly. There were mixers all over the counter and one of Jane's friends held two bottles of liquor in each hand.

"Oh my God, she's here, our little freshman!" he said.

"Welcome to Wednesdays," Jane laughed.

I walked in, smiling and tentative. I felt naked. All six of them were staring at me — no, probing. Sometimes you can just feel when you are being judged.

But I kept my composure and laughed along with them as they told jokes and gossiped about everyone they knew, about who said what stupid thing and who did what unbelievable thing.

They asked what drink I would like and read me the list of mixers. I didn't plan on drinking but I asked for an appletini because it was the first thing that came to mind. I held it all night. Finally, when they were drunk and I thought they wouldn't notice, I went to the bathroom and dumped out my drink in the sink. But they caught me, and when I returned they said, "Oh, the old dump-it-in-the-sink trick. Did you guys see that?" They kept asking me, drunkenly, "So who are you, Hannah? Give us the dish. We want to hear all your dirty secrets." I'd try to change the subject, not because I had dirty secrets, but because I was worried that if we got into it, they'd see how really innocent I was and I'd feel more naked than I already felt.

But what caught my attention most was their continual mention of the word "Wednesdays." It became more than just a day of the week when they talked about it. It was like a name. I asked them what "Wednesdays" were. Jane laughed and looked at Steve and said, "You explain."

Steve told me that last year they had all started drinking together on Wednesdays. Once everybody sort of knew about it, they started calling themselves the "Wednesdays." He told me they were trying to find a new member, so they wanted me to come tonight. Then another guy leaned forward and said, "This is an audition." They laughed it off like they'd been joking, but even with all that popcorn-fluff I could feel that kernel of truth at the bottom of the bowl.

I kept smiling, but said that I should probably leave.

I lay in my bed that night trying to think what they reminded me of. I was stumped. I couldn't figure out what had gone so wrong. I tried to put together the pieces: they were judgmental, funny, exclusive. They had a name....

And then my heart sunk as I realized what I had done. I had allowed it all to happen and hadn't seen the signs, because I'd thought college would be nothing like high school. It hit me then exactly who they were — they were the "Jumps."

Jane never invited me again. She spoke to me cordially on occasion, but I mostly tried to avoid her. She set up a lunch date to check on me out of obligation, and then cancelled the day of the lunch. I was relieved.

I have a new group of friends now. I don't feel naked in front of them. I don't have to drink an appletini. They are not perfect, but being with them feels like sticking my hand into fresh soil. It feels tangible, authentic, and organic. It feels like how I thought college would feel. It feels like home.

~Hannah Greene

A Place
to Call Home

Unselfish and noble actions are the most radiant pages
in the biography of souls.
~ ·David Thomas

I didn't quite know what to expect the first time I drove down to St. Vincent's. I had volunteered on a whim when I decided to stay behind in Baltimore for the summer following my freshman year of college. Right before freshman year, my family moved from Pennsylvania to Maryland. Going "home" over the summer wasn't exactly an option for me—staying at school to work made more sense. When Marya, my boss at the campus community service center, asked me if I'd be interested in driving a van of students bringing sandwiches and drinks into downtown Baltimore every Tuesday evening, I thought, "Why not?" I figured it'd be a good way to help pass the time until school started up again.

Loyola College's Care-A-Van program normally runs from September to May, when the regular academic year is in session. Student and adult volunteers travel down Baltimore's winding Interstate 83 until they reach this open lot situated right next to St. Vincent's Church. Some people call the place Tent City on account of the makeshift houses erected using some rope, tarp, and two trees. Father Jack calls it People Park. Regardless, if you've never had an encounter with a homeless person before, the lot next to St. Vincent's would be the place to start.

Traditionally, volunteers arrive bearing ham and cheese sandwiches and containers filled to the brim with iced tea and water. In the winter they bring hot chocolate. During the summer, we brought lemonade — lemonade, sandwiches, as well as some good company and conversation.

It was desolate. The grass that once blanketed the lot had died off, replaced by a morbid, dusty brownness. Cars zoomed by the place, kicking up dust in their panic to get to the safety of the highway. Sometimes people stopped at the red light glanced out their windows at the people there; staring emptily, apathetically, they often returned immediately to the comfort of their cars' front windowpanes. "This is it," I thought. This was pathetic, sad: an empty, ominous, dirt lot, decorated with a few dying trees here and there and boxed in on three sides by asphalt. St. Vincent's stood on the fourth side, mocking the conditions there. For any religious homeless folk, the irony of having God so near and yet so far must have been unbearable.

And then there were the people. They lived in blue-tarp tents held up by some sticks and white rope; the Boy Scouts would've been proud. Others slept on benches, their clothes folded up in piles underneath, covered by today's newspaper, which doubled as a blanket in the night. One man rested on an old, musty mattress, dressed only in boxers and an undershirt. No pants; no socks; no shoes. Father Jack would later tell me that the guy had AIDS, as well as a drug problem. No dignity either, I suppose. I was numb.

"Would you like water, iced tea, or lemonade, sir?" What the hell was I doing here? Me, a nineteen-year-old preparatory school graduate. I had both my parents, a car, a nice life; I was the quintessential Prince of Suburbia, and now I was hanging in downtown Baltimore.

I tried starting conversations with some people. How do you talk to a person who's homeless? I was nervous — I thought they all resented me. I hated being "well off." I shouldn't have, but I couldn't help it. What could I possibly do for anyone here?

This one guy — his name was Eartle, which was easy enough

to remember, since it sounded like "Myrtle Beach"—was lounging against a tree that still had some life in it, using its leaves to provide shelter from a sweltering June sun. Summers in Baltimore are hot, even at 6:30 at night. I went over and introduced myself, feeling guilty because I couldn't stop my darting eyes from absorbing the scene around me: Eartle on a makeshift cot, surrounded by a couple of trash bags holding his personal belongings and an overturned cardboard box he was using as a table.

We talked; he called me Prince Andrew to remind him of what my name was. "Yep, that's me," I thought. "Prince Andrew of Suburbia." I told him I used to live near Philadelphia. He had some friends up that way. He asked what I did at school.

"I'm an editor of *The Greyhound*."

"Yeah? They came down here and interviewed me once."

Next Tuesday night I was back. Eartle was still there, under that same tree. I brought him a couple of sandwiches and hunched down next to him. He invited me to have a seat on his cot. He asked me how my week had been. "Rough," I replied. "Busy at work, and I'm taking a summer class."

"Just keep pluggin' away," he said. We sat in silence for a couple seconds. Then it happened.

"How'd you end up here?"

I shouldn't have done it. It was rude and misguided; this guy sleeps on a cot at night, and I had the audacity to ask him how it happened.

Eartle laughed. "Choices, Andrew—it's all about choices."

And then he went on and on about his life. He had served during the Vietnam War. According to him, a bullet had been lodged in his brain for some time; it was out now. He played baseball during the war on a traveling team. They went around the States recruiting soldiers. I just sat and listened.

He had been to a lot of hospitals. A lot. They all had cute nurses, though. Eartle was an expert in cute nurses. He had a million different jokes, and they were all funny. We laughed it up, Eartle and I. I learned he was Native American, and he told me stories about festivals he'd been to in Baltimore's Patterson Park. Eartle was starting to feel like a second uncle to me. Oftentimes I'd forget that I had to get up and leave at 7.

Tuesday night became the best night of the week. When work ended at 5, I was busy helping to get stuff ready for my weekly trip to People Park. I raced down I-83. After my job for the night was finished, I sauntered over to my seat on Eartle's cot. We talked baseball. We talked about journalism and newspapers. Actually, Eartle did most of the talking, always pausing every ten minutes or so to see if I minded. I never did. I just sat there and listened, and baked in Baltimore's summer sun.

I laughed to myself later on. In Baltimore, I was about two hours from my life in Pennsylvania. In a way, then, I too was homeless. But Tuesday nights were different. With Eartle, I had one good hour every week where I could just forget the world and get wrapped up in conversation about anything. I forgot that Eartle was homeless. Instead, I remembered that I had a buddy, a friend—a semblance of home.

~Andrew Zaleski

65

First Failure

I have not failed. I've just found 10,000 ways that won't work.
~Thomas Edison

I leaned my head on my hand and stared with large, blank eyes at the overhead in Professor Chang's physics lecture for electrical engineers. I was completely lost. There were drawings and equations, all in pretty colors, but all complete gibberish to me. I had no clue why semiconductors worked, nor did I care to know. Was this what engineering really was? My mind swirled.

As I sat in class scrunching my eyebrows and rubbing my temples, I became more and more stressed by the fact that I did not understand a single sentence leaving Professor Chang's mouth. How could I not understand these equations? I had always excelled in math and science in high school, and now, as I looked around the lecture hall, I seemed to be the only one drowning in the material. The other students asked intelligent questions that raised good points with the professor, while I sat back attempting to scribble everything down from the slide before we moved onto the next topic I would surely not understand.

As a freshman in college, I was actually failing a course for the first time in my life and I didn't know where to turn next. Did I really want to be an engineer? I knew they designed systems to make things work. What things? Apparently everything. Did I care why my microwave, cell phone, or car worked? No, it just worked, and I didn't care why as long as it wasn't broken.

I picked my college major back in freshman year of high school. I excelled in math and science, knew I wanted to make a difference in the world, and discovered the profession of environmental engineering with the help of my guidance counselor. I was entranced by the fact that it was an up and coming field, great monetary potential, and would help save the world, but I didn't realize what engineers actually did... until now.

Throughout my eighteen years of life, I always had a goal and I always worked hard until I achieved that goal. Because of my AP credits from high school, I was already technically at the sophomore level in the engineering program. How could I throw that all away? I would have to start at ground zero. Did that mean I would need an extra year of college? What would my parents think? And if I wasn't going to be an engineer, what was I going to do? I felt my whole world crashing down around me in that lecture and began to feel like I was going to hyperventilate.

I left the class and immediately ran over to my advisor's office. I let her know that I simply could not be an engineer. I had to drop the physics class immediately. She informed me that I was too late. I was too far into the course to drop and no matter what, the grade would be going on my permanent GPA.

Oh dear God, I was going to have an "F" on my pristine report card. An F. An F! F for big Fat Failure! I knew I had to go home and call the only people who could possibly make me feel better, my mom and dad.

As I dialed the number, I felt the tears welling up in my eyes, debating how I would tell them that their perfect straight A student was failing a class!

The phone rang and then my mom answered. With my throat tightening from the tears I was holding back, I managed to squeak out "Hi, Mom."

"Honey, what is wrong?"

"Mom," I sniffled, "I'm failing physics and I don't want to be an engineer anymore."

"That's it? Oh dear, sweetie, you almost gave me a heart attack. I thought you were pregnant or something... which, if you ever are, we will work through as well. Okay, what happened?"

I explained to my mom about how lost I was and how engineering was not what I expected. She explained that I was being harder on myself than I needed to be. It was okay not to be perfect all of the time, and she and my dad would support me in whichever career path I chose. She recommended I go to the career advising center on campus to take some career tests to give me ideas on other options.

Feeling like a huge weight was lifted from my shoulders, I followed her advice. I took a few career tests and realized that there were jobs out there that I never even knew existed. I wondered how seniors in high school could possibly be expected to mark a box on their college applications signifying what major they were choosing, when we truly hadn't been exposed to more than a quarter of the possible occupations that existed.

Each test actually pointed me in the direction of teaching, a career I thought was an easy way out before. I pondered the fact that I still enjoyed math and sharing my knowledge with others. I liked the idea of helping high school students realize their potential and I could also coach swimming, which I loved.

A few weeks later, I journeyed back to my advisor to inform her of my decision to switch majors. Unfortunately, she reiterated the bad news that I would still have to finish the dreaded physics course and it would stay on my record. I started utilizing the physics tutor lab on campus and even thought about visiting my intimidating professor during office hours. I was afraid he would think I was stupid and would not understand why I was so far behind, but my grade was on the line, so I swallowed my pride and timidly showed up at his office one day. Although at first he seemed perturbed to be taken away from his research, he warmed up to the fact that I was making an effort to succeed in his class.

After a grueling semester, with every spare minute devoted to my physics homework, I passed with a C. I began my second semester of freshman year on course to become a math teacher and graduated on time, three and half years later, on the dean's list.

Surprisingly, after one year in the "real world" as a teacher, I discovered that wasn't the profession for me either. I went through the same breakdown as I did in college, not knowing what I wanted to do next. Over my summer break, I took a part-time job at a local radio station and decided radio was more fun than teaching. I realized that failing is part of learning and that it's okay not to have your whole life figured out, as long as you work hard and rise to whatever challenges you face. I'm now in my third year as the human resources manager at the radio station group, wondering where my career path will take me next.

~Emily Ruffner

66

Mono-derailed

Always act like you're wearing an invisible crown.
~Author Unknown

My fly was unzipped. And six hours later, after traveling through twelve sorority houses and meeting hundreds of girls, my fly was still unzipped.

Mortifying, I know.

But it was only Philanthropy Round.

"I have the rest of formal recruitment (rush) to make a good impression"—those were the famous last words of a casualty of recruitment.

After winter break, I came back to Northwestern with new clothes, an iPod dock and speakers, and mononucleosis, an ugly gift I wanted to return. Having mono is never in vogue, especially during recruitment season.

However, the kissing disease was not going to stand between me and the Greeks. I wanted to join a sorority. How many more weekend nights could I spend in the Mole Hole (an all-male wing) of Allison Hall, watching guys drink beer and play video games? I was tired of being one of the guys. I needed to get out of the Mole Hole and relocate to a lighter, brighter, and prettier place—the sorority quad.

I started recruitment with a lot of enthusiasm. I smiled, I laughed, and I met a lot of great people.

I was awed by the sorority universe; its inhabitants wore cute, coordinating outfits and sang songs. This place even had its own time zone, called "Panhell Time."

Being the ambitious freshman that I was, I attended all my classes—including 9 A.M. calculus—when I had mono. To do this, I had to sleep whenever I was not in class. But adding the demands of sorority hopping to my schedule left me little time for catching Zs.

And naturally, my enthusiasm for recruitment slowly waned.

At one house, a girl ambushed me for trying to kidnap a sugar cookie.

Does she think I'm too fat to be eating a cookie? Turns out it was against the rules to leave the house with anything given to you. This included, but was not limited to, sugar cookies.

At another house, I forgot my purse. I asked my recruitment counselor if I could go back and get it. She sighed loudly, and reluctantly said she would take care of it.

Wouldn't it be a lot easier and quicker if I went into the house to get it? It was my purse, and I probably knew where to find it. Ten minutes later, my counselor came back with my purse and a puss on her face.

I didn't know that once a recruitment party is over, you can't go back in the house. Not under any circumstance. This includes, but is not limited to, retrieving your designer handbag that houses your credit cards, IDs, money and other life necessities.

At another house, a girl asked, "How are you today?" as I came in. It seemed like an easy question to answer, but it wasn't.

"Do I say the truth?" I wondered.

I feel like death.

"Or should I lie?"

I feel sororerrific!

"Well, I don't want her to think I am a liar so I'll go with the truth," I decided.

Big mistake.

"Actually, I'm not doing so well," I replied. "I have mono, umm... but don't worry, it's not contagious. Well, unless we share a drink or something like that, but that's not going to happen so..."

Alissa, shut up and just shake her hand!

I extended my hand to shake the active's hand.

The look on her face was priceless, but not nearly as priceless as the looks I got when I showed up to another house covered in snow.

I was walking under an awning on my way to the house and a snowbank fell on my head. It hurt. My dress was soaked, my hair frizzed. A mix of snow and tears made my mascara run down to my chin.

At this point, things were really starting to get ugly, and when I say "things" I really mean me. I tried to beautify myself before the parties, but nothing in my wardrobe went with mono. I didn't have the strength to pull my hair taut to blow dry and straighten it. My face, no matter how much blush or bronzer I used, remained pale and greenish. The blue bags under my eyes made me look like a junkie.

And my normally sparkling personality was dulled by mono too. I was either exhausted from not sleeping or groggy from napping. My conversational skills suffered.

One night I overslept and was late for one of the parties. I rushed to get ready and ran to the house I was supposed to be at. The girls were already inside, so I decided to ring the bell. I rang and rang the bell, but no one came to the door. I saw all the girls inside, happily chatting, but no one saw me through the window. Defeated, I walked back to the dorm.

The next morning I was not asked back to that house, among many others.

That was when I officially withdrew from recruitment.

I was sad, but life went on.

A few months later, I received an invite to attend a chapter's informal, spring recruitment. I was apprehensive about going, but unlike winter recruitment it was only one day, one chapter house. Plus, I had made a full recovery from mono and so had my appetite. The allure of an ice cream social was too strong to pass up.

I went, I got a bid, and I accepted.

It has been almost two years since then, and as an active member,

I have never had any regrets about the way things turned out. This year, when I was talking to freshman girls during recruitment, I told them some of my recruitment horror stories. I told them the stories mostly because they're funny. But I also told them because recruitment is about sisterhood, and the most sisterly advice I could think of is to hold your head high, even when snow falls on it, and never leave the bathroom without double checking that your fly is zipped.

~Alissa Piccione

Opportunity Cost

A penny saved is a penny earned.
~Benjamin Franklin

Some people learned everything they needed to know in kindergarten. Call me slow, but it took me until college to figure out one of life's most practical lessons.

It was my college economics professor who introduced me to the term "opportunity cost." When you choose one thing, it's a tradeoff at the expense of something else. If you go to the football game, you can't go to the movies. If you have dessert with lunch, you can't have it with dinner. If you go to law school with student loans, you'll be working for twenty years to pay them off. It's a lot more than a theory; it's one of the practical realities at the heart of almost any decision we make.

At the ripe age of nineteen, I had my eye on a summer term abroad. I knew my parents didn't have the means to send me to Europe; they were barely sending me to college. But I had a choice: Accept this limitation as my destiny or figure out a way to pay for it.

Working as many as three jobs each summer, I had managed to cover state school tuition and board for both my freshman and sophomore years. Having been living within my means, I decided it was my turn to live outside of them for a change. So into the debt pool I dove, head first. *Voilà*, I was heading to Europe.

I had barely enough money for my flights, tuition and board at the University of Dijon, and "living" expenses. I even opted out of meals on the airline to save a few bucks. Lucky for me, my sister gave me a travel pack of butter cookies. They were dinner and breakfast on my flight over.

I had to cut similar corners (if you call eating a corner) to subsidize my journey. For instance, baskets of baguettes were abundant for breakfast at the convent in Dijon where our student group stayed. God forgive me, but I'd snatch what extra pieces I could to bring back to my room for later. (Initially I just gorged myself, but I learned soon enough that I was no squirrel.) How else did I sustain myself? Besides careful choices every step of the way and the kindness of friends and strangers, I found the answer in peanuts. I'd buy a bag a week and ration them—for lunch, for snacks, for dinner.

Don't feel sorry for me. I traveled almost every weekend—to Nice, Venice, Lauterbrunnen, and Paris twice. The accommodations were modest at best and I was mostly hungry, but that's not what I remember. It's the canals, the horn blowers in Wengen, and sleeping on the pebbled beaches in the south of France that I recall.

When I returned home, I was different. Surprisingly not as skinny as you'd have expected, but I had a resilience and confidence knowing that I had made my own way. When I shared the grisly details with my parents and sisters, they asked why didn't I call—why didn't I tell them I needed more money: all I needed to do was ask. Today, our country is in the midst of a credit meltdown, and I am reminded of my summer abroad, the loan I took and repaid, and all the peanuts I ate that made it work. It's what my economics professor said: It's not that we can't have what we want, but whatever we want has a cost—a price we must pay. Or, as my business law professor put it, there's no such thing as a free lunch. And when I think back to my summer opportunity, I know what it cost: Courage, sacrifice, and peanuts.

~Kathryn Z. West

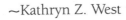

Working and Learning in the City that Never Sleeps

I've always worked very, very hard, and the harder I worked, the luckier I got.
~Alan Bond

Going to college in New York definitely has its perks—as long as I've been a student at NYU, I can never recall being hard pressed to find a mouth-watering restaurant, any kind of shopping I could ever fathom, or something to do on a weeknight. It's an exciting life in the city—always moving, always on your toes, always something to do. NYU prides itself in providing a particular type of education—one that goes beyond the classroom and takes advantage of its vast resources in what is arguably the greatest city in the world. As the admissions brochures describe, New York is as much our classroom as it is our playground, and the meaning of this became clear to me in my sophomore year.

Although spending one's college years in New York is an exciting, enriching experience, it certainly does not come without its pressures. New Yorkers are go-getters by nature, always looking to "one-up" the competition and prove their worth. NYU students are no different. From the time I enrolled in my freshman year, I noticed that my fellow students were driven to get ahead. Many had jobs and internships by their first semester, some even holding two at a time. And by my second semester, it seemed as though I was the only one without any kind of professional, pertinent New York experience related to both my major and expected career goals. As someone who had always been an overachiever throughout my schooling experience, this was troubling for me. Was I suddenly just that unmotivated? Was I destined to become a professional failure? I knew that there was only one way to prove myself: it was time for my first New York internship.

I was lucky enough, at the beginning of my sophomore year, to find a position that interested me—an internship at a small PR firm specializing in classical music and the arts. As a communications major who was looking to break into the classical music industry, the job seemed like a perfect match. I sent in my resume, nailed the interview, was offered the job, and accepted. After providing them with my class schedule, the company quickly e-mailed me back with the hours they expected me to work:

"Dear Oren: We're very excited for you to join us. As per your availability, we'll see you on Mondays from 10-6, Wednesdays from 1-6, and Fridays from 10-1. Looking forward to seeing you on Monday."

It was not what I had bargained for. They had literally scheduled me to work every hour that I was not in class—and I had a full class schedule lined up for the semester! I felt trapped into one of two options: I could either trail further behind my classmates, without any kind of practical job experience, or I could have the hardest semester of my life. Of course, I could have taken a step back, spoken with my new employer, and explained that a 16-hour workweek was simply not an option for me at the moment. Instead, I chose option two—the hardest semester of my life.

If I thought it was going to be a difficult semester, I clearly had no concept of exactly what I was getting myself into. My semester was a whirlwind—one of running to the subway immediately after class in order to get to my internship and one of working tirelessly on projects at the office only to return home to do the whole day's homework at night. By the end of the semester, I was exhausted. Not only had I worked myself to death, but my long hours of juggling office work with schoolwork made it impossible to go to concerts, hang out with my friends in the city, and do so many other New York activities that I had enjoyed my freshman year. In short, I bit off more than I could chew, all in the name of growing up—too fast, in hindsight.

Don't get me wrong—my internship was a wonderful experience. I learned so much about Public Relations, the classical music industry, and what it takes to work in a real, thriving New York office. I made numerous professional contacts, developed important business skills, and even made a few friends at the office. The company appreciated my dedication and the long, hard hours that I poured into my numerous work projects. In fact, I was consistently praised by my boss as one of the best interns she had ever employed.

Needless to say, though, I took a semester off of interning after my first experience, but was pleasantly surprised to receive a phone call in mid-February. It was from one of the clients of the PR firm I had worked for—a well-known New York orchestra.

"Hi, Oren. The folks over at your last internship had forwarded me your resume after you left, along with high recommendations. We're looking for a summer intern in our Marketing department and are wondering if you might be interested."

That's how I was offered my second New York internship. And after much thought and plenty of discussion with the company, regarding scheduling (among other things), I accepted. Now, as a second semester junior, I haven't interned for a full year and don't plan to for another semester. After all, I already have two internships under my belt and can only hope that I am well on my way to "one-upping" the competition and proving my worth in the city that never sleeps.

~Oren Margolis

69

The Basics

After enlightenment, the laundry
~Zen Proverb

I've studied hard, my grades are high
With college as my goal.
I anxiously await the day
To see the good times roll.

I know my trig and algebra,
The gods of ancient days.
I've read the classics every year
And all the Shakespeare plays.

I know the rules of chemistry;
I speak in Español.
I've studied what the country thinks
As shown in voters' polls.

In choir I was a baritone,
In drama played an elf.
In shop I built a china hutch
And polished every shelf.

I quarterbacked and threw for points,
In baseball pitched the ball.

I ran the anchor leg in track
In soccer—did it all!

Count on me to lend a hand,
To play an active part,
To run the errands, paint the props,
To give it all my heart.

I've done it well—the grades, the sports
And volunteered my time.
A part time job for extra cash,
I've learned to "save a dime."

At last my independence comes,
I'll strike a carefree pose.
But one thing has me so confused—
It's how to wash my clothes!

~Cynda Strong

70

Reporting Home

A wise man changes his mind, a fool never.
~Spanish Proverb

As far back as I can remember, I've only wanted three things in life. I wanted to be a journalist, I wanted to be happy, and I wanted to go away to school. I loved my small Long Island town growing up, but as I got older, my town did as well. I felt like I needed to see another part of the world. Unfortunately after high school, I was committed to going to the community college only ten minutes from my house. I wasn't going away, and I felt like I was letting myself down.

I came to love community college, and I later realized how smart I had been to go there first. But somewhere inside I still felt like I was doing something wrong, and when the time came to think about transferring to a four-year school, I refused to look at home. I applied to the University of Rhode Island, Emerson College, Northeastern University and Cornell University. In the end, I decided to attend Cornell, though at the time it didn't seem like a hard decision. Cornell was one of the best in the world. It was Ivy League and it was located in a beautiful part of upstate New York. It seemed perfect.

There was just one small catch. Cornell didn't have a journalism program, so I had applied as a general communications major. I didn't realize until later how much of a mistake that was on my part.

Before I knew it, the time to actually leave had approached and I said goodbye to Long Island and began my trek upstate. I moved into my townhouse apartment and adjusted pretty quickly. It didn't seem so bad at first. I was getting along with my roommates exceptionally well, and we already had made a solid group of friends. I didn't think life could get any better.

However, the glamour started to wear off. I began to miss some of the little things I had taken completely for granted back home. I couldn't understand why I was missing such inconsequential things. They hadn't started to bother me until after classes started. I think it was then that I realized what was wrong.

The major problem was my change to a communications major from journalism. I had always known that I wanted to be a journalist and to write for a living. Writing was my passion, and I thrived under the pressure of deadlines. I had even thrived at my community college and gained a reputation for being a really good movie critic. But I had also been paying attention to the world around me, and I wasn't stupid. There wasn't much of a demand for print journalism, as more newspapers were going under, and more people were looking for work in the field.

The economy wasn't in the best shape either, and I knew in my head that if I wanted to make money in the future that I couldn't stick only with what I loved, so I decided to branch out in the general communication field. I figured that with training in Public Relations and Advertising I would then be set later on should I not find a journalism job. I would at least be making some money. I had convinced myself that this was what I needed to do and that I would love these other fields because they were still communication.

I was wrong.

As I started studying these topics further in depth, I realized how much they didn't thrill me. As I walked out of class and started doing my homework (always reading assignments) I wasn't feeling satisfied. My fingers weren't working over a computer keyboard. The letters weren't fading from incessant typing. I wasn't typing at a speed of almost twenty words a minute like I had done when I had deadlines where I had to crank out a 500-word article in forty minutes. I wasn't typing at all. I wasn't even writing the old fashioned way with pen and paper. And I was miserable as a result.

It was the fact that I wasn't being true to myself that made me miss the little things and want to go home. What had only been a little homesickness became an overwhelming despair. I just sat and cried nonstop in my room. It didn't help that I saw everyone else being so happy with that what they were doing. I realized that this just wasn't for me after all.

I kept my feelings to myself for as long as I could. But eventually they became too much for me to handle on my own, and private crying turned into crying on the phone to my mother every night. I was stuck with something I wasn't happy doing, but I felt as if I shouldn't give up this opportunity. I was the first one in my immediate family to leave for school. My mother had found money she didn't have to get me to where I was. A degree from Cornell could mean a world of options after graduation. A degree from that school would be my ticket out of the life I had known. How could I drop my golden ticket in a garbage can and turn my back on such a promising future? I felt I couldn't, no matter what the cost was to my happiness.

Eventually I realized I couldn't stick it out doing something I didn't want to do merely because of a possible end result. After all, I was always taught that money can't buy happiness.

So five weeks after I had unpacked my bags, I started repacking them. I filled out a withdrawal from the university, and knew that it was the right thing to do when my academic advisor signed it and said, "If you want journalism, then this place isn't for you." I started saying goodbye to the friends I had made and stopped going to the classes that held no interest for me.

But I stopped crying that week. I started to smile again, and that alone told me that I was making the right decision.

So maybe I won't have a degree that reads Cornell University.

But I'll be doing something I love.

And it won't change the fact that Cornell University is an amazing school, or that they wanted me.

I did manage to take away one truly valuable lesson from my

time there. Above all else, do what you love, and don't let anything stop you from going for your dreams.

~Lauren DuBois

A Price Worth Paying

Who goeth a borrowing
Goeth a sorrowing.
~Thomas Tusser

During the summer after my sophomore year of college, I interned in Washington, for then-Senator Al Gore. Although I was ecstatic about this opportunity, my parents were less than thrilled by it. Practicing conservatives, they were disappointed that I'd be working for a Democrat—and going unpaid for it. Furthermore, they regretted that I was walking away from a highly competitive internship program at a statewide bank. The program, which lasted four summers, was designed to groom me for future employment with the bank, and I had participated for only one summer.

But they let me go. I think they knew how excited I was, and on some level, they must have believed that living and working in Washington would be a good life experience. It certainly proved to be.

While I was in Washington, I learned some very practical lessons, like how to live on a meal allowance of only $10 a day, and why I shouldn't park by a yellow curb on a busy Washington street. I became an expert at using public transportation and navigating the city. Quickly, I discovered that I needed to walk confidently and carefully, no matter the time of day.

At work, I saw the value of a strong role model, and I realized that if you aren't being challenged by the work, you owe it to yourself and your colleagues to speak up. By reading the Senator's mail (my job one afternoon each week), I learned how complex any one issue is—that everyone has a story, and that every story deserves an audience.

But the hardest lesson came during the last days of my six-week internship. Senator Gore's staff had invited me to stay on for another six weeks, and I was delighted by this prospect. My parents had agreed—until I received mail back home from Lord & Taylor, a high-end department store in my hometown.

When the envelope arrived, my father felt compelled to open it, particularly because it resembled a bill. What he found certainly didn't please him. So he picked up the phone and dialed Senator Gore's office.

When the receptionist buzzed me to say my father was on the phone, I knew that nothing good could be happening. He wouldn't normally call me there.

"Hello?"

"Kathleen, it's Dad. Get in the car and get home now."

Uh-oh. I was in deep.

He continued.

"I opened the bill that came from Lord &Taylor. You owe them over $250. You need to get home now and make some money."

"But, Dad!"

"Kathleen, it's not up for discussion. Drive home this weekend. And on Monday, I expect you to call the bank and see what you can line up."

When I hung up the phone, I was angry, ashamed, and heartbroken. I had been looking forward to those next six weeks. I had fallen in love with Washington—everything from Georgetown, where I lived, to the Russell Building, where I worked. I was energized by the city, and for the first time in my life, I had felt so grown up.

But someone who is grown up also knows how to manage her money better. Even though I hated that my parents were insisting that I come home, I also was slowly realizing that making no money (while spending a fair amount on rent, food, transportation, and entertainment) was more than ridiculous.

Before I had left for D.C., I had felt that I needed some new clothes. Instead of talking about this with my parents, I had gone to Lord & Taylor, opened a credit account, and charged some dresses. My plan had been to line up a babysitting gig when I returned to college in the fall. Then I would pay off the dresses little by little.

I clearly had no understanding of how credit worked. I did not realize that the longer I waited to pay, the more additional fees I would accrue. My plan to pay only the minimum each month was pricey and irresponsible.

As a financial manager, my father realized that I was in dangerous territory. While he did not plan to bail me out, he did intend to set me on the right path.

To make matters worse, as I drove home from D.C. that weekend, I hydroplaned and was in a bad car accident. Thankfully, no one was hurt, but my car was definitely worse for wear. You can only imagine how excited my parents were to see my damaged car pull into the driveway.

That Monday, I called the bank and spoke with a woman I knew in Human Resources. Liz said that she could not re-enroll me in the intern program—I had forfeited that opportunity when I opted out for six weeks—but that she did have a short-term job for which she thought I was well qualified.

"Kathleen, what I really need is someone who can help us edit our credit training manual."

"Your credit training manual?"

"Yes, it's used by our customer service representatives in all the branches. It explains the ins and outs of all of our credit products—like credit cards, debit checking cards, mortgages, etc. Essentially, I need someone to help edit what we have developed so far."

As I contemplated what Liz was saying, I couldn't help but wonder if this was some sort of a joke... or if my father had already spoken with her. It was all a little too ironic. But the good news? She clearly wasn't looking for a subject matter expert.

"Sure, that sounds like something I would enjoy. I'd like to hear more about what it involves."

We talked more, and I started the next day. By summer's end, I had made some money and had learned a lot about credit. I had a whole book to show for it (as well as some decent paychecks).

Eighteen years later, I am grateful to my father for intervening as he did. I am glad that I learned about credit during college, and not years later. The lesson could have been much more painful than it actually was. To this day, I maintain only one credit card and pay it off in full each month!

~Kathleen Whitman Plucker

Flexibility

He who trims himself to suit everyone will soon whittle himself away.
~Raymond Hull

In many ways, I was your average eighteen-year-old: I hung out with my friends, was permanently attached to my cell phone, and pretty much lived for Free Cone Day at Ben & Jerry's. However, in other ways, I was unique. Like clockwork, I dusted and vacuumed my room every other Sunday. My closet was color-coded, my shoeboxes were labeled, and God help the person who de-alphabetized my bookshelf. I didn't drink. Though I loved nights with my friends, I had also been known to spend Fridays studying. You might say I was somewhat compulsive, as well as an overachiever, a trait that family and friends alike warned me I would not be able to continue at college when living with another person.

Bearing this in mind, I walked into my dorm on orientation day with a smile fixed on my face. Never mind the fact that some clever person had already crossed out "Welcome to Sherrill!" and edited the bulletin board to read "Welcome to hell!" I was going to be laid back and flexible and normal, for once in my life.

Unfortunately, the edited bulletin board was like a prophecy. I quickly realized that Sherrill, for whatever reason, was the designated "party dorm" for the year. But this was college, right? And so I said nothing, and each morning I took my toothbrush and walked down the street to the library where there was a small, infrequently used bathroom that was not covered in vomit. Each night I attempted to get some sleep before my 8 A.M. class, despite the drunken singing pulsing through my wall, gritting my teeth and telling myself I was becoming a better, more tolerant person.

As part of my "be flexible" campaign, I had also sworn to be a good roommate. I would be accommodating, respectful, and an all-around cool girl. Unfortunately, I hadn't planned on rooming with Party Girl. She was out until 2 A.M. and slept until ten, sighing irritably as I crept around the room at 7:30 getting ready for my morning classes. Giggling and attempting to whisper, she and her friends would stumble into the room in the wee hours of the morning and ransack the refrigerator. Somehow, it was always my Hot Pockets that got eaten first.

I began spending as much time in the library and as little time in my room as possible. I took to going home every weekend, figuring that if I let my roommate have the place to herself on the weekend, maybe she would be a little less crazy during the week. Finally, it came to a head.

I had just returned to campus after a weekend at home. After unpacking my duffel, I went to our mini-fridge and took out one of my bottles of water. I lifted the bottle to my mouth and took a big gulp. Fire shot down my esophagus. Hacking and gagging, I spit out what I could and looked at my bottle in shock. From her position at her desk, my roommate turned around and looked at me condescendingly.

"You should have smelled it before you drank it. That's vodka."

I stared at her in disbelief. Finally, in a high voice, I said, "But it's my water bottle!"

She shrugged, already turning back to her computer. "I needed a place to store it over the weekend."

The next day found me in the first year dean's office; nearly hysterical from another sleepless night and the tension of the past month, I exploded. Sobbing, I babbled about transferring, dropping out, anything to get away from my roommate and my dorm. I figured the dean wouldn't care, but I had to tell someone, and she seemed kind.

To my great surprise, she reacted with empathy for me, and rage towards my roommate.

"That's unacceptable. I heard the situation in Sherrill was bad, but I had no idea it was this bad. Please don't transfer. I'm going to do whatever I can to make this better for you."

Somewhat mollified, I left, hoping the insanity was at an end. Unfortunately, I was wrong. Part of "making it better" entailed the dean talking to our resident assistant, and eventually my roommate herself about her lifestyle. My roommate cornered me by my wardrobe the next afternoon. Red-faced, she shouted about how I had gotten her in so much trouble, how everybody hated me, and how I was such a freak. Bursting into tears, I grabbed my cell phone and ran out. I called my mom and told her to come get me—I was coming home; I couldn't make it here.

I had never been so happy to see my mom take control of a situation. She spoke to the dean and the head of housing, supporting my story and providing a calm backdrop to my tearfulness. Eventually, it was decided that the best thing to do would be for me to move dorms and deal with transferring later. I no longer felt safe with my roommate, and so the head of housing handed me the keys to a single room in a nearby dorm.

I can barely remember moving in to my new dorm. I felt like a refugee, moving out over the dinner hour while the rest of my building was at the dining hall. It must have been ninety degrees as we hauled the paraphernalia of my life down two flights of stairs, across the parking lot, and up another four. By the time we were done, I no longer cared if I went home or not. I just wanted to shower and sleep.

And sleep I did, for the first time in a month. And the next night. And the next. My new floor was the polar opposite of my old dorm. The bathroom, though small, was clean, and my room, a corner nook on the fourth floor with a slanted ceiling, was my own. I barely left it, even for meals. After my experience in Sherrill, I felt like I could never get enough time to myself.

Eventually, though, things changed. Secure in the knowledge

that I had my own room to return to, I began to go out. The topic of transferring slowly faded from conversation. I made friends and joined clubs. My grades soared, and by May, I had a 3.9 GPA and a firm grasp on my $20,000 per year academic scholarship. I had survived my first year of college.

In hindsight, I see I made the quintessential college-student mistake in August—I tried to become someone I wasn't. Sure, everyone wants to be a good roommate, and I was extra-concerned with being flexible, knowing my own rigid personality. But the fact remained: I was uncomfortable with my roommate's drug-and-alcohol lifestyle, and that of my dorm, and it took me a month to realize that that was okay. Becoming more flexible didn't mean I had to live with something that was unacceptable. I'm confident now that I'm not a freak; I am someone who recognizes her right to feel comfortable and safe in her own space.

Oh, and my ex-roommate? I didn't see her at any of the honors ceremonies last May, and I never saw her at any of the great school-sponsored events because she was too busy getting hammered. She gained a ton of weight from the drinking, became very unhappy, and finally made the decision to transfer.

~Ashley Mie Yang

Chapter
8

Campus Chronicles

Professors and Mentors

Mentor: Someone whose hindsight can become your foresight.

~Author Unknown

I Survived
PSYC 497

The dream begins with a teacher who believes in you, who tugs and pushes and leads you to the next plateau, sometimes poking you with a sharp stick called "truth."

~Dan Rather

I had to take the class; all Psychology majors did. Psychology 497, Applied Research, was a graduation requirement. And it had to be passed with at least a C.

I heard about this course as soon as I transferred to Coastal Carolina University. Rumors about the infamous class circulated campus. I noticed seniors wearing navy blue T-shirts displaying the message, "I Survived PSYC 497." It was also the primary discussion topic for Psychology majors. They complained about the weekly deadlines, off-the-cuff oral presentations, the final paper, and, most of all, the professor.

"Dr. Piroch is evil," some students said. "She never smiles. Ever."

"A couple of my friends had to take her class twice before they passed," others commented. "I've heard she's the hardest professor here."

For two years I listened to the nightmarish tales of Dr. Piroch. I successfully completed all the other requirements of my major, knowing that the worst was yet to come. I would still have to take a course with the Stephen King of professors.

I enrolled in 497 in the spring semester. I attended summer school the year before so I would only have to juggle two other classes that term. I had prepared the best I could but I was still very nervous, and for good reason.

"Welcome to Applied Research," Dr. Piroch boomed on the first day of class. "In this class, you will design your own research study. You will conduct your research under my supervision, write a paper in accordance with APA guidelines, and then report your findings to your peers and other members of the Psychology faculty."

So far, what I had heard was true. She was assertive, stern, and a bit intimidating. And she did not smile. Not one time during the first session. But my anxiety was slowly giving way to excitement. I wanted to do well in 497. I wanted to impress Dr. Piroch.

I decided to conduct a correlational study on the relationship between the number of alcohol establishments in a college community and campus crime rates. Dr. Piroch seemed to like my proposal. She said it was unique.

For the next several months, I reviewed prior studies and wrote multiple drafts of each section of the paper. I consistently turned in drafts early and was able to make necessary corrections before they were graded. I had weekly conferences with Dr. Piroch to ensure I was on the right track. And, as required, I gave weekly, impromptu speeches in preparation for my final presentation.

I volunteered to present on the first day. For fifteen minutes, and with the help of two graphs and a note card, I explained the purpose of my study, the colleges and universities I had chosen, and the statistics I collected. I proudly informed my audience that I had found a positive correlation. It was slight; but it existed.

Throughout my presentation, I made eye contact with all members of the audience. But my gaze kept drifting back to Dr. Piroch — I saw her scribble notes and wrinkle her forehead. But when I finished answering questions from my classmates and other professors, I saw her smile. Dr. Piroch stood up, clapped her hands, and smiled at me.

A few days later, I went to collect my paper and find out my final grade in the class. On the way, I thought about how many of Dr. Piroch's students had misunderstood her. They confused her passion for the subject with being rigid, dry, and overly serious. Sure, her expectations were elevated. But they weren't unreasonable. And she set the bar high because she knew that some of her students just might reach it.

I noticed my name, written on a manila envelope, hanging outside my professor's door. I opened the envelope and found my paper and a typed letter. It read:

Your grade on this paper is an A, and that's also your final grade for this class. Your work habits, achievement goals, and desire to learn will all serve you well no matter what you choose to do in the future. Your presentation was excellent and you responded well to the seven minutes of questions that were asked of you. It has been my sincere pleasure to have you in this class and to have you as a major in our department. I've enjoyed getting to know you. In addition to being an outstanding student, you are also a truly fine person with a lot to offer. I wish you the very best in your future and hope you have some time to relax this summer. Please keep in touch with me.

I wish I could say that I have kept in touch with my professor. But I can say that she has touched my life. Dr. Piroch is, without a doubt, the best teacher I have ever had. She is the reason I went to graduate school and one of the reasons I became a teacher. She encouraged me to write. And by teaching me to never be satisfied with a first draft, she made me better. I am proud of all I accomplished that semester and especially of the fact that I made Dr. Piroch smile.

~Melissa Face

One of Our Own

While we are mourning the loss of our friend,
others are rejoicing to meet him behind the veil.
~John Taylor

It was seconds before 11:00 A.M. on a Friday and a student was waiting to see me. As I went out to greet him, in walked another student, Daniel, a member of the student organization for which I served as advisor. The organization was in the process of selecting a new executive council, and Daniel was coming to arrange an interview. He was in the process of interviewing for the Executive Director position, the highest one within the organization. I commented to someone earlier that day that he was the type of worker and leader that I wish I could be—he was dedicated to the organization, would do anything asked of him, and never expected anything in return. He was quiet, yet with a twist of sarcasm and a smile that could light up a room.

He had an undying love for Freddie Mercury and the music group Queen. In fact, so much that in one of his classes he and one of his friends used to somehow coerce their teacher into letting them play one of the group's most popular songs, "Bohemian Rhapsody." Sometimes they listened to it, sometimes they acted it out, and sometimes they sang it. Oddly enough, he had just as strong of a love for Elmo. Yes, the Sesame Street character. I don't know the story behind this admiration, but it's only fitting that he'd appreciate a character that you couldn't help but like.

As Daniel walked in, he saw that I was about to begin another meeting and offered to come back later. I joked, "No, don't worry about it, you won't take that long." He came in, I explained where we were in the selection process, and we arranged a time for his second interview on Monday. He seemed excited to be asked back for a second interview because it obviously meant we liked him. A few comments back and forth and then I got up from my desk as he grabbed his backpack to leave.

The last thing he said to me before we wished each other a good weekend was, "Thank you for what you said Tuesday at the induction ceremony. Everyone needed to hear that." He was referring to a speech I had given earlier that week, when we inducted new members of the organization, that touched on everything from challenging themselves to reach their full potential to welcoming them to an organization that had quickly resembled a family. Simple enough. He was on his way out the door, I was in a hurry to start my other meeting so I could finish a busy Friday and head home for the weekend.

I received a call the next night about 7 P.M. Daniel had committed suicide. Surely this must be a sick joke, I thought. I had just seen him a day earlier and he seemed fine. He had worked for our office for three years, and I'd never known him to even be in a bad mood, let alone suicidal. Daniel was the model member—he did anything and everything he could, he always saw the good in people, and constantly challenged them to reach their potential.

I was shocked, as was everyone who learned of this incident. I began going through my mental Rolodex of lessons learned in graduate school... how to motivate students... how to academically advise a student... how to resolve conflicts... how to counsel a student with an eating disorder... how to conduct research and work with a budget... how to counsel a suicidal student... how to give career advice... nowhere could I find anything that taught me how to react and deal with losing one of my own students.

Not only that, but I certainly didn't know what to tell the other students. I stayed up until 1 A.M. that night talking with about twelve of our members, and we ranged from tears to questions to laughs as we exchanged our favorite Daniel stories. We had always viewed him as a happy-go-lucky student with a bright future, but did we miss something? Did we say something to drive him to this? Why did he do this? Did he leave a note? How did he do it? Does his family have any information or were they left with as many questions as we had? Could we have stopped it? Where do we go from here? So many questions, so few answers.

If you work on a college campus long enough, you experience several student deaths, but it's usually not anyone you know personally. Maybe a student you know in passing, or maybe you help someone cope with the loss of a friend. Here was a guy who we now know battled depression for several years, yet nobody ever caught onto it. He never mentioned it and certainly never showed it. He was always optimistic and seemed to look forward to tomorrow.

I've often sympathized with football coaches who lose players who collapse during workouts. I've always wondered how that would affect their coaching in the future. They can throw out whatever politically correct answer they want about it being the same kind of practice they always run, and that they'll try to move on as a team, and that they won't change their coaching style at all in the future. Surely they must feel some guilt. I'm sure they'd question whether or not they expected too much from their players, or if they pushed them too far, or if they should have treated them differently. I could never imagine how they handle that and are still able to move on. Now I understand.

It was a situation that nobody can plan for or justify. Personally, I was able to survive because I had supportive colleagues, supervisors, and students. The students kept thanking me for my support, but in reality, they were giving it right back. We shared stories, laughs, thoughts, questions, and tears. We knew there wasn't any problem that, together, we couldn't conquer.

I only wish Daniel had felt that way.

~Jim Bove

Just What I Needed

Give people enough guidance to make the decisions you want them to make.
Don't tell them what to do, but encourage them to do what is best.
~Jimmy Johnson

In college, people don't tease each other like they do in high school.

I learned that the hard way. Some people gain the freshman fifteen; I gained the freshman forty-five. I had struggled with my weight in high school—people taunted me in the hallways, called me names like "hippo" and "lard-butt." But in college, no one said a word.

Instead, they whispered to their friends and giggled as I went for more French fries or scarfed a piece of chocolate cake in the dining hall. They didn't need to say anything; the way they looked at me said it all.

I dealt with a lot of issues that year—adjusting to life away from home, making friends, finding the right classes to take. Food became my way of dealing with my problems.

By sophomore year, I found a supportive group of friends and learned to manage my weight, shedding almost thirty pounds. But I never forgot what it was like to be on the outside, to feel like you were all alone and no one cared about you.

One night early in spring semester my second year, a friend

dragged me to a party at a freshman dorm. He wanted to flirt with some girl he knew from his hometown. I reluctantly agreed to go.

The dorm had a cafeteria on the first floor, and the rooms upstairs smelled of stale pizza, cinder blocks, and grease. When we got inside, about twenty people were crammed into a tiny space with fluorescent lighting and crusty wall-to-wall carpeting. Generic indie rock blared from a set of small speakers, and everyone was crowded around a mini-fridge playing a drinking game.

In an instant I recalled all those miserable, awkward parties where you sit around with people you don't like and guzzle crappy beer in the hopes of having a good time. Afterwards, I used to raid the vending machine and binge-eat under the covers so my roommate wouldn't see.

"I can't do this," I said quickly to my friend.

He nodded, understanding how I felt. "It's cool, give me a call later."

As I was about to leave, I noticed a nervous-looking guy leaning against the wall a few feet apart from the group. He was staring blankly ahead, looking unhappy.

"Hey Max," someone shouted to him. "Come party with us!"

"Give me a minute," he answered.

"Don't be a buzzkill!" a girl shouted back.

"Why does that kid even hang around here?" muttered another girl sitting on the floor.

I wasn't sure if Max heard her, but when no one was looking he slipped out the door.

For some reason, I felt compelled to follow him.

"Hey, wait up!" I shouted.

I chased him down the hallway, nearly tripping over another group of freshmen who were camped out on the floor.

"What?" he asked flatly.

"I never really had fun at those either," I admitted.

"Oh yeah?" he said, his eyes full of mistrust.

"I'm just trying to help, that's all. When I was a freshman, I was really unhappy too."

"What makes you think I'm so unhappy?" he demanded. "And why do you even care?"

I started to feel a little guilty. I realized I had my own selfish reasons for helping Max. I wanted to be the cool older kid who steered him away from a bad party and bad people—the friend I wished I had as a freshman.

"Look man," I said finally, "I don't know anything about you, I just saw you and it reminded me of how I used to feel. I should have left you alone. I'll see you later."

I started to walk away.

"Wait, wait," he said, motioning me towards the stairwell. "I'm sorry. You're right, I don't like those people. The truth is, I don't know who else to hang out with. It's been really hard here. Everyone says college is the best time of your life, but so far I've been really unhappy. I hate this place."

"Well this might not make you feel better," I said, "but we all go through it."

"Really?" He looked at me.

"I wasn't lying when I said I had a hard time as a freshman. Trying to make friends, adjusting to life away from home... plus everyone made fun of me because I was fat." I paused as I remembered eating alone in the dining hall downstairs. "People at this school can be really hurtful; it doesn't matter that they're smart."

"Yeah, I hear that. Can you believe what that girl said?" Max said, referring to the girl on the floor. "I've never even talked to her!"

"Don't worry about those people," I assured him. "You're gonna find people you actually like. I promise."

"Okay," he said, "I have a hard time believing you, but I hope you're right. I should go back to my room. See ya."

"Okay, bye." I watched him stroll away, looking at the ground. Suddenly, he turned his head.

"Hey! What's your name?" he asked.

"Craig!" I shouted.

"Nice meeting you, Craig, I'm Max." I could tell there was something different about the way he held himself.

I smiled and said, "Nice meeting you too, Max." I realized he was really saying, "Thank you."

I only saw Max a few times after that. But when I did, he seemed to be in better spirits. From what I could tell, he had made some new friends. I don't know if what I said that night helped him, but I'm glad I did what I did. Not just for Max, but for me, too. I realized how far I had come since freshman year, and I was proud of both of us.

~Craig Raphael

Teacher Student

The years teach much which the days never knew.
~Ralph Waldo Emerson

I was working my way through college, cramming four years of college into ten, as my friends teasingly tell me. One year, spring rolled around and I needed to finish several elective classes. One of the few that both sounded interesting and meshed with my work schedule was Medical Anthropology.

I remember two things from the class. The first is a vague sense that I liked the class, the second was a woman, who I will call Pat, who I met in the class.

I noticed her immediately as I entered class the first evening. She was the only person in the class with white hair.

The only path that did not make me walk between people in conversation or across the front of the classroom was one that led to an open seat directly beside her. Thankfully, I took that path.

Pat smiled, and greeted me cordially. She was one of those people you would describe as having "never met a stranger." People with that demeanor often make me uncomfortable, but for some reason I was instantly at ease with Pat.

After that night, we always sat beside one another and talked about the deepest and oddest things, sometimes even as the professor was lecturing. I do remember professorial glares or throat clearing directed at us. When they occurred, Pat would put her hand on my arm and say, "Hush, we have to be good now," and then laugh.

One night I asked Pat why she was there. "I mean, why aren't you taking it easy? You have earned the right to slack off. Why take this class?"

Her response was immediate. "Because I love Anthropology. I always wanted to get a degree in Anthropology, but my parents and my friends threw a fit. They told me it was a wasted degree. 'Be sensible,' they said. So they talked me into taking elementary education classes and getting a teaching degree."

"That does sound sensible," I said.

"It was!" she replied, laughing. "I led a very sensible, safe life. I became a teacher, married my high school sweetheart, had children, and we saved for a retirement, promising each other we would eventually travel. But I knew in my heart we wouldn't. We were too settled."

She continued: "I never took any risks. I never let those dreams I had as a girl come to the surface, but they were there, buried away. Don't get me wrong, I had a good life, but not what I dreamed."

"So how did you get here? What made those dreams come back? The opportunity and time to take classes?" I asked.

"Well, about three months before my husband was to retire, he died unexpectedly of a heart attack. I fell into a funk for two years. I felt my life was over. Then one day I woke up, and simply said, 'Pat, you can't go on like this. This is not living.' So I got out of bed, opened the curtains, and decided I was going to live. I realized that one of the things I missed was the sense of giving and being needed. I had felt that as a teacher and I wanted to feel it again. So I went right down and applied at the Peace Corps—I figured I could teach English to children in another country and learn about a foreign culture.

"My own children thought I had gone absolutely insane, to the point of talking about having me committed, but off I went to Afghanistan. I taught in a small village for two years until, unfortunately, I fell and broke my hip. It was a rather nasty fracture, and required quite a bit of surgery and rehab, and it took me eighteen months to get back on my feet, but unfortunately I couldn't return to Afghanistan.

"By that time I was determined to live, to actually live each day, no matter what. I decided I would do the things that were important to me and I would not squander another day of life—it is too precious a gift. So I enrolled in college to get that Anthropology degree, and here I am, at seventy-one, working on my degree."

I never encountered Pat after the course was finished. I have no doubt, though, that she got that degree. In the process, the wise old teacher taught a young man a lesson in life. Living the lesson is harder than teaching it, I have found. But I haven't forgotten Pat or her lesson, and I have come to believe it is a lesson we all should learn.

~Daniel James

The Sun Will Rise Tomorrow

The role of a writer is not to say what we all can say,
but what we are unable to say.
~Anaïs Nin

It was the fall semester of my senior year of college and I felt like my entire college experience was a bust.

I remember sitting at a long grey table in a grey classroom with my ten classmates in NYU's new Journalism building. At the head of the table stood a tall African American man in a light colored suit and a matching fedora, my professor, James McBride. During this particular lesson, Professor McBride asked the class something along the lines of "Who isn't satisfied with their college experience?" My hand shot up immediately, as if it were spring loaded to go up at that exact moment. I looked around the room and there were no other hands up. After a short awkward pause, two of my other classmates reluctantly half-raised their hands. We were then paired off and told to interview each other about it. The purpose was to write a short piece in the voice of the interviewee.

I was paired with an Indian girl with long black hair. We left the classroom and walked across the street to the park and before I knew it I was treating the green park bench as a therapist's couch, rambling on about all of my qualms about college to a person I hardly knew. I told her I felt like my classes were not teaching me anything and that basically in three years I had hardly learned anything. I told her that since I commute to school I didn't have many friends and I felt like I was missing out on a large chunk of the "college experience." She listened carefully and took notes. I didn't know it at the time, but by the end of the semester I would be feeling a lot better about my "college experience."

Professor McBride was an amazing teacher. This best-selling writer and composer took the time to get to know each of us through our writing. His teaching method was unique. Each of our assignments was to be handwritten and double-spaced on yellow legal notepads. I remember when he gave us our first assignment and my classmate asked him how long it should be. He simply responded by saying, "Write until you're done." I always hated having specified lengths for papers because I felt that in order to fulfill the required length there were a lot of extra words mucking up an otherwise concise paper. But Professor McBride had such a novel and practical answer—"Write until you're done."

Imagine my surprise when I was handed back my first assignment, and stapled to the last page was an entire page of typed—on a typewriter, no less—comments. In my other classes I usually got a sentence, or a paragraph if I was lucky, explaining why I had gotten the letter grade I received. Professor McBride had comments on not only the flaws of my piece, but also what I did well. To top it off there was no letter grade accompanying the feedback. He said he wanted us to improve our writing and not worry about getting a grade. It was an amazing feeling not to be relegated to a single letter. Liberating, almost. After that, I wrote more freely without being regulated by the threat of a low grade.

I was no longer writing what I thought my professor wanted to read, but rather what I wanted to convey. In sophomore year, I had switched my major from Biology to Journalism (against my parents' wishes), but I had found that as I progressed through my new major, my urge to write slowly began to die. I've never had great punctuation, and most of my professors tore me down for it. I tried to learn but it never sank in. Each paper I got back usually greeted me with a B and a short quip about my less-than-stellar punctuation. All the negativity gradually ate away at the little self-confidence I had, and before long I just didn't feel much like writing and phoned in many of my assignments. Believe it or not, it came to a point where I absolutely hated writing.

But unlike my other writing professors, Professor McBride actually found good things in my writing and pointed them out to me, along with the bad. His care in reading my pieces and finding the redeeming qualities gradually began to repair my wounded confidence. All I really needed was an encouraging word. Soon, I started to enjoy putting pen to paper again. Professor McBride had given me something that I never really had to begin with — confidence in myself — and confidence that what I have to say matters. That may seem like a dramatic statement, but it is true in every sense of the word. I started to carry myself with my head up and I stopped being so self-conscious.

Unlike many of the professors I've had, Professor McBride truly tried to impart his knowledge to us. He taught us not just about writing, but about life. During one of his lectures he said to us that, no matter what happens, we need to remember "the sun will rise tomorrow." It is such a simple and obvious fact but somehow hearing it from someone I respect and admire gave it weight. These simple words have gotten me through any day where I felt like the world was crashing down around me. On those days, "the sun will rise tomorrow" became a mantra I would repeat over and over in my head.

The twelve weeks I spent in James McBride's class were the most insightful and educational weeks of my entire time at college. I learned more in those twelve weeks than I did in the past three years. As a human being, I grew quite a bit during this time. I am the person I am now because of what I learned from Professor McBride. His class is one of the few reasons that I can honestly say my college experience might actually be worth the ridiculous amount of money for tuition.

Although I said thank you and shook his hand after the final class, I don't think anything I do could possibly convey my gratitude to James McBride—there aren't words to describe it. But I wanted to try writing about him because writing is exactly what he taught me to love doing again. Thank you, Professor McBride.

~Kevin Chu

A Semester with T.S. Eliot

The art of teaching is the art of assisting discovery.
~Mark Van Doren

It was the first day of second semester during my senior year at the University of Kansas. As an English major, I was looking forward to one more semester full of reading for hours and writing inspiring essays (I know, what a dork). It was going to be the last hurrah of my undergraduate career and I wanted more than anything to go out with a bang.

Then I went to my last class of the day. It was a study on the poet, dramatist, and critic, T.S. Eliot. I knew little of Eliot, but I figured that by now I could easily handle any upper level English course. I shouldn't have been so optimistic.

When my professor walked into the class I almost laughed out loud. He looked like a stereotypical college professor, complete with a corduroy jacket and a briefcase. I kept thinking at any moment he would pull out a pipe. He had a British accent despite the fact that his hometown was somewhere in South Carolina.

Like many of my other professors, he found it necessary to torture his students on the first day of classes by making them introduce themselves to the class, giving information that no one really needs to know. One by one, each student stated their name, hometown, and major. Afterwards we were supposed to tell one interesting fact about ourselves. This task was always much harder for me than it should have been. None of my classmates seemed to feel this way as they rattled off interesting literary works that they felt somehow related to them. The biggest overachievers of the class recited Eliot's work and then went on to relate it to their life. By the time it was my turn, I was so lost I almost got up and ran. It was obvious to me that I wasn't going to fit into this class unless I learned some new vocabulary quickly.

I introduced myself the best I could. I tried to make Lenexa, Kansas, sound exotic rather than a quiet, suburban town twenty-eight miles from campus. Then, I very excitedly announced that come May I would be taking the traditional walk down the hill to celebrate graduation.

My professor, who already looked disappointed in me, lowered his head and said, "Well, you have to pass my class first. So we'll see."

I waited for him to laugh. He didn't. A giant lumped formed in my throat. I already hated T S Eliot and I had yet to read a piece of his work.

For the next four months, it was Eliot who haunted my dreams. I would read his poems five or six times and write down comments that would make me look smart. It didn't fool anyone. My reading responses were always returned to me covered in red ink. Usually my professor would kindly write at the bottom: "I think you missed the point." But I would not be defeated. I had sat through too many boring lectures and written too many papers on topics I cared little about to let one professor keep me from getting the ultimate prize: my degree.

So I did the unthinkable. I gave my assignments everything I had. I stayed in on Friday nights and spent hours in a quiet corner of the library reading everything I could about Eliot. I wrote and rewrote my final paper until I was sure it was the best thing I had ever written. It had to be — it was worth seventy percent of my final grade.

I patiently waited for my grades to be posted. I would wake up at six every morning and quickly log on to the computer, hoping that I had passed. I couldn't eat or sleep. Forget having fun, all I could think about were the works of Eliot. His poems raced through my mind days after our final class. I would go for runs and recite "Ash Wednesday" with every step I took.

Finally, the day came. Just before graduation, my grade was posted. There next to the name of that horrific class was the letter B. It might as well have been an A, because I had never felt more proud of myself.

I didn't have the heart to sell back my T.S. Eliot books. We had been through so much that I felt I couldn't part with them. I keep them tucked away in my closet for now. I'm not ready to re-read them yet. I'm worried the nightmares of that semester will return. But I happily look at my diploma and remind myself that with hard work and determination, I can always overcome even the biggest critic.

~Kathleen Ingraham

A Lucky Break

Those who have succeeded at anything and don't mention luck
are kidding themselves.
~Larry King

I was late, and I was yelling expletives at my dashboard.

I couldn't believe I was running late for the interview. I'd gotten all dressed up—a tweed skirt, purple shirt, and conservative black heels—trying to look my best, and now I'd gone and blown my chance by driving the wrong way and getting totally lost. I passed a sign that said I was entering New York, a surefire way to tell that I was heading in the wrong direction since my interview was in Connecticut.

Finally, I found it. I pulled up in front of the red brick building and walked in, looking around, trying to get my bearings. I've been to what feels like one million auditions, and yet I'm still surprised when an interview makes my stomach churn. The elevator opened and I stepped in.

I stood outside the door, glancing at the sign. "Chicken Soup for the Soul" it read. I swallowed hard and turned the brass knob....
"Hello?"

• • •

My summer internship at Chicken Soup for the Soul was a total coincidence—something I now think of as a very lucky break. My friend's sister, Valerie, was looking for a temporary replacement for a few months and she knew that I was a writer, liked kids, and—most importantly—needed a job. I passed a writing sample along to the publisher, and before I knew it I was doing daily coffee runs for everyone in the office. I was a twenty-year-old intern doing intern things and receiving a weekly stipend. I spent the first few weeks doing my job—which was anything anyone needed done around the office.

And then things changed. Valerie left for her few months. With an insane twenty-eight books in the works for the next six months, eight of them for teens and preteens, my responsibilities multiplied. I was looking through stories sent in by contributors. I was choosing the ones I thought were really heartfelt and incredible. And when it turned out that I had an innate sense of how to rework a story without losing its original flavor, I was given the ultimate gift—the go-ahead to edit some of the teen stories.

I loved it. One day, I came home from work and changed my outfit—I was going out on a date. My date picked me up and we went to dinner, where I spent at least fifteen minutes recounting my favorite stories from *Chicken Soup for the Soul: Teens Talk Middle School*. I was over-the-top excited to tell him about one girl's crush, one boy's embarrassment, and another girl's triumph. I felt like I knew each of the contributors personally. I realized while I read and edited those stories that I was completely enthralled by what I was doing.

Somehow, it only got better. Bill, who is the CEO, Bob, who is the President, and Amy, who is the Publisher, took me under their wings and taught me everything they knew about publishing. I learned how to create a book from start to finish—from conceiving of the title, to soliciting the stories, to designing the cover and the interior, to reading two thousand stories to pick the very best 101 to create an initial manuscript. Our California staff taught me how to work with the contributors to sign their permission forms and edit their stories. I learned how to create and proofread a layout, and how a book gets sent to the printer. It was amazing to hold a finished book in our hands that had only been an idea a few months before.

We finished *Chicken Soup for the Soul: Teens Talk Middle School* and moved on to *Chicken Soup for the Soul: Teens Talk High School*, and my name went on both of them as a co-author. I almost had a heart attack as I ascended the escalators at Barnes & Noble months later, eventually stepping off to find the books sitting on shelves, with my name on them. I think I'm still in shock.

I have continued working part-time for Chicken Soup for the Soul while I finish college, and when I came back during my winter break to work full-time for a month, it was more like a homecoming than anything else. I was overjoyed to see new books—books I had spent my summer immersed in—lining the shelves of the office.

Before Christmas, Amy made her way over to my desk. "Here," she said, "Merry Christmas!" In it was a little Christmas present, but most importantly, a card. It read, "Merry Christmas and Happy Hanukkah" and written underneath it in blue pen, "We love you! Amy, Bob, and Bill."

• • •

I went into that interview thinking I was getting myself into a summer internship just like any other summer internship. Instead, it turned into one of the most fulfilling summers of my life, and has continued to be my own personal Chicken Soup for the Soul success story.

~Madeline Clapps

What Doesn't Kill You

Men fail much oftener from want of perseverance than from want of talent.
~William Cobbett

"**D**on't be a drama queen."

I fought to control my face and hold back the tears. My freshman year with Dr. Peters had gone from bad to worse. I was drowning in homesickness and roommate problems, on top of all the academic pressure; and now, my grandmother had died, hundreds of miles away. I'd never felt more alone.

A week crept by between my grandmother's death and her funeral in early February, and I desperately needed to be with my family. But all I saw in Dr. Peters' face was disgust. "You can't just go running home all the time," he told me.

Far from "running home all the time," except for Thanksgiving and Christmas, I'd tried to tough it out, hoping it would soon get easier. Now this.

Unlike friends in other majors, I couldn't tell myself this was just one bad professor. I was a music major in viola performance, and Dr. Peters was my principal teacher. If I stayed, he'd continue to be my daily reality for another three and a half years.

I'd been a successful player in high school, and Dr. Peters himself had recruited me very aggressively and gotten me scholarship money. But as soon as I arrived on campus, he'd started attacking my self-confidence as if that had been his goal all along.

I understood he might be demanding, or want to toughen me up. In fact, that was one reason I'd chosen his school. But this was something else.

For a long time, I was sure the fault was mine. I'd practice longer and longer—sometimes staying in a practice room until three in the morning. At my lessons, I'd literally shake, and start playing wrong notes. "You're not working hard enough," he told me.

I was over my head in a required math course. He didn't care. I had a major paper due in honors English. He didn't care.

Sometimes, I was sure I'd played well, but the most I could hope for was silence, or maybe—once in a blue moon—"That wasn't too bad." The slightest mistake was all he seemed to hear—or care about.

I tried talking to him about my self-doubts. All he said was, "I'm not surprised. This isn't for everyone. If you can't handle it, feel free to go. Don't waste your time and your parents' money."

I couldn't talk to older performance students in the viola studio—there weren't any. The few surviving older students were all majoring in music education, and the expectations for their performing capabilities weren't nearly as stringent. And all anyone ever said was, "He's just like that." My mother suggested maybe his being hard on me was really a backhanded compliment, because he expected more of me. But whatever I did, it never seemed to be enough.

My semester auditions had gone well, and I got good seats in the best ensembles, but I became convinced I was just awful. It had gotten so bad, in fact, that I wasn't sleeping. I'd drop into bed later and later, and then toss and turn—sometimes until dawn started to lighten my room. I rarely got more than three hours of sleep at a stretch. Of course, not sleeping didn't improve my performance, confidence, or mood. I got sick—a lot.

Every Friday afternoon, the school of music had sort of an "open mike" session. It was an opportunity to get used to performing. I should have been playing at least every month, but I kept putting it off. Except for my required ensembles, I was a performance major who avoided performing.

I'd started calling my mother and sobbing—sometimes in the middle of those sleepless nights. She tried to convince me to see a doctor, but I just got hysterical and told her I couldn't afford to take time off from practicing.

Then, I got the bright idea of transferring—I even contacted one of the other schools that had accepted me out of high school. But by re-audition time, my confidence had bottomed out so badly I knew I'd bomb it. That's when other potential careers suggested themselves. I called home one day and informed my parents I was switching to animal husbandry. Another time it was pre-med. I'm sure they thought I'd lost my mind—and maybe I had a little.

The breaking point came with Grammy's death. She had always believed in me, and it was thanks to her I was able to buy my first viola. I went home the middle of that long week, went to the funeral on Sunday, and didn't return until the next day, which meant I had to cancel my weekly lesson time.

Dr. Peters' angry e-mail greeted my return. I tried to apologize and explain, at my rescheduled lesson, that the only way I could have gotten back in time was if one of my parents had driven all night to get me there, but it was beyond his comprehension.

Somehow, I limped through cold, cloudy skies, and slush, to the end of the second semester. Spring turned snow to mud, and dead branches into leafy hiding places for birds' nests. Still, I was cold inside, and my dreams lay in tatters. The more I played, the more mistakes I made, and the worse I sounded. But it was too late to do anything but finish the semester and hope I didn't fail out. I had the summer to decide what to do, come fall.

One last hurdle remained—I had to play a solo piece for the string faculty. My grade on that jury performance could mean the difference between passing and failure. I practiced and practiced, but was sick with dread.

The morning of my jury, though, something came alive inside me. I knew when I woke from a restless sleep, and felt the sun on my face, that I was "back." I went to the music building and warmed up, then walked in to face Dr. Peters and the rest of my jury.

Somehow, once I started playing, the music took over. As I finished, my chest felt lighter. The jurors' marks ranged from Bs to an A-. Except, of course, for Dr. Peters, who gave me a D on the jury and a B- for the semester. For a performance major, he might as well have failed me.

I'm still not sure why I went back for more in the fall. I'd been accepted into a big summer music festival before my second semester "crash," and going there reminded me of my dreams. But, while Dr. Peters was a gifted teacher, our relationship stayed rocky my entire four years. Other people, including faculty, praised my playing. He rarely did, and on the eve of my grad school auditions, told me I was wasting my time, and would embarrass myself. Gee, thanks for the send-off!

I don't know how I did it, but I took the first audition anyway, and was accepted on the spot. After that, it got a little easier. Everywhere I auditioned, I heard the positive comments I'd been missing for so long. I graduated on time, with my performance degree, and now I have an amazing teacher who actually seems to like me.

As I was preparing to graduate, several faculty members told me nobody had expected me to last past the first year. It was only then I found out I was Dr. Peters' first performance graduate in fifteen years!

The music business is tough and full of rejection. Though I'm still trying to stop Dr. Peters' verbal abuse from running through my head every time I play in public, I'm finally at the point where I appreciate the truth of the old saying that "what doesn't kill you makes you stronger."

~Marcela Dario Fuentes

Chapter 9

Campus Chronicles

Family Bonds

When you look at your life,
the greatest happinesses are family happinesses.

~Dr. Joyce Brothers

Finding Common Ground

Call it a clan, call it a network, call it a tribe, call it a family.
Whatever you call it, whoever you are, you need one.
~Jane Howard

Everything I had worked towards for over five years came down to this. It was finally my graduation day. As I took my seat, I worried about tripping; I scolded myself for wearing heels. I welcomed the new set of fears, however. They were replacing the ones I had about my visitors.

My parents were sitting out there with all of the other proud families. They weren't sitting together, though. Mom and Dad had been divorced since the days I had started my academic journey learning the ABCs in first grade. I had enticed them to come from Wyoming with their significant others to my December graduation in Arizona. I hoped the warmer winter weather would reduce the chill that I thought still existed between them.

I wasn't oblivious to the reasons behind the tension. When my parents divorced, my four younger siblings and I stayed with Mom. I was aware of the sacrifices Mom made for us as a single parent. All of her focus had to be on her five kids, her own dreams set aside while she struggled to help us grow up. I knew that Mom had put off her own college dreams when I came into the world. In the past few years, I had seen firsthand how important she thought college was.

When I graduated high school and applied to community college in Wyoming, she did too. We were college freshmen at the same time, even taking English 101 together. I still lived at home that first semester. I would see the light shining under her bedroom door as she worked into the night on her essays. That was after working a full shift at the supermarket, as well as taking care of the kids. A diploma in my hand was my way of saying the battles she fought were not ignored. No way did I want Mom to miss the result of her quiet influence on me.

As a child, I created my own conflict with my dad. I had cut myself off from him, often staying with Mom when my siblings went to visit. As the oldest, I was so hung up on being part of the team with Mom that I thought aligning with my own father would be a treacherous act. Later in high school I realized that letting Dad into my life did not dishonor my mom and her strength in any way. We slowly started to learn about each other's lives. I learned that he had traded in his textbooks for tools, and spent what could have been his own college freshman year working at the mine when I came into the world, and he never went back.

It had taken a few bumpy roads to get there, but by the time the trip to my college degree was ending, I had begun to understand the pride he had for his eldest daughter. I wanted to nurture that by sharing this important day.

There were already too many important moments missed because of my childhood rift with Dad. Years ago, I refused to attend his wedding. I spent years avoiding his new wife, Debbie, while I grew up. But fate had thrown Debbie and me together.

It was when I had started to let my dad back into my life and let go of the past. My high grades in community college allowed me to score a summer job at the plant where she worked. Debbie taught me to drive a forklift and she showed me how to keep the automatic bag machines running. When I moved to Arizona, she sent money the semester I couldn't make tuition. I wanted her at my graduation too.

This was the grand family history that my mom's significant other would have to contend with during my graduation dinner. His name was Phil, and I didn't know him very well at all. When I moved to Arizona, I could barely pay my rent, much less afford trips home. Besides, Phil wasn't just new to me. After dating long distance for years, he had recently made the move to Wyoming, just in time for this little celebration.

This was going to be some evening.

Alphabetically, I knew my time was near when I heard "Gunderson." With the last name "Haapala," I'm almost always the first H. I was glad to see the professor announcing the graduates. I had enjoyed his class that semester, thankfully one of the smaller ones. He probably wouldn't even need the pronunciation of my name that I'd written out.

Gunderson was shaking hands on stage and I shifted in my seat.

"Tina Ha—uh—Har-ja-la."

I turned as red as my cap and gown at this mispronunciation. I stood and crossed the stage and shook hands, a smile on my face anyway. I could pick out the applause of my family—a little extra "woo-hoo" from Mom and Phil, and, when I glanced up, I could see Dad and Debbie smiling and clapping, my dad just a little bit taller than the parents surrounding him.

That was it. I was officially a college graduate. Now on to bigger challenges—like dinner.

We settled in to the big table at the steakhouse and hid behind menus. Talking about food and ordering from the waitress kept the chitchat at a decent level. But then the lull while waiting for our drinks turned awkward.

"So," I said, filling the silence, "I can't believe that professor mispronounced my name. I must not have made much of an impression in his class." The class was Conflict in Communication. I was hoping not to need the tools from chapter ten tonight.

"Oh," Dad said, "I've had to deal with that for a long time."

"It's okay," my mom said, "we're the only ones who know he messed up. Nobody else would know how to pronounce it anyway."

"It's a hard name," said Phil. "I still have a hard time spelling it."

"I've gotten used to just spelling it for people," Debbie said. "'Yes,' I tell them, 'it really is...'"

"...Two As!" Mom and Debbie said, almost at the same time. Both laughing, too.

I watched from across the table as Mom and Debbie laughed over the shared struggle of having a difficult last name. Everything was fine. I didn't need to worry. I exhaled, silently thanking Professor What's-His-Name for his stumble. That night, it helped my family land on common ground.

~Tina Haapala

Family Matters

In time of test, family is best.
~Burmese Proverb

For me, getting into college was the easiest step. I knew that I had the GPA, the SAT scores, the activities, and the winning essay to get me in. It was once I got to New York City and entered my dream school, New York University, that I was presented with the biggest challenge.

See, I was born and raised in a small town (in the sense of people, not of land) in southwestern Pennsylvania where any day of the week there are horses trotting alongside tractors and people make eye contact and smile (and not because they are crazy or are trying to hit on you). Since my freshman year of high school, I knew that I wanted to go to school for journalism in a city, but I always thought that it would be in Pittsburgh. All of a sudden, I became restless at the thought of staying in Pittsburgh and sticking to what I had known my entire life.

After hours of researching cities (Chicago? Phoenix? New York?), I decided that New York was the place for me, having only visited the city once before. The summer before my senior year, I set up a trip to visit Fordham and the ultra-expensive NYU and from the moment I set foot in one of NYU's buildings (because there really isn't a campus), I knew that this was the place I wanted to be indebted to for the rest of my life.

There were people who doubted me along the way. I remember

very distinctly at my graduation party all of my naysayer relatives who quipped, "New York City? Why would you want to go to school there?" And my honest reply, "Why wouldn't you?" My uncle even told me that I would never make it more than two months in the city. I attribute the fact that I'm in my junior year and happily expecting to graduate from here to this dare that he set out for me, but I admit that it wasn't always easy along the way.

Within the first month, I was in tears when I called home, and part of it was the stress of the city. I couldn't handle the fast pace; the people were so different; the classes were all required; and my roommates were a disaster. I swear that universities place you with whomever they feel you will get along with worst. My family, though they were miles away, pushed me to find better, to do better for myself.

I got involved. I fixed up my resume and found a job on campus. I joined clubs. I found friends who were interested in the same things as me—exploring one of the greatest cities in the world. And this worked well until my second year, when at the beginning, I fell into the same rut and the same issues popped up again. My family became the constant in my life that I relied on to make it through the weeks until I could be at home again. I remember calling home and saying, "Only a month until I'm home again. Only two weeks until I'm home again. I'll be home tomorrow!"

And then, during the winter break sophomore year, it clicked for me. I missed the camaraderie of my house. I missed the feel of a home, with people who loved you waiting inside when you walked in the door. But I knew deep in my heart that even miles away, my family would always be there—always cheering me on when my friends and I weren't talking or the critiques were too tough to handle, telling me stories about what happened in their day. I still have a hard time understanding it when people will brush off the fact that their parents want to talk to them and ignore the phone call. I'd drop almost anything to talk to my family.

My junior year, the sadness never started. I am happier and more successful than I ever imagined I would be. One of the first assignments for my journalism class was to write about the place I loved most, the place I couldn't wait to visit—my family dinner table. But I didn't write it as that freshman and sophomore who needed family contact like she needed air. I wrote about a place full of memories and full of love. It can take a long time to get to that place where you're happy with yourself, especially away from everything you know, but once you get there, you try to hold onto it for as long as possible.

~Katie Jakub

83

Bully for Me

A brother is a friend given by Nature.
~Jean Baptiste Legouve

My big brother was a brat.

For eighteen years, I felt like Kyle was The Enemy. Always teasing and tormenting me. Only eighteen months my senior, he knew which buttons to push and he pushed them just for the exquisite purpose of pushing. That and, of course, the reactions from me he loved to induce. In fact, I found it hilarious that people talked about older brothers looking out for their sisters, protecting them. Older brothers fought off their sisters' bullies. Huh? My brother was the bully.

When we were little, his roughhouse shenanigans caused my only black eye, stitches in my lip when I bit through it once, and even a nosebleed or two. I often wished I were an only child!

We ended up attending colleges two thousand miles apart, and that was fine with me. Yet, oddly, that's when we began communicating.

Through the miracle of e-mail, we kept in constant touch. My fingers flew over the keyboard; mostly I whined. Freshman year was not an easy adjustment for me, as I dealt with serious homesickness, impossible roommates, difficult classes, looming career decisions, and... dating. At a particularly low time, I cried to Kyle about my shattered confidence, my broken heart, and the particular jerk who broke it. Shredded it. Stomped it into dust.

And that's when it arrived.

I hefted the thick package delivered to the dorm one day. "What's this?" I muttered as I tore into it.

The box revealed a sweatshirt. "Phi Delta Theta? That's Kyle's fraternity." I frowned. Why would he send this? I shoved it aside and dug deeper.

Envelopes. A stack of letters. And they were all addressed to me. I opened the one on top.

"Katrina," it said, "your brother showed me your picture and I think you're awesome, beautiful, absolutely drop-dead gorgeous."

I rolled my eyes. "Yeah, sure." I opened another letter. And another. Eighteen in all.

Each one was from a different guy. They complimented. They gushed. They invited me on tantalizing dates. They... wooed me. And they tried to convince me to make a trip out to Knox College and meet them.

"This is over the top!" I snickered. Before long, I was laughing out loud.

And then it hit me. As president of the frat house, Kyle was initiating (or hazing?) freshman pledges. Knowing Kyle—and know him, I did—he'd decided to kill two birds with one stone. He had a parcel of boys to keep busy, and he had a sister who needed a boy. Who needed a boost to her trampled-on feminine ego.

I loved it. I didn't care about the motive. I liked what the guys said and I liked getting fan mail. Mostly, I adored the idea that my big brother had pulled it off. Forget e-mail. I picked up the phone.

"Kyle, the box came and I can't believe what you did."

But Kyle wasn't accepting compliments. "Oh," he mumbled, "I was just tired of reading your woe-is-me e-mails." His voice deepened, gruffer. "Were their notes all clean? I warned the guys, 'Nothing off-color or you're going down.'"

"The letters were perfect," I whispered into the phone. "Just perfect."

Big brothers, I decided, really did protect their sisters. And mine fought off the biggest bully I'd ever encountered—my own self-doubt.

~Katrina L. Hatch as told to Carol McAdoo Rehme

84

Speak Your Heart Today

*Siblings are the people we practice on, the people who teach us about fairness
and cooperation and kindness and caring—quite often the hard way.*

~Pamela Dugdale

I t was a Saturday afternoon and Joey was picking on me, always
a first priority on his older brother to-do list. "Noooo! Please
don't flush Snoopy's head down the toilet!!" I pathetically
pleaded, ready to give anything in return for my favorite stuffed
animal's life. I had already witnessed him decapitate Snoopy's head
medieval-style, but this was just too much.

His sinister cackling grew louder and eyes wider as he reached
for the handle. I panicked. "Mom! Heelllp meee!!" My mom had
heard me cry wolf before and generally preferred us to handle our
own disputes, but this time she heard my desperation. "Hey, what's
going on in here?!" she demanded as she hurried into the bathroom.

Joey stood calmly with a goofy grin on his face and hands on his
hips, looking quite proud. "Hi Mom! Snoopy wanted to learn how to
doggie paddle so I showed him." She paused for a second and tried
not to laugh. Then she rolled her eyes and stepped up to Snoopy's
porcelain coffin. "I promise to give Snoopy stitches and a bath, but
you two have to promise me to make up and say sorry." She shot me a
look knowing in her secret motherly ways that I had done something
to taunt him. I sheepishly looked down. How did she always know?

By bedtime neither one of us had said sorry. What came next from our mom was unexpected. She sat us down in Joey's room and explained why the number one rule in our house was "Never go to bed mad." This was a phrase we had heard a million times before, but tonight it struck a chord with both of us.

"You guys need to make up before bedtime because you never know what might happen," she started. She went on to explain something quite grown up for a six- and eight-year-old, telling us about the day her mother died. "I was twenty-one years old and left the house in a hurry after arguing with my mother. That night she died unexpectedly from a heart attack at fifty-three, and I never did get to say I was sorry or tell her 'I love you' one last time. It has always been something that I regret and that's why it's our rule to never go to bed mad in this house. You need to appreciate each other today."

Our mom's story became a defining moment in my relationship with Joey. We had many more fights, but we grew up closer than any other brother and sister I have ever known. In elementary school, I was lucky enough to hang out with him at recess. In high school, he brought me with him to the cool senior parties. In college, I was regarded as his best friend. I found it hilarious and endearing that the front slot in his wallet held my high school senior picture.

Joey and I always said "I love you." It was our routine, but not in a brush-your-teeth-twice-a-day kind of way. It was genuine. I loved that no matter how many people were around when I walked into his house at college, he would always give me his trademark bear hug that squeezed the breath out of me. We also never got off the phone without saying "Love you!" We were known for our closeness and our friends teased us about it often. Little did they know that we took it as a compliment.

One night my sophomore year and Joey's senior year at The Ohio State University, we were out at our favorite bar with all of our friends. I was tired and ready to go home. "Good night sista, love you!" he called out as he came over to give me a hug. "Love you too Joey." Today, I can remember that twinkle in his eyes as we said goodbye. He did love me so much. I felt incredibly lucky to not only have such a caring brother, but also a built-in best friend who just happened to be the most popular guy I knew.

That night, the unimaginable happened. Joey went back to his fraternity house where a late night party was being held. Joey had too much to drink and made a decision to take a party drug called GHB. At twenty-two years of age, my brother was dead. My worst nightmare became my reality. Joey was taken away in an instant and he was never coming back.

I was surprised to see that life went on after that night. The world didn't stop. Family and friends went back to work and school. The seasons kept changing. I graduated from college. But my life was forever changed and there still isn't a day that goes by that I don't miss Joey. Some days it will hit me out of nowhere, feeling like someone punched me in the chest. "Is Joey really gone? How could this possibly be?"

One of my favorite moments used to be meeting people who knew Joey and watching their faces light up as they automatically became my friend by association. Now I feel trepidation when the topic of conversation leads to family and my heart skips a beat when asked, "Do you have any siblings?"

I now travel the country speaking to high school and college students about the dangers of drugs and alcohol, in hopes that I can prevent this from happening to others. Every time I walk out on stage, I feel a strength that could only be described as Joey guiding me, and I have to smile. As devastating as this loss has been, I can't express enough how comforted I am knowing that I have no regrets about my relationship with Joey. I am incredibly thankful that we never took each other for granted and always spoke our hearts until that very last night together. I would have never thought I would be able to live without him, but because we preserved our relationship while he was here, it is lasting me through his death.

~Erica Upshaw

All of Me

The only rock I know that stays steady,
the only institution I know that works is the family.
~Lee Iacocca

"I'm a homosexual!" Natasha Lyonne whined piteously, and the whole room laughed.

Twelve friends and I were crammed into one of our college's tiny, smelly lounges to watch *But I'm a Cheerleader*. People sat on coffee tables, on the floor, their heads on each other's laps, passing around a greasy popcorn bag, boxes of Tofutti Cuties, and paper bowls of vegan nuggets nabbed from the dining hall. My girlfriend, Amanda, had organized the screening. I'd told her two days before that I'd never seen it, which shocked her. She'd announced imperiously, "It's like the movie every gay girl has to see." And as I sat next to her watching it, my head on her shoulder, holding her hand, I realized I had never felt so comfortable and so much like myself.

I had dated boys in high school, but it confused me how I had no feelings for my boyfriends beyond vague friendliness. It didn't hit me until the end of senior year that I was gay. It was too late to act on this realization beyond dumping my boyfriend, so I spent most of my summer months crying to the few close friends I had told and worrying what my Catholic family's reaction would be if they found out.

My ever-patient, wonderful high school friends assured me, "Just wait till you get to college." In college, they thought, it would be easier to be out of the closet, because I'd no longer be surrounded by a conservative family and uptight classmates. Besides, they figured I might meet some other gay people.

They didn't know the half of it. My college turned out to be so overwhelmingly liberal that the Queer Community Alliance Open House contained a third of the campus, and there were even sub-groups within the queer community for people who identified as "trans" or "femme." There was gay speed dating and gender work-shops and a college-wide Drag Ball. My world had (literally) turned inside out, and I was rubbing my eyes, trying to process it.

Then, of course, there was Amanda. Of my like-minded, neo-hippie, gay friends, she was the most intriguing. I found her beautiful and fascinating and three weeks after freshman year started, we were dating. The emptiness I'd felt in my earlier relationships was replaced by the emotional intensity of our first kisses and first arguments. It was like reliving early adolescence.

But when my family called and asked how I was doing, there was nothing I could tell them.

And when dating a just-out-of-the-closet Catholic proved to be too much for Amanda to handle, I didn't know who to turn to. I stayed in my tiny single for a week, skipping class, sleeping con-stantly, and eating food from the vending machine instead of facing Amanda in the dining hall. I called home, wanting to break down and be comforted, or have Mom say something sage-like that would make me buck up and move on. I knew, though, that they would never react with sympathy if I told them about Amanda. All I could manage was, "I'm feeling kind of down."

The year went on, and I had good friends who helped me out of my break-up slump. We went to parties and held our own movie nights, and eventually I felt like myself again. Only, I felt like that self was erased the minute I picked up the phone to call home.

I was quiet and moody after every phone call. It was exhausting to carry on the ever-lengthening lie of what my college life was like. Even my friends told me, "You have to tell your family."

I knew that I had to, but I didn't know if I could.

What scared me the most were my parents' faces after I'd initially say the words, "I'm gay," before they could censor themselves. I knew what I'd see: horror, disgust, and disappointment.

I thought it over obsessively. I would wait until the summer, when I was home with them, so we'd have time to talk it through before I left for school. I would tell them after our June vacation, so that the vacation wouldn't be ruined, but before August, because two of my too-young-to-know siblings would be away at camp. I found a friend whose family wouldn't mind having me over in case mine kicked me out. But the day came, and I knew I couldn't go through with telling them face to face.

I got out a piece of paper and poured out the story until one piece of paper became eight. I wrote about figuring myself out in high school, about getting to college and being overwhelmed, about Amanda. I told my parents I was spending the night at a friend's, stuck the letter on the table, and drove away like my old Acura was a race car.

My hands shook as I drove home the next morning. I replayed everything my parents could possibly say in my head and prepared stock responses. I just wasn't sure if I'd be able to get them out.

Somehow, Mom and Dad were in the yard as I pulled up the driveway. I got out of the car slowly, and shakily, I said, "Hey"

Before I could make it to the front door, I was embraced. That's when I lost it.

Dad stood there and watched me as I sobbed for all the time I had spent worrying and hiding and trying to be someone else.

Finally, he said, "Do you want some eggs?"

I nodded, and we went inside.

Coming out wasn't over that day. There was a lot that my parents needed explained, and some things took them years to fully accept. For me, knowing that they loved me, no matter what, was a step in the right direction. And when I called them from college the following year, it would not be as a liar or as only one side of my personality. I would be all of me.

~Eve Legato

86

Euro-Trip

You don't choose your family. They are God's gift to you, as you are to them.

~Desmond Tutu

I had just finished college and, like the multitudes of new grads out there, I was going on a two-month backpacking trip to Europe. The itinerary included England, France, Italy, Greece, Austria, and Germany. I spent the first three weeks with a friend and the rest of the time I was on my own. I swam in the Mediterranean Sea off the beaches of Nice and Positano. I explored the Roman Coliseum and the Vatican with friends I made at the hostel. Then it happened. After gazing at an awe-inspiring sunset in Santorini, I went to an Internet café and opened an e-mail from my mom.

The e-mail read, "Your dad and I haven't been on a holiday in a while and we want to come meet you in Europe."

"Oh no!"—that was my first thought. This was my trip, my independent adventure, my solo dance.

But there was no stopping my parents. My self-discovery trip of eating bread with peanut butter and meeting random strangers at the hostel was over. The one saving grace was that traveling with my parents meant I was no longer on a measly budget.

We decided to meet in Venice. I found my dad waiting for me by a flower stand in the small square near their hotel. I gave him a hug, and he pointed to the window where my mom was watching and waving anxiously. This was going to be interesting, to say the least. I couldn't remember the last time I traveled with both my parents. I spent the last four years at school more than 5,000 miles from home.

My original plan was to head to the hills from *The Sound of Music*, better known as Salzburg, after being in Venice. However, Mom and Dad wanted to visit Italy and France. I would have to backtrack. Places that I thought I wouldn't revisit for at least five years, I was going back to only three weeks after I had left. My parents' idea of planning included printing off itineraries from guidebooks and following them. I had thrown out my guidebooks after visiting France and Italy to lighten my backpack. I was traveling without any plans or real guides. Adventure was my tour guide. But now that I was traveling with Mom and Dad, adventure had moved on.

One of my favorite places in Italy is Cinque Terre (the English translation is Five Lands, or Five Fishing Villages.) So just ten days after my first visit to Cinque Terre, I returned to the five coastal towns with my parents. We rented a villa with a kitchen where my dad could cook. On our first day, we spent two hours looking for the fish market. No fish was found, and at 3 P.M., the *gelateria* owner told us the fish market was already closed. We were too late. "Fish market *abierto* in the morning." he said. The next day, my dad went to buy fish at dawn—I've never seen him so excited. We ate fish for brunch at 11 A.M.

On the beaches of Monteresso, I watched my father walk barefoot in the sand, the waves brushing over his feet. At that moment, he was more than just the guy who chauffeured me around, the guy who taught me to ride a bike, and the guy who told me to do my homework; he was a real person. I lay on the beach and talked "life" with my father. He told me not to be too cheap with my money. "Sometimes in an effort to be frugal, you may cost yourself more money in the end," he said. My previous economical traveling diet of bread and cheese had left me with sunken cheeks. After a week with my dad eating gelato and pizza in Italy, any weight I had lost was easily (and deliciously) regained.

When I was young, my dad told me an old folktale about a man who lost his horse. The moral of the story is that what you perceive to be something bad may turn out be a blessing in disguise.

Initially, I thought my parents intruding on my Euro-trip would be a disaster. I was wrong, and my parents coming to join me was actually a precious gift. Three weeks after we returned from Europe, my dad passed away suddenly due to a heart attack. I cherish that time we had on the beach together, and the image of him walking along the waves in sheer delight will forever live in my memories.

~Sharon Cheung

87

My Mom Followed Me to College

Living involves tearing up one rough draft after another.
~Author Unknown

L et me begin with the answer to your first probable question: why in the world would your mother follow you to college?

I have a high-functioning form of autism known as Asperger's Syndrome. To make it short and simple, I can do the work required of a college student, but I'm really not ready for the independence part of it. However, I wanted to be able to use my gift for writing to make a living someday, and thus began our college search.

We visited Taylor University in Fort Wayne, Indiana in the spring of my junior year of high school and spoke with Dr. Dennis Hensley, the professor who developed their Professional Writing program. It was this visit that convinced me and my parents that our prayers had been answered. It was a small Christian college with a strong writing program, one that would teach me not only how to write, but how to make a living at it. There was only one problem: the school was 1,000 miles away.

To most families, the how-far-away issue would be a minor one, but for my family it meant some major life changes and sacrifices. In order for me to go to this school, my mom would need to be there to support me while my dad financially supported us from Texas, where he serves as a police lieutenant. In order for us to still have family time, my mom would need to limit her work to school weeks only, which would allow for us to be home during holidays and summers. In order to cut costs so that this could happen, we would have to sell our house and move into something very inexpensive.

This was much easier said than done, but after everything was "in order," we left my dad, my two brothers and their wives, and my two nephews in Texas and moved into a second-story apartment just down the street from the school. My mom got a job as a part-time clerk in our college's bookstore. I began classes. All seemed well and good, until October 13th—a day that will be etched in my mind forever.

It began as any other Monday. Classes at nine. Chapel at ten. Then came the announcement of a special meeting at noon. This meeting would announce the closing of our school on May 31st of the next year. Hold on, I thought. This can't be happening! Colleges don't just close up like that, do they?! Didn't they know the sacrifices our family had made to get me here? The sacrifices the rest of the students' families had made to get them here? What about them? What about us?

There were lots of questions but not a lot of answers. There was much crying and disbelief, but not much consoling. Time stood still that day at TUFW. And the next. And the next. It was announced that the main campus in Upland, Indiana, would not be closing its doors. Some departments would be moving, but they had not decided which ones. My mom wrote a letter, pleading with them to keep the Professional Writing program and Dr. Hensley. Concerned parents and students called—some irate, some just wanting answers. All were concerned about the future of our school, formerly Fort Wayne Bible College, then Summit Christian College, and finally Taylor University Fort Wayne—a school that taught its students the importance of ministering to the community. This loss would affect not only our school, but also the entirety of the Fort Wayne area.

My story has a happy ending. Dr. Hensley and his Professional Writing program, along with nearly all of the students in it, will continue, uninterrupted, at the main campus next fall. Although the move creates a few new bumps in our road—uncertainty about living arrangements and a job for my mom—my dream of becoming a professional writer is still alive. And while I'm sad about the loss of TUFW, I can truly say that I am happy to have had the opportunity to attend, if only for one year.

~Joel Copling

88

Don't Forget

*My mom is a neverending song in my heart of comfort, happiness, and being.
I may sometimes forget the words but I always remember the tune.*
~Graycie Harmon

As I stare through the window into complete darkness, I wrap a blanket around my shoulders for warmth. It's my first night in my dorm room and everything gives me chills—the unusual creaks, the frightening shadows, and the new voices in the wind. I know this is the time to get educated and serious about the future that is within arm's reach. But do I want to grasp it? Do I want to leave the world I know behind for another that is completely foreign? I haven't had a sense of insecurity until now.

A couple of months ago, I was prepared for finals, graduation, and the day I would keep my promise—move out as soon as I had the chance. Of course, I used that threat when I was angry or couldn't get my way. Expecting to see horrified faces after the announcement, my parents had grinned instead. Now that I'm here, I know why. This is something I was not prepared for and they knew it. Well, it's too late now. Prepared or not, I'm here.

I miss watching *Happy Days* with my dad on Saturday mornings and Get Smart with my mom on Thursday nights. I miss the times my dad took me fishing and my mom took me shopping. I miss the cheesy home videos I produced with my siblings and the sneaky missions that always failed because Mom and Dad knew everything. Now, all those moments are only memories.

I need to let my parents know that I was wrong. Sitting at my desk with my laptop open, I address an e-mail to a radio station my mom listens to every morning before work. I request a special song Carrie Underwood wrote that I can relate to, called "Don't Forget To Remember Me." It's my way of telling my parents that I, too, do not want to be forgotten.

•••

The next morning, my mom got ready for work as usual. She stumbled out of bed and turned on the radio. She was alerted by the speakers' conversation. "You know how I was upset a couple weeks ago because I sent my little girl to school for the first time? A college student e-mailed us and said that she misses her parents and everything they have done for her. She also requested a special song in honor of them. So we want to thank Candace for that e-mail, because it really eased my worries about my little girl growing up and forgetting about the things us parents do for them."

The song began to play while my mom frantically ran over to my dad and woke him up. "Honey! Honey! Did you hear that? Was that our Candace? Our daughter who couldn't wait to leave home?" My dad, just barely opening his eyes, replied with, "If it is, that was very sweet of her." My mom saw her phone had a text message on it from me saying, "I miss you Mom!" My mother smiled and knew that the radio announcers were talking about me.

I got a call from my mom that night. I was so excited to tell her that I survived my first day of college, and we talked for about an hour. Just when we were about to say our goodbyes, I added one last plea: "Mom, don't forget to remember me."

~Candace Jewell

89

Makes Me Happy

The turning point in the process of growing up is when you discover
the core of strength within you that survives all hurt.
~Max Lerner

War was raged in our house in late July with less than a month to go before my first day of college. It was a battle of wills, my mom's and my own, over where I was to attend. She wanted me to attend the prestigious nursing school to which I was originally accepted, and I wanted to go to a small, private writing college with a student body of fewer than 300 students. Every night for two weeks, we argued, yelled, bickered, and gave silent treatments until both parties went to bed with regrets and frustrations.

It was mostly my fault. Since my junior year of high school, I had aimed toward being a nurse. I took all the science and anatomy courses, applied for nursing scholarships, and even worked as a volunteer in my town's local hospital. My goal, or so I told everyone, was to work on Mercy Ships, healing the sick and being Superwoman to the world.

Yet, as graduation and college neared, it all sounded hollow. Treating the sick and healing the hurt was a noble endeavor, but not what I was meant to do for the rest of my life. I could picture myself in scrubs, making rounds, and taking temperatures, but I couldn't picture myself happy. It wasn't the future I wanted.

Then, it dawned on me. I had been creating and writing stories for as long as I could remember. Even at four years old, I had my dad write as I told him the stories I had molded in my mind. It was my outlet, my element, and my medium of expression. I had written for my high school's newspaper and attended a writing camp over the previous summer. I loved it, and writing was what I had always pictured myself doing as a hobby. Now, it had become much more than a hobby. It was going to be my career. It had to be.

Try telling your parents you have decided to give up a secure medical career for the unstable life of a writer. I can almost guarantee it will not go over well.

My dad acted as mediator between his feuding females, trying to make one see the other's point of view. Neither side budged, and as time grew shorter, so did our tempers. Just saying the word "college" was enough to set off a whole new round of yelling. The tension was thick enough to cut, and the phrase "elephant in the living room" came to mean so much more to me.

It finally reached its breaking point when my mom informed me that if I did not attend the nursing school, she would not pay for any college expenses.

My desire was put to the test. Was writing really that important to me? Would I be willing to put in the effort and personal sacrifice to do what I loved?

For several days, as my mom's ultimatum settled in, I wrestled with those questions. The more I thought and tried to picture what my future would become, the more I realized that writing was not only what I wanted to do, but what I needed to do.

What cemented my decision was when my dad quoted Thurmond Whitman, who said, "Do not ask what the world needs. Instead ask what makes you come alive. Because what the world needs is more people who have come alive."

On August 1st, Mom and I sat down at the dinner table and I told her that she had every right to choose where to spend her money, just like I had every right to decide where I wanted to go to school. If it was her choice to not finance any of my college education, then

I would take a year off to work and earn money so I could go to the college I wanted.

I withdrew from the nursing program and began to prepare myself for a year of work and penny-pinching. It wasn't a joyful choice, but it was a step toward achieving my dreams of writing for the masses.

Yet standing by my decision to be a writer had proven my conviction to my mom. She had seen through the years how writing had affected me and now realized that it wasn't just a passing whim. Finally, we were at peace, and she decided that if writing was what I really wanted to do, then she would support me both emotionally and financially. Her support has meant the world to me.

Before that time, I had never stood up against my parents on any major decision. Choosing which college to attend allowed me to become a separate and complete adult away from my parents. College doesn't just give you an education, it helps shape the person you become. I am now finished with my first semester as a Professional Writing major and I cannot wait to see what comes next.

~Nan Johnson

Do Good

*If you want others to be happy, practice compassion
If you want to be happy, practice compassion.*
~Dalai Lama

It was time to pack up and move out on my own for the first time in my life. I was scared to death.

I was headed to Moravian College in Bethlehem, Pennsylvania, and had spent the entire summer preparing for this life-changing event. Change was never something that I handled well. Just before graduation, each student in my high school's senior class was required to present a "Senior Speech." This speech was to be the culmination of everything we had learned during our high school career. I cried through every single speech and was a blubbering fool during my own. I spent every moment of my summer vacation with as many friends as I could, for fear of never seeing them again once we parted ways for college. I had a breakdown every few weeks about leaving home, and couldn't imagine life without my family and friends.

During these breakdowns, my dad was with me every step of the way. He listened to my fears and comforted my tears. I remember countless walks through the neighborhood with my dad in which we discussed what I would do when I finally got to college. My dad had visions of me partying it up with new friends, but I had visions of sitting all alone in my dorm room.

Moving day quickly arrived. We made it to Moravian College

without any major problems and for a few hours I forgot about all of my worries. I was having fun setting up a new room, getting to know my new roommate and exploring a brand new campus.

But then came the time for my family to go back home and leave me all alone with an entire school full of people who I didn't know. I was crying, my mom was crying, I'm pretty sure I saw some tears in my dad's eyes, and maybe even in my brother's. We were strong however, and they made a quick getaway so as not to upset me any more than I already was. My roommate and I spent the rest of the day doing Freshman Orientation activities and I was feeling pretty good by dinner time. I had met some nice girls on my floor and two girls that my roommate knew from high school.

As I was climbing into my bunk bed that night, I saw an envelope sticking out from beneath a box on one of my shelves. I grabbed it and took it into bed with me. My name was written on it in my dad's handwriting. As I opened the card, I began to cry once again. My dad had written a chronology of all the memories that he loved about me. He also wrote how proud he was of me for making it to college. He assured me that I would have a great time there and also wrote two simple words at the very end of the note that have since become my life motto: "Do Good."

That's all he asked of me — "Do Good." Not, "Get On the Dean's List" or "Stay Out of Trouble" or "Don't Waste My Money by Flunking Out in the First Semester." Just, "Do Good." I knew that was something I could handle.

A new chapter of my life had begun and even though it was scary, I knew that all I had to do was try my best and I would make my family proud. It was also a chance to go after my big dreams. And boy, did I pursue my dreams that first year of college!

I have since graduated from college and I continue to dream big dreams, but they have gone from dreams of that cute boy in class and that cool frat party across campus to dreams of scoring a high-paying job and buying a house of my own. I still cherish the card that Dad gave me and take it out from time to time to remind myself of how two simple words gave me the courage to overcome my fear of being out on my own, and instead have one of the best years of my life.

~Jennifer L. Cunningham

Chapter 10

Campus Chronicles

Personal Growth

Insist on yourself.
Never imitate.

~Ralph Waldo Emerson

Becoming an Athlete

Endurance is one of the most difficult disciplines,
but it is to the one who endures that the final victory comes.
~Buddha

I stood on the scale in the shellhouse and looked at the lever hanging in perfect balance. This isn't going to work, I thought, nudging the balance of the weight up a few notches and stepping off the scale.

"One hundred thirty-seven," I reported to my crew coach. Without looking up from her clipboard, she recorded my weight. I went to join my teammates.

As I sat on the ergometer rowing machine and tightened the straps around my shoes, I thought about what I had just done. It wasn't the first time I had lied about my weight. But it was the first time I had ever lied about weighing more than I actually did. I picked up the handle, took a deep breath, and started to row.

During my first week at the University of Washington I saw a flier recruiting students for the school's world-class crew program, which had a long history of winning championships and producing Olympic athletes. No rowing experience was required. At the initial meeting, the coaches told the assembled freshmen that they were looking for girls who were tall, strong, and relentlessly athletic.

At 5-feet-7-inches, I wasn't very tall compared to the other girls.

I had just enough coordination to be an average runner and softball player at my small, rural high school, but not enough natural ability or drive to excel. The crew coaches said they wouldn't turn anyone away who showed up for practice every day and worked hard, and I knew I could at least do that. I wanted so much to belong somewhere, I didn't care if I wasn't an exact fit.

The freshmen on the novice women's team met in the basement. We'd check the board where each person's name was written on a Popsicle stick and assigned to a position in a boat, and then we'd stretch on the concrete floor between the long rows of rowing shells stacked horizontally on racks.

Even though I liked being out on the water, I didn't feel I was part of the team. Secretly, I knew that I'd never be a real athlete like the other girls. The coaches knew it, too. But it wasn't as though they didn't give me a chance. Sometimes, I'd show up for practice and find that the Popsicle stick with my name on it had been moved up to the second boat on the board, and my stomach would knot. On the water that day, the coaches would watch the boat carefully, timing the 500-meter sprints through the Montlake Cut between Lake Washington and Lake Union, to see how my presence changed the boat. If I could make the boat go faster, I could take that seat. The coaches never said anything to me about it, but the next day my Popsicle stick would be back in the lineup for the last boat.

When it was cold and dark and raining, I showed up for practice only because I knew if I didn't, the coaches might not let me come back. I'd do an extra workout sometimes, burning so many calories I'd have to eat five or six meals a day just to have enough energy to get through practice. I prayed that I'd gain weight.

One hundred thirty-seven, I thought as I rowed on the erg after weighing in. I realized that over the course of the winter, I had quietly abandoned the eating disorder I'd been flirting with in high school. I could tell my body was getting stronger, and I suspected I was becoming an athlete.

That spring when we switched to 6 A.M. practices, enough girls had dropped out that my eight was reduced to a four-person boat. The coaches moved me up to the stroke seat.

"No matter how bad it hurts, you're not going to die," our coach yelled from the small motorboat as she followed us on Lake Union. "Remember, this is what it's like to work hard!"

Days when I had a fight with my boyfriend and wanted to hide from the world, I dreaded going to another practice. But now I had to show up every day for the other girls in the boat—they couldn't go out on the water without me.

While the girls in the other boats had regattas and championships to look forward to, my boat wouldn't be going to those events. Our biggest race of the year would be the Windermere Cup on Opening Day of boating season where we'd be racing against local rowing clubs and colleges. By the time we maneuvered our shell into the starting position on the day of the race, two solid rows of motor boats, pleasure boats, and small yachts lined the course in a straight path to the finish line 2,000 meters away just beyond the Montlake Bridge. This was the moment we'd been training for all year long.

The race was a blur of color, of trying to hear the coxswain scream instructions to us over the roar of the crowd, of seeing the shells on either side of us pull a few seats ahead and then move out of sight. After gliding across the finish line, I turned to look at the girls in my boat. We had worked together as a team and had pulled as hard as we could, and we still finished last. They all had big grins on their faces, just like me. I felt like an athlete.

At the end of the season, I went out with a teammate a couple of times to scull in a two-person boat, but by summer, I had given up rowing. At the start of my sophomore year, I didn't go back to practice. I knew that the way my body was built, I'd never be able to physically compete with the bigger girls, and I didn't think I'd be missed.

Later, I learned from a friend that my coach had known all along that I'd lied about my weight when I was on the team. I wondered why my coach had never said anything. Maybe my coach had more faith in me that I gave her credit for. She might have sensed that being on the crew team was my refuge.

I don't know if the crew coaches meant to teach me the most important thing I would ever learn about being an athlete—the lesson of endurance. I think they were just trying to produce good rowers who knew how to want something and how to work hard every day to reach a goal. But I carried this idea of endurance—of my own capacity for enduring and for surviving—through my junior year when I ended a bad relationship, and through the year after that when I struggled to the finish line of a marathon senior year of college. No matter how badly it hurt at the time, it wasn't going to kill me.

This is what it feels like to work hard, I thought, after I had graduated from college and pushed through the last miles of an Ironman Triathlon to finish third in my age group. It feels good.

~Jennifer Colvin

The Brilliance of Blond

If you are ashamed to stand by your colors, you had better seek another flag.
--Author Unknown

I felt the sweat drip down my neck as I sat in the black salon chair. It was hot out, but the air conditioning should have prevented the small bead from seeping out of my pores. It dripped down my back and pooled somewhere above my pants. Suddenly, I began questioning the decision I was about to make. Was I a blonde or was I a brunette?

I had decided having blond hair was more of a burden than a blessing my freshman year in college while sitting in the math center, waiting for one of its many tutors to sit down next to me and begin lecturing me on what most math majors see as black and white. Listening to the math tutors speak always reminded me that math is everything I'm not. I will never be math. In math, answers are right and wrong, and in my bleak situation, they were wrong more often than not. Put simply—math is a brunette, and I am a blonde.

My calculus class had not been agreeing with me for a large portion of my second semester. During every lecture I was tempted to get up and scream, "Boring!" I have taken more interest in twiddling my thumbs than I ever did learning the ins and outs of level one calculus. I planned to switch to an English major but I still had to pass.

A skinny young man with glasses slipping down his nose took a seat to my left. I have forgotten his name, but his demeanor has stuck with me. He put one foot on the table and leaned back in his chair, his far-too-short khakis hanging above his ankles, and his brown hair glistening for all the wrong reasons. Mr. Math Tutor was in dire need of a shower. He spoke as though he was God's one and only gift to earth, and I found myself rolling my eyes as he listed his credentials for my edification.

As we delved into the world of derivatives and anti-derivatives, it became apparent to both my tutor and me that if the world depended on my mathematical knowledge for survival, we were going to need to find another planet to live on. He looked over at me with frustration, his forehead wrinkled and his eyebrows raised. He then asked me what my major was. I lied and told him English. Even the thought of uttering the word "math" evoked the same feelings one has when dry heaving.

"What are you going to do with English? It seems kind of pointless," he said, as he cracked his knuckles obnoxiously. I looked at him with disbelief. This bold statement was escaping the mouth of the person who had just told me he was one class short of graduating, but was not going to take that class or get his math degree. While I may not have been great with numbers, I was more than capable of multiplying UNH's annual tuition by four.

I was beginning to get annoyed as he continued to prod me with questions about my uncertain future. He made mention of the current economy in reference to something he had seen on the news, and proceeded to say, "But you wouldn't know anything about that. You don't look like the type who watches the news."

Until that point in my life, I wasn't aware there was a specific look to those who watched the news, but I knew exactly what he was referring to when he said it: I have blond hair, therefore I'm stupid. There I was, slouched over in my chair, nearly in tears, all because of the color of my hair. I shot him a look that most of my friends describe as horrific. It's the only facial expression that I cannot reproduce on command, and though I have never seen it myself, I'm sure it conveys the appropriate feelings.

My tutor then explained to me that he was currently reading *The Heart of Darkness*, something, I'm sure, he figured a feeble-minded blonde like me had never heard of. I explained, "I read that when I was a sophomore—and it blew," before leaving the tutoring center and dialing my mother.

In tears, I explained to her my frustration with being reduced to nothing because of my hair color. "Everybody here thinks I'm dumb," I said to her.

"You're not dumb, Nikki," she reassured me, like I didn't already know.

The truth is even my parents thought I was a little "flighty," simply because I didn't have my life planned out, and occasionally "dreamed out of reach." When looking at their faces as I told them I wanted to be a math teacher, one would have thought I'd won a Nobel Prize. Clearly my one and only plan had not worked out, and finally years of people assuming my intelligence level was somehow correlated with the gene that made me a blonde had finally come to a head. I was sick of people talking to me like I was hard of hearing or avoiding intelligent conversation with me for the sole reason that I looked as though I could not understand it. I had reached a point in my life where I was sick and tired of trying to change a stereotype, and I thought it was time for me to be a brunette.

"So you're going darker?" my hairdresser said to me as she ran her fingers through my hair.

"Yes," I said. "I'm in need of a change."

She went over to mix up the new color, and as she walked away, Mr. Math Tutor's long face popped into my head. I began to think of his sudden appearance as a sign. I could see his pockmarked face and pursed lips, and atop his head was a mass of brown hair. This young man had underestimated me; he had prejudged me as a bimbo. He was a dumb brunette! It was in that instant that I turned around and called out to my hairdresser that I had decided on a simple trim and the color would not be necessary. That moment, I decided being a part of the endangered species called "Natural Blondes" was brilliant in itself. Mr. Math Tutor saw the world in black and white. Mr. Math Tutor was math. I am not math. I am blond.

~Nikki Yuskowski

Diagnosing the Problem

You must have control of the authorship of your own destiny.
The pen that writes your life story must be held in your own hand.
~Irene C. Kassorla

The envelope was finally in my hand.

I had applied as a joke, not thinking anything would happen, but now the envelope was in my hand. My brother had just been accepted to a college in Chicago and my parents were ecstatic—so I applied to another school in Chicago just to humor them. I thought, "There's no way they have enough money to send me there," and "there's no way they'll accept me with my grades."

"We are please to inform you that Joel Alonzo has been accepted to study Journalism at Columbia College Chicago."

I had been accepted—my heart hit the floor.

I had heard stories of people getting accepted to college and dropping to their knees, screaming praise to the heavens, but all I felt was fear. I didn't want to tell anyone but I didn't want to leave home.

The day finally came. My mom's minivan was packed to the top with clothes and boxes. Somewhere between Springfield and Bloomington, in the middle of our five-hour drive, I started crying. My mom looked at me and put her hand on my leg.

"You'll be fine, and your dad and I will always be just a phone call away," she said. I looked out the window to hide my tears. I kept crying until we pulled off the highway at Wendy's. We were halfway there, but I was already gone.

A few months later, I was slowly getting into the routine of things, but the feeling of homesickness hadn't gone away—it had only grown. Chicago is a big city with many things to see, but I had withdrawn into the small comfort of my dorm room. Even on weekends, I would stay home on my computer.

"Hey man," my roommate Brian, from Vermont, would say. "We're all going bowling—you want to come with us?"

"No thanks," I would reply. "I'm just going to stay around here, do some homework."

"Dude, it's the weekend, you can do that later."

I faked laughter. "Ha ha, no thanks man, maybe some other time."

"All right," Brian would say. "Suit yourself."

Suddenly, the kid who loved nothing more than going out and having a blast had turned into a home-bodied introvert, staying home and watching re-runs of *Everybody Loves Raymond*. If only I knew that was just the beginning.

It's difficult to describe to people how I felt on the inside. During those years of my life, I wasn't in control of my body—it was like watching myself in a movie, completely unable to control what I said or did. My speech was tightly regulated along with my slang. Whatever was cool to say at the moment was what usually came out of my mouth. The same was true for my laughter—a canned kind of laughter, the kind of laugh a boss gives one of his employees after telling a joke just to shoo him out of the room.

It seemed no matter what I said or what I did, I was destined to come off as inauthentic, so I just kept my mouth shut. I started toying with the idea of suicide.

Everyone I met seemed to have a different solution:

My grandma would say, "You're in a new town—it's the jitters, it'll go away. Have you met a nice girl yet?"

My buddies would say, "Screw it man, whatever. Have a beer."

My mom would say, "You miss your mom, that's what it is."

But nothing seemed to fit. As much as I wanted to jump off the nearest skyscraper, I had to figure out why I felt this way.

I immersed myself in psychology literature. I would identify with some things:

Manic-depressive — that sounds like me, sort of. I do get "depressive" sometimes and at other times feel a little crazy.

Attention deficit disorder — maybe that's it. I can't focus at all.

It wasn't until late at night, while on the Internet, that I found a website dedicated to people suffering from depersonalization. It fit me exactly, and I cried three times that night.

I woke up the next morning and called a doctor I had found listed on the website.

"Hi, this is Bobbie," a woman answered.

"Hi Bobbie," I said, anxiously. "I was wondering if you could, um, schedule me an appointment." I was so nervous I could hear my teeth grinding into one another.

"Yes of course, how about tomorrow at noon?"

"That's perfect, I'll see you tomorrow," I said.

"Yes — we'll take care of everything then."

I got off the phone and took a breath. She said that everything would be taken care of. It felt like I had surfaced for air for the first time in years.

That night I slept like a baby.

~Joel Alonzo

The Freshman Fifty

In order to change we must be sick and tired of being sick and tired.
~Author Unknown

Long before I entered college, I had heard of the "freshman fifteen." The term usually refers to the extra pounds put on by first-year female college students. I had always written the expression off as more of a joke than an actual phenomenon, and assumed that I had little to worry about. After all, I was in the best shape of my life and, more importantly, a man. So it certainly would not happen to me, right? Wrong!

Like most freshmen, college was my first time really away from home, my first true taste of absolute freedom. There was nobody to tell me what to do. I could stay up as late as I wanted, and sleep in as long as I wanted. I could attend class when I wanted, or skip class when I wanted. And most importantly, I could eat what I wanted, and eat as much as I wanted. And that's just what I did.

I grew up in a household where I had to ask if I wanted something to eat. Otherwise, with three siblings, the refrigerator and cupboards would always be empty. My family hardly ever ate out, and if we did, almost never at a fast food restaurant. Also, I was a dedicated member of my high school's wrestling team, which meant that if I wasn't losing weight, I was probably watching my weight. So for most of my teenage years I was counting calories and had but an ounce of fat under my skin. But then during my senior year, after I had wrestled my final match, I promised myself two things. First, I would never again, under any circumstances, eat another rice cake for the rest of my life. And second, I would never again worry about what I ate.

For a person who had not a care in the world about his food intake, college was an absolute paradise. I had the option of a meal plan that consisted of nineteen meals a week, or one with fourteen. Knowing that I would probably not be up in time for breakfast most days, I chose the latter. I also had the option of eating at one of several vendors that served up quick meals, or an all-you-can-eat style buffet. Not worrying about what I ate, I almost always chose the latter.

The buffet had everything that an American teenager could ask for: a taco bar, a pizza bar, a salad bar, a hamburger stand, a chicken stand, a Chinese food stand, a sandwich stand, and a dessert bar with a wide variety of ice creams and baked goods. If my mouth watered for a double-layered taco with every topping imaginable, I could have it, and I did. If my taste buds desired a triple cheeseburger covered with chili, I could have it, and I did. If my stomach craved a sundae with four scoops of ice cream and a half-pound of hot fudge, I could have it, and I did. And most of the time I had all of those things in just one sitting. Looking back, I spent more time in the dining hall than I did in the library.

When I went off campus I was no better. I frequently ate at the local fast-food restaurants and was constantly snacking on junk food. And I don't even want to think about the amount of empty calories I drank at the never-ending house parties. In just four months I probably consumed more calories than I did in the first seventeen years of my life combined.

I had gotten fat and hadn't even realized it. Sure, my clothes felt a little tight, but it was also the first time I had done laundry myself, so I assumed that they had shrunk. It was not until I returned home during winter break that I recognized the truth. I went to a wrestling practice at my former high school and within minutes the jokes started. My teammates were relentless and even my coach asked about my weight. "So I gained a few pounds," I said. Then they made me step on the scale. I was well over 200 pounds, which wouldn't have been that big of a deal, except that only a year earlier I wrestled in the 152-pound weight class. In less than a year I had gained fifty pounds. I had transformed from a lean muscular middleweight into a short chubby heavyweight. It was embarrassing. I felt as if I had let myself down. I could only imagine how much weight I would have gained if I had chosen the plan with nineteen meals a week.

When I returned to school for the spring semester I decided to lose some weight. I did not forget the promise that I had made to myself and continued not to worry about what I ate. I just did not eat as much. Instead of three fried chicken breasts with lunch, I would only have two. Instead of two slices of pepperoni pizza with dinner, I would only have one with a salad on the side. Instead of four glasses of soda, I would have two glasses of milk.

Slowly but surely my weight dropped. I never went back to the body I had my senior year of high school, but I came to the conclusion that I never would, and was content with that fact. I did manage to learn a valuable lesson that would stick with me for life—with absolute freedom comes a great deal of personal responsibility. There is a vast difference between not worrying about what you eat, and taking care of yourself. Everybody has a choice between abusing their body with food or being generally healthy. Now, I choose the latter.

~J. M. Penfold

Inspiration on 57th Street

The difference between try and triumph is a little umph.
~Author Unknown

I love the way sentences fit together, and the excitement I feel when I find the perfect adjective is something close to the way a kid feels on Christmas morning... plus I'm a bit of a talker. So it's not surprising that I decided very early on to become a journalist. Being much more attracted to glossy magazine pages than the ink-smeared pages of a newspaper, I chose to study magazine journalism in the frozen tundra that is Syracuse, NY, at Syracuse University.

For my introductory magazine journalism class, our little group knew from day one that we would spend the semester completing and agonizing over the infamous twenty-page term paper on the exploration of a magazine we selected.

My professor assigned me my first choice magazine to profile: *Cosmopolitan*, the magazine for the "sexy single girl." The research turned out to be fun as I poured over back issues and library books detailing the magazine's history. I explored everything, from the type-faces to the cover lines to the advertising—to the seemingly impossible acrobatic sex positions. The formula established by Helen Gurley Brown turned out to be genius, and I dreamed of what it would be like to meet Editor-In-Chief Kate White, to momentarily turn myself into a sponge so I could soak up any advice she could give me.

I sent snail mail letters to the New York City offices and surprisingly received an e-mail response within a few days. I was lucky enough to have secured interviews with the Senior Features Editor and one of the Account Managers. I attributed my success to the electric blue paper I used to send my letters.

Spring Break couldn't arrive fast enough as I Googled the staffers and wrote up interview questions, endlessly preparing for the in-person interviews ahead. That morning, I navigated the subway all by myself and reached my final destination without a hitch. My breath caught in my chest as I reached the top of the stairs and crossed the threshold. I had been to New York before, but never had the air felt so crisp, never had I felt so exhilarated by my favorite city. Quickly returning to earth, I briskly walked to Starbucks for some liquid courage.

Following a pep talk from my mother, I made my way to the Hearst Corporation building on the corner of 57th and 8th. I'm not too sure if anything could have prepared me for what I found once inside. The lobby was immense and pristine, complete with a cascading waterfall running next to the escalator that seemed more like a stairway to heaven.

Everyone looked like they were on their way to somewhere important, even if it was simply to go scarf down some lunch before getting back to work. They were dressed immaculately, and I stopped to wonder if The Closet filled with designer garb actually existed; I laughed to myself as I realized that surely this wasn't the result of a journalist's salary.

And how could I forget the view from the 38th floor? It was indescribable. I looked out the glass windows to find that the skyscrapers seemed to go on for miles, and the enormity of the city below really took hold of me.

From my interviews, I gathered that these people working in this glorious monstrosity of a building weren't just here through the process of osmosis. Everyone possessed a creative vision, the talent and the moxie necessary to climb their way to the top of the building, so to speak.

I realized that I could find a place for my exploding excitement for the perfect sentence structure, the fabulous story idea, and the revealing interview in this competitive industry; it is a hunger and a thirst only satiated by success, and I was determined.

I felt at home, I felt a sense of purpose, I felt invigorated, and I left the building with an extra bounce in my step. If my goals hadn't been affirmed before, they most certainly were now, and I couldn't wait to work my little *tuchus* off until I reached the very top.

And as of right now, I am playing the sponge in my classes, while I generate online content for my internship, when speakers come to the university, and just about whenever else I am able to learn something from my experiences. When I graduate, I will head out into the real world with a bounce in my step, armed with knowledge, a notebook, and of course, a collection of my favorite adjectives.

~Samantha Morgenstern

96

Conceiving, Believing, and Achieving

Discipline is the bridge between goals and accomplishment.
~Jim Rohn

In college, I kept my leisure activities to a minimum. No television, partying, or socializing for me. I was determined to succeed and leave my mark on the school and at the same time, increase my knowledge about my chosen career in filmmaking. Somehow, someway, I wanted to be the absolute best I could be.

My journey actually began when I interned at Paramount Pictures the summer before beginning school at the Academy of Art University. I didn't care about earning the credits, but was interested in the inner workings of the entertainment industry. The internship taught me the difference between the professional world and the college world.

I took the work ethic learned from the three-month internship and applied it to college. Not only did I do well in my classes, I also purchased numerous books on filmmaking and studied just as much during my free time as I did in my required courses. I wanted to focus my efforts and achieve success according to my own standards. So I asked myself three questions:

1. What is my goal?
2. Can I accomplish it?
3. What actions must I take to reach it?

At the end of the first year, I attended the school's annual film festival showcasing the best work of graduate students. I discovered that film awards were given out to the most outstanding projects and at that moment, I found the answers to my questions:

1. Win the school's Film Award.
2. Sure. Someone wins every year, so why not me?
3. Produce a high-quality short film.

To my amazement, this goal fueled me for the next few years and propelled me to learn as much as possible about storytelling in order to produce a project that deserved an award. The odds of success were against me, as only two percent of graduates had ever won an award, but once I focused on achieving this goal within the time-frame of college, it set in motion an extraordinary self-transformation. I felt an enormous amount of energy and passion that was dormant before I set my sights on the prize. Partying, socializing, and drinking were unimportant compared to the possibility of winning an award, something that would increase my chances of finding work in the real world and also give me a great sense of accomplishment.

I wrote ten short screenplays so that I could understand screen-writing. I produced half of them as short narrative films, and one of them ended up as my thesis film. It was fairly complex and ended up costing $15,000. Surprisingly, we only had a crew of two people, just the Director and me, because he was afraid of working with other people besides the actors. I don't know how we did it, but we constructed sets, built miniatures, found costumes, and even created special effects—extremely daunting for two people. Somehow we managed, even though it took us two years to complete the project.

When we finally submitted it to the film festival, it was my last year in college and my last chance to realize my dream. I felt confident that our film would win at least one award in the category of Writing, Producing, or Directing. To my surprise, it didn't win in any of those. Instead, when the director of the Motion Picture Department announced our film, he said it excelled in every category of filmmaking and because of that, they created a new award, called the "Special Jury Prize." It was the first time the award was ever given and remains that way to this day. I set out to achieve my goals early in college and found enormous rewards by conceiving, believing, and achieving my dreams.

~Joe Lam

97

Never Forget

The only truly dead are those who have been forgotten.
~Jewish proverb

We make the sixty-kilometer trip from Krakow to the town of Oœwiêcim, more commonly known as Auschwitz, its German name. This is the most humbling and sobering day of my life.

As I enter Auschwitz through the main gate, I look overhead and see the words "*Arbeit Macht Frei*" or in English, "Work Shall Set You Free." I imagine the millions of innocent people who marched to their deaths underneath this twisted phrase. Here, the orchestra made up of prisoners would play as thousands of other prisoners would march out to start their day of forced labor. Many times this labor had no purpose at all, only to slowly and painfully kill the prisoners.

Once past the gate, Auschwitz opens up into rows and rows of barracks and Nazi offices. Today it is a museum with each building housing a separate exhibition. One of the most moving is the "Physical Evidence of the Crimes" exhibition. In it are the belongings that were taken away from the prisoners as they entered the camp. Included in this display is a long room filled to the ceiling on both sides with shoes of the victims. As I walk along in silence, alone with my thoughts, I make out a child's rubber boot. I stop and put my hand on the glass. I have no idea what is to come. Once I leave that room, I turn a corner and there is a whole separate display of children's shoes, the grizzly evidence taking up about a quarter of the room. I walk on to see the suitcases, crutches and prosthetics of the victims, each collection more disturbing than the last.

As I leave the physical evidence display I cannot remove the image of the child's boot from my mind. Why the children? Why couldn't they be spared? I look up and I see a tall chimney. My heart sinks into my empty stomach because I know what is before me. I walk into the gas chamber and immediately have a rush of fear. I don't want to be in this room but I know I have to continue on, in remembrance. There is only one small light in the middle of the room. The windows circling the entire room around the top have metal grating on them that serves two purposes: to keep the victims from escaping their death and to allow the sinister, cowardly men to watch. Today these windows give me a per-spective—a perspective on evil. The chamber feels like death. The next room isn't any better, since it holds the crematory. The trolleys poised at the open doors of the four cremators. It is now that I feel I must get out, and I will run if I have to.

The next location I come to in this eerily silent place is the Death Wall. Here, in a small courtyard, is where the guards would line up whomever they felt deserved to be shot and killed. Many times the prisoners were made to wear blindfolds, unable to see the trigger being pulled, unable to brace themselves for their untimely death. I can feel the sadness, the ruin, and the lost opportunities. Today at the base of the wall there are memorials—flowers and candles—for the victims. But behind the colorful display there is still the black concrete wall. The contrast is extraordinary. I cry silently, out of view from my fellow travel companions. I will never forget those who came before me into this space. I will never forget those who did not have the chance to leave this place.

We take a short taxi ride to the other camp in the complex, called Auschwitz II, or Auschwitz-Birkenau, named for the town in which it is located. This isn't a museum. It is left as if the camp was liberated yesterday. The barracks come into focus, as far as the eye can see, some 300 of them. The barracks that were constantly being filled with new prisoners. The barracks that hold at least 400 people. Long lines of latrines and washrooms are also still intact. The gate, the Death Gate, which the trains went through in order to reach the sorting platform, is still here. Even the train tracks that cut the camp in half are still here for all to see.

Today, I can walk freely around the camp and feel the sorrow. I almost wish I were in an organized group so as to distract me from the sadness. When I walk into the wooden barracks I know that I am not alone. There is no light. The only light sources are the five small windows on each long wooden wall. In some parts of the barracks it is pitch black. Yet I feel their eyes on me; I feel their eyes on my soul. I immediately sense the multiple presences within the wooden structure. It was almost as if there is a crowd of people around me, although I'm really only accompanied by three other human beings. The crowd I feel cannot be seen.

As I continue to walk, I come upon the destroyed ruins of the gas chambers and crematoriums. Auschwitz-Birkenau was established in order to deal with the overcrowding in Auschwitz I. It also played an integral part in The Final Solution, the mass extermination of the Jewish people. Two shattered fragments remain of what used to be four chambers. Whether it is only in my imagination or reality, a smell becomes apparent, the smell of death and burnt debris. It is as if the Nazis have just departed.

As I walk back to the Death Gate, along the train tracks that carried millions of innocent people to their death, the cold no longer seems to matter. The almost two-hour bumpy, cold drive from Krakow becomes trivial. I can't imagine complaining about anything ever again. These people didn't have the time to complain about the cold. Staying alive was their goal and they had to put all their energy into that. The courage that was shown by the prisoners in these camps is astonishing. I can't imagine having to be that strong. To say goodbye to your family, knowing full well that in fifteen minutes they would be murdered and then burned, is mind blowing.

I try to think of things to do to make everything better but there is nothing. It is too late, the atrocities have already been committed and the genocide has already taken place. I have done my part, though. I have seen it and learned from it. I have changed inside, even if just a little, for the better.

~Savannah Cole

No Quitter

Effort only fully releases its reward after a person refuses to quit.
~Napoleon Hill

By my junior year of college, I was hanging on by a very thin thread. My scholarships were gone, I was up to my eyeballs in debt, my grades were horrible, and I hated every minute of school. For the first time ever, I was not in love with college. I was, instead, over it. I had started college one hundred and fifty percent sure that I was going to finish and head to medical school. All I wanted more than anything was the title "doctor" in front of my name. Except now I was not seeing "doctor" in front of my name, I was seeing "failure."

I hated the life of a pre-med student, and the idea of going to medical school was not even remotely appealing anymore. I had struggled through all my science classes—failing chemistry, both inorganic and organic, more than once each—and I was barely able to survive my biology classes. Still, I refused to give up. Gloria Panzera was no quitter.

I took a creative writing class in the spring of my junior year in order to avoid a meltdown that was sure to follow the existential crisis I was in. I never thought that switching into this course, simply to be in the same class with my friend and roommate, would change my life as a college student. This particular semester I was taking almost all science classes and had decided I needed a break from heavy-duty reading. I had switched out of an American literature course to take this creative writing course. For the first time in the three years I had attended college, I was excited to go to class. I couldn't wait to get to my desk to start working on a story or read my classmates' work. I was in college student heaven.

Looking back I should have taken this change in attitude as a sign, but instead I stubbornly continued along the same path for another year and continued to fail and retake science classes. I was no quitter. Because I had room for electives in my schedule, I continued to take creative writing classes since they brought me happiness and were cathartic in a way I could never explain.

The semester before I was supposed to graduate, I met with my benevolently blunt academic advisor for a credit check. "I don't know why you keep taking these classes, but you're on your way to being an English major if you want," she stated. I didn't know what to say. She continued, "If you go through this upcoming summer and through the fall, you could graduate as an English major." I left confused and depressed because I was not getting any better at my biology classes, was looking at graduating late with a horrible GPA, and was wondering what the heck I was supposed to do with a Bachelor of Arts in English.

I knew switching meant many things. It meant I wasn't going to medical school. I wasn't going to be a doctor and I wasn't going to graduate in four years. It also meant I was quitting—quitting the goal of being a medical doctor. When I had started school four years before, I had not been encouraged to study anything other than medicine. "Why would you leave university with so many bills if you're going to just be a teacher? You're going to be paying those bills forever," my dad had repeated to me many times throughout my college career. After long days and months of talking to my friends and family, I decided I needed to switch.

That semester of being an English major was the greatest semester of my college career. For the first time since I had started, I knew I was where I was meant to be. I wasn't worried about not graduating. My existential crisis was over. For the longest time, my friends and family would ask me, "What are you going to do with all those science classes?" And for the longest time I didn't have the answer. But when I started teaching high school seniors and college freshmen I suddenly knew why I had experienced those four years of unhappiness and failure. I had students who talked about how their parents wanted them to be engineers and doctors, but they weren't so sure. They really thought philosophy or literature or music was more their cup of tea. I suffered those four years of college so I could help others who also felt they needed that doctor title. I was put through those classes so that I could tell my students to study their passions and forget about living life for anyone other than themselves. If they wanted to be the greatest guitarist in the world, I said go for it. Work hard, find your niche and you'll be successful—as successful as a doctor.

I wanted that doctor title more than anything when I started college, and when I graduated with my English degree I didn't think I'd actually attain it. It wasn't until I started graduate school and decided I was going to go for my Ph.D. that I realized I would have that doctor title and my happiness wasn't going to be the price. After all, Gloria Panzera is no quitter.

~Gloria Panzera

Transferring by Bicycle

Nobody can go back and start a new beginning,
but anyone can start today and make a new ending.
~Maria Robinson

T he whole college application process made me so nervous that I made it as simple as possible and applied to one place, early decision. By December of my senior year, I was thrilled to be going to a school for smart people in upstate New York. Their winters were cold and long and by the time the sky cleared we'd be packing our bags for summer. I didn't think weather would be that important. I wasn't concerned that the town was so small that the main attractions were the Conoco station, Bluebird's restaurant and Sidney's Hardware. Without a car or a need for a screwdriver, I figured leaving campus would be a rare event. Besides, I was looking forward to the excitement of fraternity parties, shyly talking to guys who would likely scare me.

My sister and brother had gone to colleges on the West Coast and came home glowing. I chose to stay on the East Coast and by Thanksgiving, I came home groaning. I did make close friends, but even dear friends couldn't lighten the load of long hours reading French novels and writing uninteresting term papers — taking breaks to run on cold, icy sidewalks.

I had always turned to exercise when things were upsetting

me, and a good bike ride often seemed to help. So after surviving one very long year, I decided to take one very long ride and pedal my way across the country. I researched the possibilities and found there was a bike route crossing the U.S. on back roads designed to teach you history as you rode. I signed up to join a group of sixteen strangers who over eighty days would pedal from Lightfoot, Virginia to Reedsport, Oregon. My family thought being a camp counselor might be a better option. I disagreed.

So one hot, sticky morning, at a Virginia campground, I met my group for the first time, all of us ranging in age from sixteen to sixty. We traveled roughly sixty miles a day, carrying a sleeping bag and panniers of light clothing. We always had a roof over our heads in the form of churches, elementary schools, and community centers.

We ate breakfast and dinner at old time cafes with pies under glass covers decorating the counter. We rose early, learning our individual routines as the days passed along with the states. We'd cycle in twos and threes, matching personality and pedaling speed. I chose 26-year-old Robyn, blond and freckled studying to be a horse vet and we adopted 16-year-old Scott from Alabama.

The three of us watched out for each other. Often we were victims of both weather and terrain. The Virginia Ozarks and Kentucky Appalachians greeted us early on. The roads weren't switchbacks, but often just straight up. Coal trucks chugged up, coming dangerously close, treating us like annoying flies. Thinking about the ride one day at a time helped in the beginning. We just had to make it to the evening meal, which was often grilled cheese and sweet fruit pie with a dollop of whipped cream.

Kansas blew in after Missouri. The headwinds pushed against us as we inched from one corn stalk to the next. I both loved and hated the challenge. But somehow the simplicity of sun and sweat was actually a cool breeze compared to the treacherous first year of college. For ten weeks, I was on one beautiful bike ride.

Windy Kansas flatlands soon rolled into the Colorado mountains and a blue water sky that kept me looking up. My New York childhood sky was lower and heavier. I breathed differently out west.

I had more air at a higher altitude. We were empowered as we flew down mountain passes, smiling recklessly.

Cyclists traveling west to east would alert us about life ahead and we'd do the same for them—where to find hot showers, where to find the cookie lady passing out Snickerdoodles, and take a left to swim in a clear lake. Every ten days we had a rest day where we bought little boxes of detergent to wash our sweaty shorts and T-shirts so they felt brand new. We took naps and went bowling.

Wyoming, Montana and Idaho escorted us into Oregon where we started pedaling more slowly. Our last day of pedaling went late into the night. We stopped in a redwood forest, lounging against our bikes, using them like pillows—their comfort and security had taken us so far. We told each other bedtime stories created from our free wheeling journey. It was like we were mourning before dawn. We talked about returning to our lives as engineers, students, teachers and artists. Like seashells picked up on a vacation beach, I wanted to pocket the joy and simplicity of feeling the wind at my back every day.

Although I'd traveled thousands of miles, the distance covered on the inside felt just as far. Finally, I was old enough to realize that sometimes it is more important to do what we want than what we should. I knew I needed to live under a wide-open sky, far enough away from family to feel the freedom of my own personal choices. I wanted a big school, to get lost enough to find my own way, and I wanted to live in a town that was alive. I didn't want to read stories in French. I wanted to write my own stories in English. And so it was, I transferred colleges by bicycle and graduated from the University of Colorado. The wide-open blue sky is a daily reminder that the "decision" to go the long way took me to a better place. And "deciding" to arrive somewhere "early" is often just too early to know for sure.

~Priscilla Dann-Courtney

Les Rastas Dorés

There is a bit of insanity in dancing that does everybody a great deal of good.
~Edwin Denby

Still feeling the effects of seasickness combined with a stifling vomit-scented basement cabin, I abandoned my restless sleep and surfaced from the bowels of the ferry, relieved as the fresh air and salty breeze immediately invigorated my dulled senses. I perched on a bench with my travel companions, four girls also in my program, excited to witness our arrival in Ziguinchor, the capital of Casamance, the southern region of Senegal, Africa.

What was I doing, surveying a remote corner of Western Africa from a ferry, about to embark on a ten-day journey through Casamance? A year earlier, I had confidently decided that I would spend my year abroad in Paris. But somewhere in the process of sifting through various French programs and discovering West African history, culture, and literature in my classes at Georgetown, I realized that a) I couldn't really afford a whole year in Paris, b) I wanted to focus on African and European studies, and c) I would probably gain far more by living in a country so vastly different and unfamiliar to me. I solidified my plans to study in Dakar for the fall of my junior year, followed by the spring semester in Paris.

Upon exiting the shelter of the guarded port, a trail of vendors and self-assigned guides followed us through the sleepy city, down wide, dusty avenues lined with over-sized trees and decrepit colonial buildings, bright colors peeking out from behind scratched paint and political graffiti. Gradually the parade of helpers dispersed and we began fielding invitations to various "spectacles." Though wary of committing to anything, we did make tentative plans with Patrick, a fellow American we'd met earlier on the ferry, to meet in "Kola..." (the end was some mumble we couldn't quite decipher). Patrick's Senegalese friend, Souleyman, the incarnation of relaxation as he zipped through the streets on a moped with his bleached dreadlocks flying in the wind, promised an animated performance.

Settled in the standard Senegalese taxi—windshield cracked, rear view mirror missing, pictures of religious leaders taped on all surfaces—our driver didn't get far based on "Kola..." and pulled over for directions, followed by a rapid slew of Wolof. "A spectacle?" the man on the street asked us. "What did these men look like?" After describing Patrick (the more memorable character, we assumed), he exclaimed, "Ah! Souleyman! *Avec les rastas dorés, laissez moi vous le montrer, il est mon frère!*" which meant "With the golden dreadlocks, let me bring you to him, he is my brother!"

Whether or not they were in any way related by blood or the veins of friendship, which often run deeper in Senegal, we put complete faith in this helpful man. He guided us through an increasingly crowded neighborhood, clay alleyways darting and dipping between houses—all to the sound of drums somewhere in the maze of cement.

Finally, we approached the source of the sound: a courtyard filled with five men drumming intensely and nearly thirty people of all ages dancing, clapping, and whistling, forming circles around toddlers and elderly women alike, displaying their skills. With our entrance, the crowd erupted into shouts, the drummers running towards us, drums still in hand, children grabbing our hems, twirling in our tracks, everyone ecstatic to share this ceremony with foreigners.

Bouncing subtly to the beat, I stood back and watched the dancing rage on, entranced by the involvement of everyone in the community. Suddenly out of a shed jumped what can only be described as a giant, brown furry mascot-like creature who started breaking it down as the beat grew faster and louder.... As if on cue, fat rain drops began to fall on our faces and arms and legs, in sync with the rhythm reverberating through the earth and the skies, falling faster and harder with each strike.

Determined to keep celebrating, the group of thirty people raced for the door of the one-room, tin-roofed house. Crammed in the stifling room, the drumming continued and this time Souleyman was intent on seeing us dance for everyone. My stomach dropped. I do not dance publicly. As much as I was loving this amazing display of animist culture, the rehearsal for a male circumcision ceremony to be performed the next day, I had yet to become even slightly comfortable with the dancing constantly expected of visitors. Not wanting to offend these welcoming people, but also seized with the fear of making a fool of myself, I attempted to appreciate the atmosphere while strategically avoiding Souleyman's pushes into the circle. My three friends each took their turn in the center and I searched frantically for a way out.

The last push was inescapable. Thrust into the circle, thirty pairs of expectant eyes on me, I found some source of movement or rhythm to fill thirty seconds of dreadful dance. I wish I could say I suddenly burst into an impressive choreography and led the group in cheer, or at least found pleasure in my contribution to the ceremony, but the feelings of fear and extreme discomfort never really left me. Beyond the anxiety, I felt deeply disappointed in myself for not enjoying the opportunity to take part in a unique experience. With great relief, I rejoined the circle as an onlooker, my heart finding its regular beat again as the drumming continued.

The rain continued to pound on the tin roof, a staccato accompaniment to the music filling the room. As darkness began to creep in through the window, we realized it was time to leave and find our way back to the hotel before it was impossible to navigate the drenched streets of Ziguinchor. We entered the night under the persistent rain, skipping over and through muddy puddles, guided by our new friends. The main road was devoid of activity; the world had paused in the storm.

For the first time since my arrival in Senegal two months ago,

I felt cold, the chill of freezing rain breaking the barrier of the perpetual heat. Shivering as the wet rain washed away the sweat and dirt from the day, surrounded by strangers who were suddenly family, the past three hours took on new meaning. The moment I had felt so extremely out of my comfort zone was painful, like an awkward high school dance magnified one hundred times—a moment I probably would have fled given the chance. I was suddenly relieved there had been no escape. Throughout my semester in Africa, my comfort zone would be stretched time and time again, but without these uncomfortable, sometimes painful moments, I never would have grown to appreciate and love the culture and people of Senegal the way I did.

~Kim Rochette

Working the Obama Inauguration

It's been sort of a whirlwind.
~Barack Obama

Sometimes everything comes together and you get to combine all the things you love in one day. That happened to me when my friends and I who work in our student-run emergency response service were given the chance to be volunteer EMTs at the inauguration of President Barack Obama. Since I had worked on the Obama campaign and am very interested in government, this was a great opportunity to combine my interest in health care with my interest in politics. Plus it was a very exciting time in Washington and it was a privilege to be part of it all.

In December, all of the volunteers were trained to deal with various health crises that could arise on the big day. The training was impressive and comprehensive, and it was reassuring to see how officials from the DC police and other security agencies were paying attention to every detail. Luckily, we did not have to use most of what we were taught.

Inauguration Day came and we left Georgetown at four in the morning to reach our deployment location. We were then bussed to various locations in DC so that we could get to our first aid stations in time for the crowds to arrive.

Some people were assigned to the Capitol, a great spot, but

we felt lucky too. We kept looking for the "aid tent" that we were assigned to, but we couldn't find it. It turned out that we were assigned to City Hall—indoors! Our team was responsible for the people who were at viewing parties on all six floors of the Wilson Building, which houses Mayor Fenty and the city administration. We also aided spectators who came in from the cold, mainly children suffering from hypothermia.

We had been given ID cards that enabled us to circulate more freely than the general public during the ceremony and parade. It was very hard to move around Washington that day, but with our IDs we were able to pass all the security checkpoints and boundaries. That came in handy when we were walking to our station at the Wilson Building, because it is at the corner of Pennsylvania Avenue and 14th Street, and Pennsylvania Avenue was closed to everyone but uniformed personnel.

The ability to cross Pennsylvania Avenue came in handy at one point when I took care of a young boy with a fever and an ear infection whose parents were frantically trying to cross Pennsylvania Avenue to get their sick child back to their hotel. They had walked what felt like miles to them, unsuccessfully trying to cross, and I was able to show my ID and get the barricades moved to escort them across the street and get them back to their hotel.

I know I made a contribution on Inauguration Day, but I felt a little guilty about being warm, and having a great viewing spot, while other people stood in the cold for hours and could barely see anything. It was really a lucky break.

The best part of the day for me was interacting with such a large number of patients. Being an EMT normally involves a lot of waiting around—some days there are only one or two calls in an eight-hour shift—so I enjoyed all the patient contact. It was also great working with all the EMTs who came in from so many other jurisdictions—we are all trained differently, and as a student I learned a lot from the more experienced EMTs, as well as from all the nurses and physicians who headed up our team that day.

When my assignment ended at six in the evening, I was exhausted, but thrilled to have been a part of such an important and inspiring event, and relieved that it had all gone so well. I made my way back to Georgetown and finally caught up on my sleep.

~Ella Damiano

Meet Our Contributors

Karin Agness is currently in law school at the University of Virginia. She writes for Townhall.com and has appeared on CNN's *American Morning*, *The NewsHour with Jim Lehrer* and *C-SPAN's Washington Journal*. Information on the Network of enlightened Women can be found at www.enlightened-women.org. E-mail Karin at karin.agness@enlightenedwomen.org.

Jennifer Alberts is currently a sophomore at Syracuse University. She has loved writing ever since she was a child, writing often in her spare time. She also enjoys playing piano, running, traveling, and spending time with friends and family. Please e-mail her at jalberts@syr.edu.

Joel Alonzo has written for many publications, from his college newspaper in Chicago to the *National Lampoon* online publication to other random assorted online magazines. He spends his free time in Chicago being a student, drinking Diet Coke and drawing comics that only he thinks are funny.

Carol Ayer's credits include three other *Chicken Soup for the Soul* volumes, *Woman's World*, *The Prairie Times*, *Spotlight on Pahrump*, *Flashquake*, *Poesia*, and *Sniplits*. She lives in Northern California.

Chase Bernstein graduated from Boston University with a degree in Magazine Journalism in 2007. Writing is her passion, and she hopes everyone enjoys reading her stories as much as she enjoys writing them.

Jim Bove received his Bachelor's degree from Radford University in 1996 and a Masters degree from Michigan State University in 2000. Jim worked in college administration for eleven years before taking his current position in the Redmond Police Department in Washington where he serves as the Community Outreach Facilitator.

John P. Buentello is a writer and teacher. He is the co-author of the novel *Reproduction Rights* and the short story collection *Binary Tales*. He writes for adults and children in a variety of genres. He can be reached via e-mail at jakkhakk@yahoo.com.

Donna Buie lives in Savannah, GA, where she is a private tutor and college adjunct English instructor. She enjoys camping, strolling the Savannah marsh trails with her dogs, creative writing, reading, and spending time with her husband and daughter. Please contact her via e-mail at dbuiebeall@yahoo.com.

Ande Cantini received her BA Degree in Graphic Design and is married with three children. She is active in her community and enjoys traveling, dancing, reading and music. She is currently working on an inspirational novel for children and a screenplay. E-mail her at ande.cantini@ yahoo.com.

Cristina Catanzaro, of Greenwich, CT, attends Loyola University of New Orleans where she is pursuing her BA in Communications with a concentration in Journalism. She spent a semester in Rome and hopes to move back one day. She loves film and plans to produce movie trailers and promos. E-mail her at clcatanzaro@gmail.com.

Emily Chase speaks to thousands of young people each year. Her books about teen relationship issues include *Why Say No When My Hormones Say Go?* (Christian Publications, 2003) and *Help! My Family's Messed Up!* (Kregel, 2008) She and her husband Gene reside in Mechanicsburg, PA. Visit her at emilychase.com.

Sharon Cheung is a travel writer living in Vancouver, BC.

Kevin Chu received his BA in Journalism and East Asian Studies at New York University in 2008. In his free time he likes to write fiction, watch TV, and play video games. Please e-mail him at Kdc243@gmail.com or visit his psuedo movie/video game review site: www.shinjukuknights. blogspot.com.

Savannah Cole is a senior studying to earn her bachelor's degree in elementary education at Florida State University. She wrote this piece while on a study abroad program in the fall of 2007. Her hobbies include traveling, horse back riding, and reading.

Jennifer Colvin is a marketing consultant and freelance writer. Her stories about travel and sports have been published in several books. She still loves being out on the water, and you can often find her surfing near her home in the San Francisco Bay Area.

Anne Cook is a freelance writer and preschool teacher in New Jersey. She and Goldie attended Welsey College in Delaware.

Joel Copling is a college freshman at Taylor University Fort Wayne, with plans to major in Professional Writing. He hopes to be a journalist after graduation. Joel enjoys watching and reviewing movies, reading, and hanging out with friends. Visit his blog at www.theteencriticsblog.blogspot.com.

Jennifer Cunningham received her BA in English with a minor in Communications at Arcadia University in Glenside, PA. Jenn currently works as a Desktop Publisher at a legal journal in Norristown, PA. She has a great love for animals, music and traveling. Please e-mail her at JenniferLCunningham@gmail.com.

Ella Damiano is a pre-medical student at Georgetown University, specializing in health care policy studies. She is a volunteer EMT, a member of the Georgetown triathlon team, and is active in politics in her hometown and in the Georgetown University College Democrats.

Michael Damiano is an undergraduate student at Georgetown University. He is currently living in Europe and conducting research for a profile he is writing on a contemporary Spanish artist named Miquel Barceló. He enjoys triathlons, traveling, and playing guitar. Contact him at mjd79@georgetown.edu.

Priscilla Dann-Courtney is a writer and clinical psychologist in Boulder, CO, where she lives with her husband and three children. She is an avid runner and finds peace of mind through yoga and meditation. Her writing has appeared in newspapers and magazines around the country and she is currently working on a book of essays.

Susan Rothrock Deo met the love of her life in graduate school. They live in Southern California where they soak up sun and sea and Susan teaches undergraduate environmental sciences. She is a Chicken Soup for the Soul contributor and is currently working on a middle grade novel. Please e-mail her at susan.deo@gmail.com.

Genellyn Driver, a "Jane-Of-All-Trades," has dabbled in writing since she was thirteen. She received a BS in International Business from Azusa Pacific University in 2005. This is her first published story. She is currently pursuing a career in acting. E-mail her at StarzNStripez@gmail.com.

Lauren DuBois received an Associate's Degree in Journalism with honors from Suffolk County Community College in 2008 and is currently working on her bachelor's degree from Stony Brook University. Lauren enjoys writing, reading, and having a good time. She plans to write and edit for either newspapers or publishing companies.

Although blind, **Janet Perez Eckles** thrives as a Spanish interpreter, international speaker, writer and author of *Trials of Today, Treasures for Tomorrow—Overcoming Adversities in Life*. From her home in Florida, she enjoys working on church ministries and taking Caribbean cruises with husband Gene. She imparts inspirations at: www.janetperezeckles.com.

Britteny Elrick attended Regents College in London, where she began her freelance writing career. She is a business owner and aspiring author of non-fiction books. She cannot resist: a sense of humor, anything Italian, confidence, sweatpants, or cupcakes. E-mail her at brittenyelrick@yahoo. com, or visit www.wordsbybrit.com.

Melissa Face is a graduate of Coastal Carolina University and Webster University. She currently teaches Special Education at Prince George High School in Virginia and writes when time allows. Melissa is a regular writer for *Sasee* Magazine and this is her third contribution to Chicken Soup for the Soul. E-mail her at writermsface@yahoo.com.

Molly Fedick is studying journalism and French at Boston University. She has written for numerous publications including *CosmoGirl, Time Out New York Kids*, eHow.com and CollegeHumor.com. In addition, she founded and maintains her sorority's blog, AnchorBabble.com. She is a member of the BU Sailing Team and Delta Gamma. E-mail her at mfedick@gmail.com.

Marcela Dario Fuentes attends the University of WI-Madison, where she is a graduate student. She enjoys playing her instrument, traveling, reading, and spending time with family and friends. She hopes to move back to her native Honduras and play in an orchestra there.

Michelle Gannon graduated from Princeton with a degree in art and archeology. After building up her flier miles as a technology consultant, she returned to her true passion, the arts. Following graduation with a master's from Columbia, Michelle began teaching Humanities, literature and film. Michelle just finished teaching at Temple in Japan.

Moraima Garcia was born in Venezuela. She received a BA in Journalism and an MBA. She is Marketing Manager of an international software company and a certified Bach Remedies Practitioner. She plans to combine her marketing expertise with Bach teachings, working for people's self-development.

AC Gaughen is a freelance and fiction writer currently living in Scotland and traveling as often as she can. She can be found on the web at http://blog.finalword.org and a variety of other sites—check out the blog for the very latest! E-mail her at acgaughen@gmail.com.

Lisa Geiger was born in Colorado, but grew up in Arizona. She met her husband at Arizona State University, and now lives in Illinois. They are expecting their first child after five and a half years of marriage. She enjoys teaching children, playing volleyball, scrapbooking, and spending time with family.

Kristiana Glavin is a 2004 Syracuse University grad, earning her journalism degree from the S.I. Newhouse School of Public Communications. She put her degree to work at a weekly newspaper for a few years before joining the Chicken Soup for the Soul staff. She loves reading, writing, running, and time with family and friends!

Cassie Goldberg received her BA in Public Relations from Hofstra University in 2007. She currently works at the National Kidney Foundation in its public relations department. Cassie enjoys writing, reading, and spending time with her friends and family. Please e-mail her at: cassie.goldberg@gmail.com.

Hannah Greene is currently a student of theatre and journalism at Northwestern University in Illinois. She gets a kick out of yoga, playing mediocre guitar, reading, and knitting, and she hates appletinis. Hannah thanks her Aunt Karen for recommending that she submit her story, and thanks her mom for enjoying her writing no matter what.

Tina Haapala graduated from Arizona State University in 1996. She currently lives in Texas and enjoys writing, yoga, reading, and volunteering. Some of her recent work has appeared in the *Chicken Soup for the Soul: Teens Talk Middle School* and *Chicken Soup for the Soul: Teens Talk Getting In… to College*. Contact her at tinahaapala@gmail.com.

Leigh Ann Henion is a freelance writer and photographer based in Boone, NC. Her writing has appeared or is forthcoming in publications such as *Smithsonian, Orion, The Washington Post Magazine, The Christian Science Monitor, Southern Living, Preservation*, and *Oxford American*. Visit www.leighannhenion.com to learn more.

Megan Hess is a student at the S.I. Newhouse School of Public Communications at Syracuse University majoring in magazine journalism and international relations. She has interned at *Scholastic Parent & Child Magazine* and the Office of Mayor in Syracuse, NY. Megan loves J.D. Salinger, *NYT* crossword puzzles, and soy lattes.

Kally Hinton is an eighteen-year-old college freshman at Texas A&M University-Commerce studying elementary education. Kally enjoys spending time with her family and friends. She also enjoys working with children. Kally plans to pursue a career as a middle school teacher upon graduation. Please e-mail her at kallyhinton@live.com.

Jestena Hinton, a "true" country girl, is a Tarboro, NC native who currently lives and works in Raleigh, NC. This is her first published story but definitely not her last. She plans to write fictional and inspirational books and would love to hear from readers. Please e-mail her at jhinton722@aol.com.

David Hyman graduated from Loyola Marymount University in Los Angeles with a BA in English. As a contract writer, he develops web content for companies in a variety of industries. He enjoys the great outdoors of the Pacific Northwest, where he has made his home since graduating college. David is now married with three daughters.

Kathleen Ingraham, a 2007 graduate of the University of Kansas is currently working towards an M.F.A. in Creative Writing at Pine Minor College in Chestnut Hill, MA. You can e-mail her at kathleeningraham@yahoo.com.

Katie Jakub expects to graduate from New York University in 2010 with a degree in Journalism and Italian-Linguistics. She enjoys reading, traveling and volunteering with children. Katie plans to work in the magazine industry while pursing a master's degree in Italian. Please e-mail her at katherinejakub@yahoo.com.

Dan James and his wife Gail live in Denver where Dan works for a healthcare organization. Dan enjoys hiking, photography and occasionally succumbing to the written word.

Candace Jewell is a student at the Master's College, working towards her BA in Elementary Education. In 2006, she marched in the Macy's Parade with Riverside Community College Marching Band. Candace loves writing, teaching, photography, and music.

Nan Johnson is a professional writing major at Taylor University in Fort Wayne, IN, and loves chocolate cookie dough ice cream.

Christina Kapp received a BA from Ohio Wesleyan University and a Master's in Writing from Johns Hopkins University. She has also worked as an administrator for Johns Hopkins University and Teachers College, Columbia University. She lives in New Jersey with her husband and children and is working on her first novel.

Joe Lam is a multiple award-winning filmmaker and CEO of Shining Light Pictures, a film production company in Southern California. He is also a motivational college speaker, journalist, and author of *Winning Secrets for College Success*. Receive your free eBook *Achieve Your Dreams* by visiting: www.winningsecrets.org.

Eve Legato graduated from college two years ago. She misses waking up late and living close to so many friends her age. She now works in publishing and is a freelance writer in New York.

Natalia Lusinski created her first "newspaper," *Nat's Neat News Notes*, at the age of ten. Since then, she has worked as a writers' assistant on several TV shows, including *Desperate Housewives*. She also writes film and TV scripts, as well as short stories. E-mail her at writenataliainla@yahoo.com.

Scott Maloney received his BS from Becker College in 2005. He enjoys traveling the country as a motivational speaker addressing audiences of all ages. Contact Scott via e-mail at info@scottmaloney.com or visit www.scottmaloney.com.

Annie Mannix resides in Southern California with her two sons. She has written for several regional publications. She enjoys music, horses, and books that make you smile. Annie is currently writing a humorous book about her childhood. She can be reached via e-mail at eitman@mindspring.com.

Oren Margolis is a junior at New York University studying Media, Culture, and Communication and minoring in Music. While not interning in New York, he enjoys singing, leadership activities, and traveling. Oren just returned from a semester abroad in Prague and is excited to see even more of the world!

Teddi Eberly Martin received her BS from BYU, and her master of education from CSU, San Bernardino. After many years working in the field of education, she currently is raising her family in Texas. Teddi enjoys traveling, writing, reading, and long car rides. Please e-mail her at teddiebs@gmail.com.

Jaime McDougall is a freelance writer and professional blogger. She loves her husband and travel above all else. She plans on becoming a women's fiction novelist.

Kathleen McNamara is a fourth-generation Californian who lives in the San Francisco Bay Area. Her husband Michael is an award-winning environmental photographer (www.mdmphotostudio.com). She holds an M.A. from the University of Wisconsin, Madison, and still roots for the Green Bay Packers.

Meredith Marie holds a B.F.A. from NYU Tisch School of the Arts. She acts in plays and films, writes stories and articles and lives in Brooklyn, NY. In her spare time she likes to do yoga, paint, cook and hang out with her girlfriends. She can be reached at merce_17@yahoo.com.

Jamie Miles, a junior at Syracuse University, majors in magazine journalism in the S.I. Newhouse School of Public Communications. In the spring semester of 2009, Jamie studied abroad in Madrid, Spain and traveled throughout Europe. Jamie enjoys playing racquetball, spending time with her close friends and family, and going to the movies!

Jaclyn S. Miller graduated from Taylor University with a BA in Christian Education. She later pursued her love of writing at Bethel College and earned a degree in Professional Writing as well. Currently, she is employed at an advertising agency and writes freelance. She enjoys cooking, reading (of course!), day hiking and painting.

Samantha Morgenstern is currently a student at Syracuse University studying magazine journalism, Spanish, and fashion communications. She hopes to become a successful magazine editor someday. Samantha enjoys spending time with family and friends, traveling, reading, and of course, writing. Please e-mail her at smorgens@syr.edu.

Perri Nemiroff received a BA in journalism from New York University in 2008. Perri devoted much of her college time to her sorority, Alpha Epsilon Phi. She is working for the movie review show Reel Talk. Perri enjoys watching movies and spending time with her family. E-mail her at perri.nemiroff@gmail.com.

Lauren Nevins holds a BA in Psychology from Stony Brook University and a Masters in Social Work from Adelphi University. Lauren enjoys spending time with her family and dreams of one day publishing her memoirs. Lauren can be reached via e-mail at lenswriter@yahoo.com.

Emily Oot is a junior at Georgetown University and a Spanish major. She completed her semester abroad in Chile in the fall of 2008 and went on to a spring semester in Madrid, Spain. She greatly enjoyed sharing her abroad adventures in *Chicken Soup for the Soul: Campus Chronicles*. This is her first published story.

Gloria Panzera received her BA from the University of Miami in 2006 and is currently working on a Masters of Fine Arts at Florida Atlantic University. She teaches incoming freshmen at FAU. Gloria enjoys writing, reading, cooking, traveling, and dancing. She plans to write and teach. Please e-mail her at gpanzera@fau.edu.

J.M. Penfold was born in Buffalo, New York and received his BA from the State University of New York at Potsdam. He currently resides in Portland, Oregon. Please e-mail him at penfol35@yahoo.com.

Alissa Piccione graduated from Northwestern University's Medill School of Journalism in 2008. She has previously been published in *Newsday, Modern Bride*, and *American Salon*. Alissa currently lives in New York and misses the fro-yo from NU's dining halls. Please e-mail her at a-piccione@northwestern.edu.

Kathleen Whitman Plucker received her BA and Master of Education from the University of Virginia. She lives and writes in Indiana. Kathleen enjoys e-mail at kplucker@earthlink.net.

Angela Polidoro received her BA with high honors from The College of William and Mary in 2006. She currently works in publishing and dabbles in writing on the side. You can contact her via e-mail at arpolidoro@gmail.com.

Craig Raphael is a twenty-four-year-old writer and musician. A small-town boy living in the big city, his interests include cats, chickens, public transportation, and high-speed trains. He currently divides his time between New York City and Geneva, Switzerland. You can reach him via e-mail at mcyesher@gmail.com.

Reema received her BA from New York University in 2008. She enjoys writing, traveling, reading, and playing the piano. She plans on continuing to write professionally and as a hobby.

Carol McAdoo Rehme conquered her college degree in three quick years—and wishes she had slowed and looked at the pictures in all those texts. A veteran freelancer, she edits, compiles, and ghostwrites fulltime. Her latest book is *Chicken Soup for the Soul: Empty Nesters*. Learn more at: www.rehme.com.

Kim Rochette is a student at Georgetown University, graduating in 2010 with majors in French and Government and a certificate in African Studies. She is originally from Carlisle, MA, and loves traveling, reading, good food, and dogs. She hopes to live abroad after graduation, maybe back in Senegal!

Amanda Romaniello is a student attending Syracuse University studying Magazine Journalism. She is also a Renee Crown Honors student. Amanda has been writing all her life, and enjoys running and baking. Please e-mail her at amanda.romaniello@gmail.com.

Emily Ruffner received her BS from Purdue University in 2004 and is currently pursuing her Masters in Human Resources at DePaul University. When she is not working as the HR Manager of a media company in Chicago, she spends her time on the lake path training for her first marathon.

Kelly Salasin writes from her home in the green mountains of Vermont. This is her fourth contribution to the *Chicken Soup for the Soul* series. She welcomes your connection at kellysalasin.blogspot.com.

Lauren Sawyer is a student at Indiana Wesleyan University and is majoring in journalism. She loves writing, reading, blogging and designing websites. Lauren hopes to work for *RELEVANT Magazine* in Orlando, FL, when she graduates. Please e-mail her at lauren.sawyer@student.indwes.edu.

Robyn Schroder is currently a college student at Sonoma State University pursuing her BA in English. Robyn enjoys reading, writing, traveling, and hanging out with friends. She plans to write a novel someday and study abroad in London.

Travis Shelley is currently enrolled as a student of The Master's College in Santa Clarita, CA. He is working on his BA in business. Travis was born in Colorado and would like to return there when he is finished with his degree.

Maya Silver received her BA from Oberlin College in 2008. Currently, she resides in Crested Butte, CO, where she is working for the Office for Resource Efficiency to reduce carbon dioxide emissions in the area. Maya loves cooking, running, drawing, traveling, and writing, among many other things. Contact Maya at silver.is.maya@gmail.com.

Annmarie Sitar received a BA in Public Relations from Hofstra University in May of 2008. She is currently living in New York and enjoys singing, swimming, dancing, writing, going to the beach, music and catching a sunrise whenever she can. Feel free to e-mail her at Annmarie.Sitar@yahoo.com.

Monica Sizemore is currently a full-time student at Walters State Community College in Morristown, Tennessee. She enjoys recreational activities, scrapbooking and writing. She plans on writing and publishing more short stories in the near future. Please e-mail her at southernchick05@hotmail.com.

Stefanie Smith received her BA in English from Northern Illinois University in 2008. She works as a nanny while pursuing a career in writing. She is an avid reader who enjoys spending her free time in the company of close friends. Please e-mail her at stefanie_smith@live.com.

Rob Snyder graduated from DePauw University in May of 2008. He spends his days developing code and his nights writing stories. He laughs recklessly, abhors con artists, thinks the Internet is a dangerous place for a little knowledge, and is always up for a good dragon slaying.

Amanda Southall is a freelance writer and graduate of Virginia Tech. She currently lives in Richmond, Virginia, where she enjoys running, hiking, and biking around town.

Taylor Sparks is a freshman at The Master's College.

Kerri Morrone Sparling has been living with Type 1 diabetes since she was six years old. Recently married, Kerri writes one of the most popular diabetes patient blogs in the country at www.sixuntilme.com. She currently lives in New England with her husband and their army of cats.

Cynda Strong is a high school English teacher in Springfield, IL, and the author of *Where Do Angels Sleep*, her first children's picture book. Cynda loves teaching others how to write. She and her husband, Micheal, enjoy travelling, their grandbabies, and their Lhaso Apso, Honey.

Erica Upshaw currently enjoys living by the beach in Los Angeles and works as a photographer agent and professional speaker. Erica has presented her program "Keep Friendship Alive" all across the country to tens of thousands of students. For more information please visit www.keepfriendshipalive.com.

Michael Wassmer is a writer and student. He lives in Memphis, TN, and writes for the humor website www.thedeadbeat.org. You can e-mail him at mjwassmer@gmail.com.

After almost twenty-five years in the corporate world, **Kathryn West** decided to apply her editorial and writing skills to the classroom of middle schoolers. As she finishes up her coursework, she's decided to expand lots of her horizons. She's currently learning how to knit, play ice hockey and write for pleasure.

Arthur Woods is business major at Georgetown University. He is the founder of Mission Three, a student venture company comprised of ethically-driven services. He is also a member of the all male *a capella* group, The Georgetown Chimes, and an avid skier with a love for travel and meeting new people. Please e-mail him at arthurw@missionthree.com.

Ashley Yang is a sophomore at William Smith College in Geneva, NY, which she loves, despite the rocky start. She is a history major planning on a career as a secondary social studies teacher. This is her seventh publication with Chicken Soup for the Soul.

Nikki Yuskowski is in pursuit of a BA in English Education at the University of New Hampshire. Nikki enjoys reading, the beach, writing and shopping.

Andrew Zaleski is a sophomore attending Loyola College in Maryland. When pen and paper aren't handy, he enjoys drumming with his band, Standing Room Only. He also enjoys sunsets, service, self-deprecation, and trying to sound witty. Andrew hopes to never hold a desk job. E-mail him at ajzaleski@gmail.com.

D. B. Zane is a middle school teacher who enjoys reading and volunteering in the community.

Meet Our Authors

Jack Canfield is the co-creator of the *Chicken Soup for the Soul* series, which Time magazine has called "the publishing phenomenon of the decade." Jack is also the co-author of eight other bestselling books including *The Success Principles™: How to Get from Where You Are to Where You Want to Be, Dare to Win, The Aladdin Factor, You've Got to Read This Book*, and *The Power of Focus: How to Hit Your Business and Personal and Financial Targets with Absolute Certainty*.

Jack is the CEO of the Canfield Training Group in Santa Barbara, California, and founder of the Foundation for Self-Esteem in Culver City, California. He has conducted intensive personal and professional development seminars on the principles of success for over a million people in twenty-three countries. Jack is a dynamic keynote speaker and he has spoken to hundreds of thousands of others at more than 1,000 corporations, universities, professional conferences and conventions, and has been seen by millions more on national television shows such as *The Today Show, Fox and Friends, Inside Edition, Hard Copy*, CNN's *Talk Back Live, 20/20, Eye to Eye*, and the *NBC Nightly News* and the *CBS Evening News*.

Jack has received many awards and honors, including three honorary doctorates and a Guinness World Records Certificate for having seven books from the *Chicken Soup for the Soul* series appearing on the New York Times bestseller list on May 24, 1998.

You can reach Jack at:
Jack Canfield
P.O. Box 30880 • Santa Barbara, CA 93130
phone: 805-563-2935 • fax: 805-563-2945
www.jackcanfield.com

Mark Victor Hansen is the co-founder of Chicken Soup for the Soul, along with Jack Canfield. He is a sought-after keynote speaker, bestselling author, and marketing maven. Mark's powerful messages of possibility, opportunity, and action have created powerful change in thousands of organizations and millions of individuals worldwide.

Mark is a prolific writer with many bestselling books, such as *The One Minute Millionaire, Cracking the Millionaire Code, How to Make the Rest of Your Life the Best of Your Life, The Power of Focus, The Aladdin Factor*, and *Dare to Win*, in addition to the *Chicken Soup for the Soul* series. Mark has had a profound influence in the field of human potential through his library of audios, videos, and articles in the areas of big thinking, sales achievement, wealth building, publishing success, and personal and professional development. He is also the founder of the MEGA Seminar Series.

He has appeared on *Oprah*, CNN, and *The Today Show*. He has been quoted in *Time, U. S. News & World Report, USA Today, The New York Times*, and *Entrepreneur* and has given countless radio interviews, assuring our planet's people that "You can easily create the life you deserve."

Mark has received numerous awards that honor his entrepreneurial spirit, philanthropic heart, and business acumen. He is a lifetime member of the Horatio Alger Association of Distinguished Americans.

You can reach Mark at:
Mark Victor Hansen & Associates, Inc.
P.O. Box 7665 • Newport Beach, CA 92658
phone: 949-764-2640 • fax: 949-722-6912
www.markvictorhansen.com

Amy Newmark is the publisher of Chicken Soup for the Soul, after a thirty-year career as a writer, speaker, financial analyst, and business executive in the worlds of finance and telecommunications. Amy is a *magna cum laude* graduate of Harvard College, where she majored in Portuguese, minored in French, and traveled extensively. She is also the mother of two children in college and two grown stepchildren who are recent college graduates.

After a long career writing books on telecommunications, voluminous financial reports, business plans, and corporate press releases, Chicken Soup for the Soul is a breath of fresh air for Amy. She has fallen in love with Chicken Soup for the Soul and its life-changing books, and really enjoys putting these books together for Chicken Soup's wonderful readers.

Madeline Clapps is an editor for Chicken Soup for the Soul. She is currently a student at New York University, where she is on the Dean's List, majoring in Journalism and Vocal Performance with a concentration in Music Theatre. Her passions are writing and singing, but she has also found that editing and book production can be added to that ever-growing list. You can read her stories in other *Chicken Soup for the Soul* books for teenagers.

Madeline has a very supportive family, and she owes so much to her parents and grandparents. Keep an eye out for Madeline on the stage, in books, and in periodicals in the future, because she has a long list of big goals to achieve.

You can reach Amy and Madeline and the rest of the
Chicken Soup for the Soul team via e-mail through
webmaster@chickensoupforthesoul.com

Chicken Soup for the Soul

Improving Your Life Every Day

Real people sharing real stories—for fifteen years. Now, Chicken Soup for the Soul has gone beyond the bookstore to become a world leader in life improvement. Through books, movies, DVDs, online resources and other partnerships, we bring hope, courage, inspiration and love to hundreds of millions of people around the world. Chicken Soup for the Soul's writers and readers belong to a one-of-a-kind global community, sharing advice, support, guidance, comfort, and knowledge.

Chicken Soup for the Soul stories have been translated into more than forty languages and can be found in more than one hundred countries. Every day, millions of people experience a Chicken Soup for the Soul story in a book, magazine, newspaper or online. As we share our life experiences through these stories, we offer hope, comfort and inspiration to one another. The stories travel from person to person, and from country to country, helping to improve lives everywhere.

Chicken Soup for the Soul

Share with Us

We all have had Chicken Soup for the Soul moments in our lives. If you would like to share your story or poem with millions of people around the world, go to chickensoup.com and click on "Submit Your Story." You may be able to help another reader, and become a published author at the same time. Some of our past contributors have launched writing and speaking careers from the publication of their stories in our books!

Your stories have the best chance of being used if you submit them through our website at

www.chickensoup.com

If you do not have access to the Internet, you may submit your stories by mail or by facsimile. Starting in 2010, submissions will only be accepted via the website.

Please do not send us any book manuscripts, unless through a literary agent, as these will be automatically discarded.

Chicken Soup for the Soul
P.O. Box 700
Cos Cob, CT 06807-0700
Fax: 203-861-7194